Economic Transition in Guinea

Economic Transition in Guinea

Implications for Growth and Poverty

Jehan Arulpragasam
David E. Sahn

Published for
Cornell University Food and Nutrition Policy Program
by NEW YORK UNIVERSITY PRESS
New York and London

NEW YORK UNIVERSITY PRESS
New York and London
© 1997 by New York University

Library of Congress Cataloging-in-Publication Data
Arulpragasam, Jehan.
Economic transition in Guinea : implications for growth and
poverty / Jehan Arulpragasam and David E. Sahn.
p. cm.
Includes bibliographical references and index.
ISBN 0-8147-0664-9
1. Guinea—Economic policy. 2. Guinea—Economic conditions—1984–
I. Sahn, David E. II. Title.
HC1030.A78 1996   96-9056
338.96652—dc20   CIP

New York University Press books are printed on acid-free paper,
and their binding materials are chosen for strength and durability.

Manufactured in the United States of America

10 9 8 7 6 5 4 3 2 1

CONTENTS

PREFACE   xi

ACKNOWLEDGMENTS   xiii

1. INTRODUCTION   1

2. BACKGROUND   5

  Abundant Resources   5
  Poor Performance   7
  The Evolution of Economic and Social Stagnation   10
  The Structural Adjustment Program   14
  Notes   16

3. TRADE AND EXCHANGE RATE POLICY   18

  Historical Perspectives   18
  Policy Reforms   21
  Economic Consequences of Reforms   26
    Reform and the Exchange Rate   26

v

Reform and the Balance of Payments   30
Reform and Export and Import Composition   36
Conclusions   39
Notes   42

4. FOOD AND AGRICULTURAL POLICY   46

Historical Perspectives   46
Overview   46
Policy Failure   49
Producer Prices, Production, and Markets   52
Consumer Prices, Retail Markets, and Household Welfare   60
Policy Reform   66
General Economic Consequences of Reform   68
Pricing, Production, and Marketing of Agricultural Exports   68
Pricing, Production, and Marketing of Food Crops   71
Rice Market Liberalization   73
Rice Consumption, Price Policy, and Food Security   81
The Multimarket Model   88
Appendix. Guinea Multi-market Model Equations   102
Supply, Demand, and Incomes   102
Prices   103
Market Clearing   103
Model Closure and the Real Exchange Rate   103
Notes   106

5. URBAN LABOR MARKETS   113

Labor Force Participation and Segmentation   114
Civil Service Reform   121
Small-scale Enterprises And Proprietors   131
Notes   139

6. MINING SECTOR POLICIES   141

Historical Perspectives   141
Policy Reforms   146
General Economic Consequences of Reforms   147
Notes   149

7. **FINANCIAL SECTOR POLICIES** 151

Historical Perspectives   151
Policy Reforms   155
General Economic Consequences of Reforms   156
Notes   160

8. **PUBLIC SECTOR AND FISCAL POLICIES** 162

Historical Perspectives   162
Policy Reforms and their General Economic Consequences   163
    Tax Reform   168
    Public Enterprise Reform   171
    Public Investment Reform   174
    Social Services and Reform   175
Notes   192

9. **CONCLUSION** 195

REFERENCES 205

INDEX 215

LIST OF TABLES

1. Area, Population, and Population Density   7
2. Gross Domestic Product, 1960–1993   8
3. Exchange Rates, 1970–1992   20
4. Foreign Exchange Budget, 1986–1991   23
5. Balance of Payments, 1981–1993   31
6. Long-term Public Debt, Outstanding and Disbursed, 1970 to 1992   37
7. Composition of Auction Imports   40
8. Characteristics of Agriculture, by Region   47
9. Distribution of Landholdings, by Size of Holdings, 1975 and 1985   48
10. Nominal Producer Prices of Select Crops, 1975–1992   53
11. Estimated Costs of Production, by Crop and Production Method
    Compared with Official and Open Market Prices, 1981–1982   55
12. Nominal Protection Coefficients (NPCs), 1975–1992   56

13. Crop Production Estimates, 1970–1993   57
14. State Purchases of Agricultural Products, Selected Years   58
15. Food Import Quantities by Good, 1974–1992   59
16. Volume of Agricultural Exports, 1960–1992   60
17. Comparison of Official Guinean Prices and Neighboring Countries Paid to the Producer for Basic Agricultural Products, 1975   62
18. Official Rice Retail Prices, 1975–1985   63
19. Percent of Entitled Ration Actually Purchased, by Household Category, 1984   65
20. Conakry Local Rice Cost Structure, 1988 and 1992   73
21. Rice Production, Imports, and Availability   75
22. Retail Rice Prices, 1985–1991   79
23. Expenditure Budget Shares by Per Capita Expenditure Quintile   82
24. Estimated Elasticities of Food Commodities   84
25. Regional Variations in Consumer Prices of Local and Imported Rice, 1986, 1987, 1992   86
26. Simulated Sectoral Effects of Tariff Increases   91
27. Welfare Effects on the Poor of Tariff Changes, Conakry   93
28. Summary Effects of a 10 Percent Tariff on Alternative Food Commodities, Conakry   98
29. Simulated Sectoral Effects of Reduced Marketing Margins   99
30. Welfare Effects on the Poor of Reduced Marketing Margins, Conakry   101
31. Participation Rates and Job Search Behavior, by Age and Gender   114
32. Nonparticipants Not Searching for Work—Reasons, by Age and Gender   115
33. Labor Market Participants—Sector of Employment, by Gender   116
34. Sector of Employment for Single and Multiple Earner Households, by Per Capita Expenditure Quintile   117
35. Predicted Sector Entry Probabilities, by Gender and Level of Education   118
36. Male-Female Comparisons of Predicted Hourly Earnings, by Sector and Level of Education   120
37. Civil Service Reform—Net Staff Reduction   123
38. Government Expenditure and Wage Statistics for 1986 to 1992   124
39. Duration of Spell without Work upon Leaving the Public Sector, by Reason and Period of Departure   127
40. A Comparison of 1990 Private Sector Earnings with the Most Recent Public Sector Earnings in 1990 Terms   128
41. Ranking in Per Capita Expenditure Distribution in 1990, by Reason for Leaving the Public Sector and 1990 Employment Status   129

42. Number of Independent Enterprises in All Households 132
43. Enterprise Type by Period of Inception 133
44. Characteristics of Enterprises 134
45. Personal Characteristics of Main Proprietor 136
46. Characteristics of Enterprise by Gender of Proprietor 137
47. Characteristics of Enterprise by Age of Proprietor and Education 138
48. Exports of Minerals 144
49. Tax Revenues from Mining, 1986–1992 145
50. Financial Sector, 1960–1992 153
51. Structure of Interest Rates 157
52. Consumption, Investment, and Savings, 1986–1992 160
53. Financial Operations of the Central Government, 1974–1993 164
54. Financial Operations of the Central Government, 1986–1993 167
55. Real Tax Revenue, 1986–1992 170
56. Primary School Enrollment, 1980–1994 177
57. Primary School Gross Enrollment Rates for Girls and Boys,
    by Region, 1992/93 178
58. Gross Enrollment in Primary and Secondary Education,
    by Expenditure Group, 1994 179
59. Education Sector Expenditures 180
60. Infant Mortality and Life Expectancy by Region and by Gender,
    1983 182
61. The Burden of Household Expenditures on Health, 1994 186
62. Health Coverage Ratios in 1988 187
63. Government Recurrent Health Budget, 1977–1991 189
64. Per Capita Government Health Expenditures, by Expenditure
    Quintiles 190
65. The Ten Major Causes of Morbidity among Children between
    the Ages of 0 and 5 Years 191

LIST OF APPENDIX TABLE

1. Multimarket Baseline Supply and Demand, 1990/91 105

LIST OF FIGURES

1. Composition of Gross Domestic Products, 1990 9
2. Exchange Rate Indices 27

3. Composition of Exports   38
4. Total Import Composition, 1990   41
5. Monthly Retail Rice Prices in Conakry, Imported vs. Domestic Rice   85
6. Average Share of Household Revenue from the Small Enterprise
        Sector, by Expenditure Quintile   133
7. Enterprise Budgets by Period of Establishment   135

PREFACE

The Republic of Guinea recently emerged from over a quarter-century under a *dirigiste*, closed economic and political system. Economic and social data from this period were never consistently compiled and were extraordinarily scarce, even in comparison with other underdeveloped countries in the world. Furthermore, information was safely guarded, once again reflecting a level of secrecy that was virtually unparalled in Africa. Some may say that if there is any blessing in disguise to Guinea's cloistered past, it is that the country has largely escaped the attention of economists. Whereas social scientists have zealously studied and perhaps overanalyzed other countries across sub-Saharan Africa, since independence only a handful of economic works have been published on Guinea (see, for example, Suret-Canale [1970], Riviere [1977], Yansane [1984], and O'Conner [1972]).

Our study represents what will surely be only one of many attempts to change this. In particular, we focus our attention on Guinea's efforts to break with its dismal economic past and reform an entire range of regulations, institutions, and markets. In order to address the scope, magnitude, implications, and results of the current economic reform program, this book looks to the past in tracing the causes of the economic crisis and the need for reform in Guinea. It also consolidates information on the reform process in progress. To do both, it pieces together a story from data and information from a variety of sources, including interviews and unpublished government data. By necessity, much of the data are estimates, where possible from the appropriate ministries as corroborated by estimates from the World Bank, the International Monetary Fund, and the United Nations. In summary, while limited by the constraints of data, this study represents an early attempt at presenting an overview of the evolution of the Guinean economy, from independence, through crisis, to reform.

ACKNOWLEDGEMENTS

The work contained in this volume was prepared with funding under a Cooperative Agreement between the Africa Bureau of the U.S. Agency for International Development (AID) and the Cornell Food and Nutrition Policy Program (CFNPP). The support of AID is greatly appreciated, especially Jerome Wolgin, Yoon Lee, and Jay Smith. Ingrid Satelmajer, who edited this book, deserves special recognition for her excellent work and tireless attention to detail. The research assistance of Elizabeth Stephenson, Jeremy Clark, and Lisa Gennetian is also appreciated, as is the work of Ding Dizon in preparing camera-ready copy and Roberta Spivak in coordinating the preparation of the book.

1

INTRODUCTION

Two stories emerge from a study of Guinea's economic reform. Guinea's recent history is one story: bold economic policy reforms have altered the nation's economic structure and carry important implications for social welfare. The other story is of economic reform itself. Guinea's reform program is an informative example of a country engaged in economic restructuring. The successes and failures of its structural adjustment program are, in many respects, typical of other African cases. In presenting the story of Guinea's economic reform, then, this book also addresses the key difficulties in undertaking structural adjustment reforms, highlighting the lessons that can be learned from the Guinean experience.

The period commencing with the establishment of the Second Republic represents a second chapter in Guinea's post-independence history. Guinea had pursued the policies of African socialism for nearly two decades. Upon Sekou Touré's death in 1986, the new leadership launched a rapid liberalization of Guinea's economy. The important changes in Guinea's economic structure have had consequent implications for social and institutional relationships. Improved incentives for agricultural production and the removal of explicit taxation of farmers have caused rural households to alter their orientation from subsistence production to producing for and buying from the market. A once-cloistered rural sector is therefore gradually establishing links with the rest of the economy and world. As a result, agricultural production has increased. Moreover, the liberalization of prices, commerce, and markets has motivated the growth and return of a private entrepreneurial class. Due to such changes as new economic relationships toward market transactions and trade, the service and commerce sectors have grown rapidly.

But has the private sector's growth from economic liberalization compensated for the effective disintegration of the vast, pre-reform public sector economy? While economic reform has resulted in apparent economic gains for some social groups, others have certainly experienced a traumatic change in their livelihoods. For example, prior to economic liberalization, a large share of Guineans, particularly in the capital, Conakry, were employed by the state, either as government officials or employees of a parastatal company. In addition to a guaranteed salary and such benefits as transport allowances and education entitlements, government employees had access to subsidized food at low prices. With structural adjustment, thousands of government employees were laid off, some with, and others without, severance pay. Has growth in the private sector managed to absorb this labor?

Economic reform has also changed the prices faced by rural and urban households. Liberalization of the trade and exchange regime led to rapid devaluation and increased official prices. For rural households, producer prices have increased for both food crops and export crops. Concomitantly, however, consumer prices in Guinea have increased rapidly. To what extent have these relative price changes, the primary instruments for structural adjustment within the economy, affected production and the supply response? What consequent effect have these price changes had on real incomes among rural and urban households in Guinea?

This book addresses fundamental questions related to structural adjustment in practice. In so doing, it focuses also on the divergence of adjustment in practice from adjustment in theory. While the benefits of structural adjustment are clear in theory, the significance of economic reform to people is obviously an empirical issue. In Guinea, as throughout the rest of sub-Saharan Africa undertaking structural adjustment programs, reform has signified important and necessary economic reorientation. However, the results of reform have not been all that was conceptualized, partly due to problems with implementing economic reforms. These problems are manifested in areas such as non-optimal sequencing of reforms. Reform implementation has also been hindered by the heavy analytical, administrative, and managerial demands required to undertake such a vast battery of economic reforms simultaneously. Some countries, such as Guinea, have simply lacked the human and institutional capital to undertake some reforms effectively. Even when institutional capacity is present, the adjustment process can be impeded by policymakers who lack the conviction that reforms are necessary and beneficial, either to them or the economy as a whole. The political will to undertake key reforms has also been lacking because losers from reform are often the politically astute and powerful, who therefore work to maintain the distortions that generate rents and privileges from which they benefit.

Time lags must also be considered when reconciling the gap between adjustment in practice and adjustment in theory. In Guinea's case, as with the rest of Africa, recognition of these lags' significance has been insufficient. Most importantly, export production lags import growth because supply responses have been slow even though production increased with liberalization. Likewise, private sector development and employment generation lag public sector retrenchment; the establishment of cost-effective and sustainable provision of social services lags the termination of the state's attempted provision of these services; the development of a new civil society and new institutions that support a market economy lags the sudden shutdown of public institutions that supported a state-run economy.

In analyzing the evolution of economic reform in Guinea, this book examines the disarticulated adjustment process, including time lags and their causes. The book also addresses the significance of this disarticulated growth pattern's effect on the welfare of households in transition. To do so, the book proceeds sectorally, following some background information in chapter 2 on Guinea and its resources, past economic performance, and recent structural adjustment program. Chapter 3, on trade and exchange rate policies, examines factors leading to the gross exchange rate distortions prior to reform, the magnitude of the distortion, and its effect on consumers. The effects of exchange rate and import liberalization on the real effective exchange rate, exports and imports, and the balance of payments are studied. Chapter 4 covers food and agricultural policies in Guinea. Command economy policies prior to reform had deleterious effects on prices, production, and markets. The extent of implicit and explicit taxation on rural incomes and production is analyzed. The chapter also examines the effect on consumers of pricing policies, differentiating between official and parallel market prices. The effect of liberalization on food consumption, consumer welfare, and urban poverty is also examined. Chapter 5 focuses on urban labor markets and how economic reforms affect the urban poor through changes in their earning potential. In particular, it examines the effect of public sector retrenchment on workers who are laid off. It also studies the role of the nonwage sector and of small-scale enterprises in providing employment and incomes in the liberalized economy. Chapter 6 highlights the mining sector's critical role as a source of foreign exchange in the Guinean economy, both before and after economic reform. Chapter 7 analyzes financial and banking sector policy changes aimed at financial sector chaos, and their subsequent effect on monetary indicators. Chapter 8 examines the public sector and fiscal policies. Upon analyzing the evolution of government finances and the causes of fiscal developments prior to adjustment, the chapter discusses the effect the main fiscal sector reforms have had on revenues and expenditures since 1986. The main elements of public sector reform—tax, public enterprise, public investment, and social service sector—are discussed in turn. Chapter 9 presents conclusions.

In general each chapter opens with a presentation of historical perspectives. Links are thus made between the policies of the First Republic, their contributions to sectoral evolution, and the subsequent need for reform. Policy reforms undertaken in each sector are then addressed. Where possible, the commitment to specific reforms is weighed against the record of actual implementation. Such a comparison illustrates the wide gap in Guinea between legislating and effectively undertaking change. Namely, although Guinea's reform program is sweeping in coverage and dramatic in magnitude, its implementation has been fraught with institutional, administrative, and infrastructural constraints inherited from the country's past. Finally, each chapter examines the general economic consequences of reforms on a sectoral basis and discusses, where possible, welfare effects on households. Although many of the reforms in Guinea have not provided immediate solutions, they are far from insignificant. In some instances, reforms are already leading to desired gains. Apparent in the successes of Guinea's economic reform is how important it has been for Guinea, as for much of Africa, to remove economic distortions and to "get prices right." Apparent in the failures and difficulties associated with reform in Guinea are problems with the implementation of policy change, as well as constraints to development that lie beyond the reforms.

2

BACKGROUND

ABUNDANT RESOURCES

Guinea is rich in resources. The national population was estimated at 5.3 million in 1988, 74 percent of whom lived in rural areas. Although there is considerable regional variation, population density is calculated at a relatively low 21.5 inhabitants per square kilometer of total land. Guinea's agricultural-based economy boasts a diversity of agroclimatic regions favorable for the strong production of a wide variety of crops. Estimates place the amount of arable land at as much as 25 percent of the nation's total 246,000 square kilometers. Actual cultivated area is currently estimated at 15,760 square kilometers, or 21 percent of arable land. Large tracts of tropical forest account for close to half of national lands, while pastures occupy 12 percent of the total area.

In addition to the natural resources needed for agriculture, Guinea is also abundant in mineral resources. It is the world's second largest exporter of bauxite, an ore from which aluminum is derived. In fact, the country has an estimated one-third of the globe's known bauxite reserves. The nation's mines also extract iron ore, gold, and diamonds.

Bordered by six other countries and the Atlantic Ocean, Guinea spans areas that are marked by their contrasts. The nation's four regions—Lower (or Maritime) Guinea, Middle Guinea, Upper Guinea, and the Forest region—vary with respect to agroecological zones, production patterns, population density, and urbanization (Table 1). The infrastructure within these regions, and particularly the distance and cost of travel to the capital, Conakry, is closely related to the nature of their economic activities and their export orientation. Conakry is the site of the only international airport and the main seaport. Some cross-border markets are also significant.

Lower Guinea, covering approximately 18 percent of the national territory, ranges from the alluvial plains and mangrove swamps of the coast to the foothill regions further inland. Lower Guinea's population is 70 percent urban, largely explained by the capital city of Conakry, which houses approximately 1 million inhabitants, namely 55.7 percent of the region's population and 19 percent of the national population (Table 1). The city's high growth rate of 6 percent is explained to a large extent by migration. As of 1983, 67.5 percent of all urban migration was to Conakry and 48.9 percent of the capital's population was born in other prefectures (GOG 1989c). Given the meager state of public urban infrastructure, including that of health and water services, the population strain in Conakry is becoming increasingly significant to an ever-larger segment of Guineans.

Conakry distinguishes itself from the rest of the country in that as many as 85.6 percent of its active population earn their livelihood from the service sector and 6.6 percent from the secondary sector (GOG 1989c).[1] This is in contrast to the national breakdown of 12.7 percent in the service sector and 1.2 percent in the secondary sector. In 1985 it was estimated that over 50 percent of all formal industrial and manufacturing activity in Guinea took place within the city of Conakry (GOG 1985).[2]

Aside from Conakry, the primary site of the nation's small commercial and industrial sector, Lower Guinea also houses the nation's main bauxite mines (CBG, OBK, and Friguia). Otherwise, the region's population is predominantly agrarian. Population density (excluding Conakry) in 1988 was 23 inhabitants per square kilometer.

Middle Guinea, approximately 22 percent of the country's total area, includes the hilly Fouta Djallon plateau ranging in altitude from 600 to 1,600 meters. The region, with an average rainfall of 1,800 millimeters, is known as the watershed of West Africa and is the source of some of the region's main rivers. Soil, however, is poor. Widespread erosion, moreover, is exacerbated by population pressure on arable land. Population density in Middle Guinea is the highest nationally. There are 25.6 inhabitants per square kilometer of total land, even though the regional rate of urbanization is the nation's lowest (Table 1).[3]

TABLE 1

Guinea: Area, Population, and Population Density.

	Maritime Guinea	Middle Guinea	Upper Guinea	Forest Guinea	Total Guinea
Total area (sq. km.)	44,288	55,528	100,879	49,374	245,857
Area without Conakry	34,995	—	—	—	236,568
Area arable	—	—	—	—	75,000
Area cultivated	—	—	—	—	15,760
1988 Population	—	—	—	—	5,279,964
Regional percentage	34.38	26.88	19.80	18.94	100.00
Percent Conakry	55.66	—	—	—	19.13
Urban	69.90	7.60	15.00	14.70	26.00
1988 Population density	41.00	25.60	10.40	20.30	21.50
Without Conakry	23.00	—	—	—	18.00

Sources: UNICEF (1990a); GOG (1989c, 1990c).

Upper Guinea covers 40 percent of the nation's land area, has an urban population of 15 percent, and, with 10.4 inhabitants per square kilometer in 1988, has the lowest regional population density (Table 1). The land is poor in quality and extensively cultivated, leading to low yields.

The Forest region, finally, is a landlocked region of mountains and tropical forest. Such geography in conjunction with bad roads effectively separates the Forest Region from the capital port. Contiguous to Upper Guinea, it is also bordered by Sierra Leone, Liberia, and Côte d'Ivoire, countries with which it engages in unrecorded transborder trade. The urban population constitutes only 14.7 percent of the total, and the population density, at 20.3 people per square kilometer, is close to that of the national average (Table 1).

POOR PERFORMANCE

Guinea's rich resources once made it the gem of French West Africa. Its mining wealth still makes Guinea better off in per capita terms than other nations in the region. Per capita GDP was computed at US$ 431 at the official exchange rate and US$ 393 at the parallel exchange rate in 1988, higher than the mean of US$ 330 among sub-Saharan African (SSA) countries (GOG 1990b; World Bank 1990c).

Much of the nation's production potential, however, remains unrealized, and growth has faltered. Real GDP estimates reveal slow growth, especially in per capita terms, during the two decades prior to 1985 (Table 2). Real per capita GDP declined by 11 percent between 1960 and 1965 and then declined by 1 percent between 1965 and 1970. Average growth in real per capita GDP between 1970 and 1980 was only approximately 1 percent annually.

The GDP story, moreover, has improved only slightly over the past decade as a whole (Table 2). The mean annual growth rate of real per capita GDP was -2.05 percent between 1980 and 1984. There is some evidence of improvement, however, in recent years. From 1985 to 1993, GDP grew at an average rate of 4.5 percent per year. GDP per capita grew at an average rate of 2.3 percent per year between 1985 and 1989 while slowing to an average rate of 1.2 percent between 1989 and 1993.

TABLE 2
Guinea: Gross Domestic Product, 1960–1993.

	Nominal GDP		Real GDP	
Year	Aggregate (billion current GF)[a]	Per Capita (current GF)[a]	Aggregate (billion 1986 GF)	Per Capita (1986 GF)
1960	11.90	3,840.00	—	—
1965	12.00	3,660.00	—	—
1970	15.50	5,000.00	—	—
1975	22.50	5,260.00	—	—
1980	33.52	7,703.16	594.54	136,630.92
1981	36.70	8,253.54	596.11	134,059.60
1982	39.18	8,611.72	609.06	133,870.30
1983	44.17	9,477.36	615.91	132,154.00
1984	48.14	10,088.97	599.62	125,665.75
1985	51.53	10,536.88	629.47	128,713.97
1986	671.15	133,979.91	671.15	133,979.91
1987	845.58	164,632.99	692.04	134,739.01
1988	1,081.59	204,847.99	733.83	138,983.91
1989	1,444.58	266,144.52	764.12	140,778.88
1990	1,820.41	326,251.14	795.54	142,575.48
1991	2,247.84	391,223.22	827.58	144,277.03
1992	2,684.28	455,223.22	851.95	144,480.26
1993	3,030.50	500,737.03	892.76	147,210.67

Sources: GOG (1986, 1990b, 1991b, and 1993a, b); IMF (1994); UNDP and World Bank (1989); World Bank (1990a).
a. Until 1986, the currency was denominated in GS, which was replaced on par by the GF in January 1986.

In 1990, 21.3 percent of GDP was accounted for by the agriculture sector; 6.4 percent by the livestock, fisheries, and forestry sectors; 23.1 percent by the mining sector, and 38.6 percent by the service sector. The remaining portion was accounted for by secondary, nonmining sectors such as construction, manufacturing, and utilities (10.6 percent) (Figure 1). This sectoral distribution has evolved over time, with the role of the primary sector in decline. Mining and the tertiary gained dramatically between 1975 and 1990, though a reduction in mining output since 1989 has reduced its share of GDP to 21 percent in 1992 (IMF 1993).

Guinea's performance with respect to traditional social indicators, moreover, is just as troubling as the broad picture of economic stagnation borne out by GDP data. Available statistics show that Guinea has not even shared in the gains experienced by other low-income nations, both regionally and globally, over the post-colonial era. In fact, Guinea is ranked third from the bottom among countries worldwide on the basis of the Human Development Index, a composite measure of national income, adult literacy, and life expectancy (UNDP 1991). Life expectancy at birth is estimated at 45, below the mean rate of 50 for the region. It is largely driven by the extremely high infant mortality rate (IMR). At 146 per

FIGURE 1
Guinea: Composition of Gross Domestic Products, 1990.

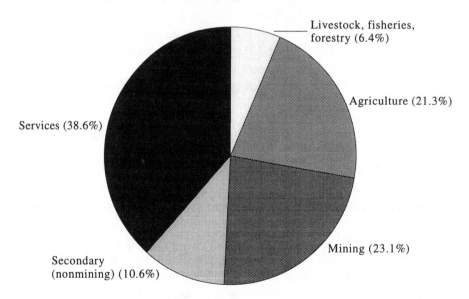

Source: IMF (1993).

thousand, the national IMR was approximately double that of low-income countries globally. It reflected the fact that Guinea's IMR had fallen by only 25 percent, as compared to a mean 42 percent decline among all low-income countries in the period between 1965 and 1988. Data on educational standards similarly reveal Guinea's relative deprivation. The primary school enrollment ratio (percentage of age group enrolled) is only 28 percent in Guinea, compared with a mean of 104 percent among all low-income countries.[4] The secondary school enrollment ratio for Guinea is also weak, currently estimated at 8 percent, compared with 37 percent among all low-income countries. Consequently, the adult illiteracy rate, estimated at 74 percent in Guinea, compares unfavorably both with the regional mean of 52 and with the mean of 44 percent among low-income countries worldwide.[5]

THE EVOLUTION OF ECONOMIC AND SOCIAL STAGNATION

The paradox of Guinea's good natural resource base and poor economic and living standards is a consequence of the nation's traumatic political history and its associated economic policies. In Guinea, politics and policy have played the primary role in leading to crises.

Under the leadership of Sekou Touré and his *Parti Démocratique de Guinée* (PDG), Guinea voted "NO" to General de Gaulle's proposed French Community on September 28, 1958. The country gained complete independence soon after, on October 2, 1958. The break with France was traumatic. Within 48 hours all French expatriates were withdrawn. With their administrative and technical expertise also went equipment, medication, and even lightbulbs. Much of the infrastructure that remained was either inoperable or unserviceable. In the face of soured relations France terminated both budgetary assistance and Guinea's favored nation trading status.

Guinea's de-linking from a major trade partner reinforced the economic inward orientation opted for in Touré's version of African Socialism. Equally significant, the severance from France completed the PDG's consolidation of political power. In the years that followed, the PDG instituted a one-party government that controlled the political, administrative, and economic spheres. The state bureaucracy extended from the cabinet to over 30,000 local party committees (PRLs). "Every citizen had to be a party member, and every village, neighborhood, factory, and office had its party committee" (Azarya and Chazan 1987, 111). Ultimately Guinea had approximately one elected official for every eleven citizens (Yansané 1990). These officials exercised control over everything from employment in state enterprises to access to foreign exchange at official rates.

The patronage system institutionalized as a result is a legacy that continues to haunt Guinean life and the workings of its economy.

The permeation of Guinean society by the PDG party apparatus, furthermore, better permitted the notorious rule of Sekou Touré. Touré's rule has been alternatively described as "totalitarian," "repressive," and "autocratic." Made increasingly paranoid by coups in neighboring Ghana and Mali and internal conflicts at home, Touré conducted frequent purges within party ranks and among his potential opponents. His vision of a "permanent plot" against his rule was reinforced by a 1970 Portuguese-backed invasion by Guinean exiles. The arrests, torture, and public hangings that followed became increasingly characteristic of a reign of terror.[6] The frightened inner circle of leadership isolated itself from outside contacts and increasingly depended upon the good auspices of Sekou Touré for its continued well-being. Many of its members were his relatives. Power thus rested firmly in the hands of one man.

With political centralization in Guinea also came centralization of the economy. The twenty-five years following independence were characterized by state *dirigisme* and control of productive assets. Banks and trading companies were taken over by the state. Land was nationalized, collective farms formed, and producer cooperatives established. The state controlled the supply of inputs and the marketing of outputs.

Productive activity was organized around a number of badly managed state-owned enterprises. Parastatals were characterized by low cost-recovery and poor productivity. Inefficiency, corruption, and insensible budgeting led to the general neglect of public utilities and services. Recurrent and capital expenditures were not targeted to maintaining and developing the infrastructure inherited from the colonial era, and the result was a gradual infrastructure decay.

To fund the state apparatus, the government imposed heavy taxes, both implicit and explicit. Taxes ranged in nature from export and profit taxes on mining companies to taxes on the production of farmers and duties and tariffs on imports. In addition to implicit and explicit taxation on production and commerce, moreover, the government effectively extracted an inflation tax. Expansionary monetary policies were undertaken to pay for government expenditures, decreasing the real purchasing power of citizens.[7] All these taxes served as further disincentives to efficient production and exchange.

Despite the large-scale taxation that introduced significant economic distortions, the government still proved unable to meet its original social objectives and obligations. For example, every secondary school and university graduate was assured a position in the civil service, a promise that expanded the government payroll to unsustainable proportions. It was estimated that as many as 50 percent of those in the Conakry work force were employees of the public sector. As a result, the government frequently found itself unable to pay salaries or to meet debt obligations. By the early 1980s the lack of fiscal discipline was only too apparent; an official government budget did not exist.

The severe government intervention, both political and economic, and the distortions that followed resulted in a disarticulation and fragmentation of the Guinean economy. Indeed, it is useful to view the country as developing dichotomies along three different dimensions.

First, the pervasive state involvement effectively squeezed out the private sector from the formal economy. Low administered producer prices and an overvalued exchange rate provided incentives for smuggling cash crops and other goods out of Guinea. At the same time, the scarcity of foreign exchange at the official rate provided some Guineans with an incentive to obtain and smuggle in goods from neighboring countries that were otherwise unavailable. Similarly, low wages in the public sector led government employees to undertake additional work in the informal sector to supplement their otherwise inadequate incomes. This phenomenon of multiple jobs (*pluriactivité*) has come to characterize life and economic activity in Guinea, and especially in Conakry.

The private sector thus faced indirect disincentives resulting from the distorting effects of state intervention. Added to these, however, were direct disincentives in the form of government laws, policing and propaganda. Members of the merchant class, referred to as *cheytane* (devil), were often harassed or restricted in their activities. Some were the victims of purges (Yansané 1990). Many others left the country.[8] Individuals in private business activity largely resorted to either kinship links with government officials or to corruption.

The squeezing out of the private sector from the formal economy thus resulted in the largely policy-induced development of an illegal economy parallel to that of the formal sector. To circumvent an overvalued exchange rate and prohibitive trade restrictions, traders smuggled coffee and cattle across the border. Domestic parallel markets offered goods smuggled in from abroad, goods produced locally and diverted from the official market, and goods stolen from government stores. A 1968 *New York Times* article (November 16, 1968) describes the following scene: "Shoppers in the state-owned Printania or Nayfay general stores idle between counters whose display spaces are two-thirds empty. Around the corner from [a] revolutionary exhortation, however, a hole-in-the-corner black market offers the goods—imported cloth, transistor radios, bicycle tires, canned foods— that long ago disappeared from the big shops" (cited in Azarya and Chazan 1987, 123). Many of these parallel market systems were in fact maintained only with the formal collusion of officials. Corruption, embezzlement, and fraud ensured the continued supply and functioning of the parallel markets, while illegally raising the incomes of poorly paid government workers.

Indeed Guinea's formal legal system collapsed and was made largely irrelevant in the face of this pervasive "unofficial" economic and social system. Laws and decrees were issued frequently by Touré, but were heeded only as long as they were being mentioned on the radio. They were easily forgotten, though, with a change in the President's or the government's priorities. However, the fact that these decrees were never rescinded added, paradoxically, to a sense of lawlessness. Citizens could never be sure as to what old law might be used against them and when (Azarya and Chazan 1987). Laws were enforced inconsistently, according to the short-term interest and gain of particular government officials, policemen, or soldiers. The casual propagation of decrees and the ad hoc manner of law enactment and enforcement, now institutionalized in Guinea, thus have their origins under Touré's First Republic.

A second polarization, in addition to the breakdown between official and unofficial activity, was increasingly evident between the rural and growing urban populations and between their respective economies during the First Republic. Seen throughout Africa, the urban-rural dichotomy is perhaps relatively more exaggerated in Guinea. Several factors contributed to this. One important dimension is the isolation of much of rural Guinea. Bad roads and difficult terrain effectively cut off many rural communities from urban Conakry.[9]

In addition to physical divisions between urban and rural, there are also political ones. With urban Conakry being the seat of the government and the powerful PDG apparatus as well as home to the largest concentration of Guineans, vested interests and political expediency have been reflected in a clear historical urban bias to policy, particularly food policy. Agricultural producers in rural areas were taxed in kind, contributing to a notable stagnation in agricultural production. Meanwhile, food prices in urban areas, supported by imports and food aid, were effectively subsidized. The urban economy also benefited disproportionately from government expenditures. Civil service jobs were concentrated in urban areas, and urban areas were disproportionately favored in the provision of government services.

A formal-informal sector division, also evident in much of Africa, further reinforced the rural-urban division. There has always been very little formal sector activity in rural areas. The high rates of inflation and the overvaluation of the currency, moreover, combined with low levels of monetization of some of the more isolated rural communities, led to much rural trade being undertaken as barter transactions. The overvaluation of the exchange rate and the distance of regional economies from the port of Conakry also fostered unrecorded transborder trade, or smuggling. It appears, for example, that the Forest region of Guinea was more integrated with the rural economies of Sierra Leone, Côte d'Ivoire, and Liberia than to the formal sector economy of urban Conakry.

The sum of geographical isolation and economic exploitation from Conakry, together with self-imposed economic isolation from the highly distorted formal sector, led to an increasingly cloistered rural sector. On the economic front, the rural population turned increasingly to subsistence agriculture as a means of protecting their livelihood and avoiding the distorted exchange economy. On the political front, farmers tried to avoid public service responsibilities that would increase exposure to state pressures. On the social front, the rural population retreated to traditional kinship forms of solidarity with a renewed reliance on traditional chieftain authority (Azarya and Chazan 1987).

Beyond the official/unofficial and rural/urban divisions, finally, the Guinean economy was also dichotomized in a third, important way. A critical split developed between the functioning and performance of most of Guinea's economy and the nation's strong enclave mining sector. The latter operated under different rules from the rest of the formal sector. Mining companies have been predominantly private and foreign, both in ownership and in operation. These companies alone enjoyed almost complete foreign exchange convertibility and thus unrestricted access to foreign intermediary inputs and supplies. The mining sector thus came to represent an independent economy within the economy. Moreover, as a result of its different rules, the mining enclave experienced very different results. Accounting for 94 percent of all Guinean exports by 1975, mining surpassed the agricultural sector and became Guinea's leading foreign exchange earner. Meanwhile, the rest of Guinea's economy continued its long stagnation.

THE STRUCTURAL ADJUSTMENT PROGRAM

The death of Sekou Touré in 1984 represented a dramatic turning point for Guinea. The establishment of the Second Republic under General Lansana Conte on April 3, 1984, signified a profound break from the ideology of Guinea's political and economic past.[10] The CMRN (*Comité Militaire de Redressement Nationale*) led by Conte endorsed the notion of a pluralist society. On December 23, 1990, a new constitution was adopted, which for the first time allowed opposition political parties to form. This constitution guarantees the fundamental liberties, duties, and rights of citizens, restricts the maximum tenure of the President to two five-year terms, and separates the judiciary powers of the state from the executive. A Supreme Court and a High Council of Magistrates were established in late 1992, and in 1993, GNF 7.5 billion was apportioned in the government budget to organize elections. Presidential elections were held in December 1993, and Lansana Conte was elected in the first round with 52 percent of the votes. Parliamentary elections were tentatively scheduled within the first six months.

In conjunction with ongoing political reform, the Second Republic has commenced sweeping economic reform. The new regime has committed itself to accepting and promoting private ownership and foreign investment. The private sector is to become the engine of growth, while the role of the public sector is to be significantly curtailed.

Economic reform under Conte commenced with the PIRN (*Programme Intérimaire de Redressement Nationale*), an interim program covering the years 1985 to 1987. The PIRN was subsequently elaborated into the PREF (*Programme de Redressement Economique et Financier*), a general structural adjustment program supported by funds from the IMF and the World Bank.

The first phase of the PREF extended from 1986 through 1988. Reform measures taken under the first phase represented a dramatic shock treatment for the Guinean economy. With a focus on removing numerous state controls and eliminating pervasive distortions, phase one of the PREF concentrated on several specific measures. In particular, it committed the Government of Guinea (GOG) to: (1) undertake a large-scale devaluation and realign its exchange rate; (2) liberalize internal and external trade by eliminating price controls and state marketing; (3) restructure the banking and financial sector by shutting down state banks and by promoting commercial banking; (4) reduce the scale and increase the efficiency of the public sector by privatizing, liquidating, and restructuring parastatals as well as by reducing public sector employment; (5) increase and reorient public investment so as to improve productivity; and (6) institute commercial and institutional reforms that would promote private sector savings and investment.

The adjustment program has brought in a significant amount of foreign assistance to Guinea, phase one being well-supported by donor funds. In 1986 the World Bank extended to Guinea its First Structural Adjustment Credit worth 38.5 million SDR. Two consecutive 13-month stand-by arrangements were arranged for Guinea by the IMF in February 1986 (for SDR 33 million) and July 1987 (for SDR 11.6 million). A three-year SDR 27.2 million IMF Structural Adjustment Facility (SAF) arrangement was also made available to Guinea commencing in 1987. Moreover, substantial bilateral, non-project assistance was also rendered in support of Guinea's reform program.[11] An SDR 9.7 million Technical Assistance Project for Economic Management was financed by the International Development Association (IDA) of the World Bank. In addition, a Public Investment Program (PIP) was compiled that covered the period 1987 to 1989 and drew in a large amount of foreign financing for investment projects in Guinea. An estimated

83 percent of all project costs, or US$ 631 million, was derived from foreign sources (UNICEF 1990a). Finally, also in the context of the adjustment program, Guinea was permitted to reschedule its Paris Club debt in 1986.

The second phase of the PREF, commencing in 1988, has had as its objective the consolidation and fine-tuning of reforms undertaken under phase one. In particular, as we will discuss in the following pages, donors and the GOG have had to recognize the imperatives of addressing a number of binding structural constraints that currently impede the reform process. Thus, in concentrating on effectively pushing forward and adhering to initial reform guidelines, the second phase also focuses on (1) strengthening local economic management and policy implementation capabilities, (2) removing sector-specific infrastructural bottlenecks, (3) improving the legal and institutional fabric for the private sector, and (4) developing a social policy that will protect vulnerable populations and those most likely to be hurt by reforms. Considering the plight of those hurt by reforms will in turn facilitate the reform program from a political standpoint.

External support for Guinea's reform continues. Phase two of the PREF has been assisted by the second structural adjustment credit of 47 million SDR approved by the World Bank in June 1988. Additional financing in support of the second phase of the reform has come from France, the European Community, the African Development Bank, Japan, and the United States. In keeping with the social objectives of the second phase, furthermore, SDR 6.9 million was made available within the context of a Socio-Economic Development Support Project. A further rescheduling of payments on improved concessional terms of US$ 205 million in debts contracted before 1986 was also agreed upon in a new Paris Club agreement in late 1992.

NOTES

1. The secondary sector here does not include employees within the mining sector.

2. Specifically, it was estimated that the city of Conakry accounted for 63 percent of the manufacturing and industrial sectors' value added and accounted for 91 percent of sectoral employment (GOG 1985).

3. Upon excluding the city of Conakry from Lower Guinea.

4. This latter figure is the consequence of a mean 43 percent increase in the primary school enrollment ratio among low-income countries since 1965. The ratio for Guinea, in contrast, experienced no growth in over 20 years.

5. The accuracy of social indicators in Guinea to date is suspect owing to lack of survey data upon which to base estimates. Nevertheless the first representative sample survey of household welfare performed in Guinea, albeit limited to relatively prosperous Conakry, adds considerable credence to the perception of an impoverished country (CFNPP/ENCOMEC Survey).

6. Accusations of attempts to topple the Government and subsequent retaliations took place several times during the Touré regime: in 1960, 1961, 1965, 1969, 1970/71, 1976, 1977, and 1980 (Azarya and Chazan 1987).

7. While the Government attempted to reign in inflation by fixing official prices, inflation reached very high levels on the parallel market.

8. By the 1970s some estimates put the number of Guineans abroad at up to two million, namely about one-third of those living in Guinea (Conde 1976).

9. Nevertheless, while geographical factors may have impeded the flow of goods between urban areas and certain rural areas, they appear to have been less of an impediment to the movement of labor between these areas. Indeed one of the most important urban-rural links in Guinea has been migration to urban areas from rural areas and the consequent flow of remittances in the opposite direction.

10. It is nevertheless necessary to recognize that, despite ideological rigidities, the severity of Guinea's economic crisis come the 1980s may well have left even the First Republic with little policy options other than some degree of liberalization. In fact there was some loosening of controls by the regime in the few years preceding Sekou Touré's death. In particular, after having abolished private trade in 1975, Sekou Touré was faced with revolt and riot among market women in 1977. Under this unprecedented grass-roots political pressure, Touré took some steps to loosen up strict market controls commencing in 1978. (These were largely ineffective, however, as discussed in the Agricultural Section to follow.) Moreover, in the first months of 1984, before Sekou Touré's death, the Government had actually instituted staff working groups to examine the possibility of an exchange rate devaluation as proposed by the World Bank.

11. France provided a loan of FF 200 million in addition to a grant of FF 55 million, Japan contributed US$ 36 million, the United States US$ 15 million, Germany DM 8 million, Switzerland SF 10 million.

3

TRADE AND EXCHANGE RATE POLICY

HISTORICAL PERSPECTIVES

Historically, Guinea's trade and exchange systems have played the most important roles in determining the stagnation and structural distortions that have plagued Guinea since independence. Exchange rate policies since independence, as well as tariff and trade policy, have contributed to depressing official exports and compressing official imports. They served to bring the economy close to an economic stall, while driving practically all private trade into clandestine channels.

The newly established government quickly withdrew from the franc zone, severing the link between the official value of the Guinean currency and considerations of supply and demand. The Guinean franc, which replaced the CFA franc, was initially set at par with the CFA franc and subsequently fixed to a gold standard.[1] The Guinean franc appreciated relative to the French franc due to domestic inflation. This, in combination with the 1969 devaluation of the French franc, led to the replacement of the Guinean franc with the Guinea syli in 1972. The syli was still fixed to gold, but at a unit value ten times greater than the Guinean franc (i.e., GS 1 = 0.036 grams of gold = GF 10).

In 1975 Guinea moved away from a fixed gold standard to a pegged exchange rate regime in which the syli was pegged to the SDR. This peg (GS 1 = SDR 24.6853) remained unchanged for the next eleven years. This monetary strategy, undertaken during a period of minimal real growth, resulted in an increasing overvaluation of the GS, and high inflation rates. The official rate sharply appreciated relative to the parallel rate (the latter is considered a reasonable proxy for a shadow exchange rate).[2] The uncontrolled increase in the money supply resulted in a rapidly decreasing parallel rate. This situation prompted much of the economy to place savings in foreign exchange.

The national currency's dramatic overvaluation as a consequence of these policies reinforced a growing dichotomy between the official public and mixed sectors, and the emerging illegal private economy. Indeed, the private sector was officially prohibited from importing during the period 1965 to 1979, and parastatal companies had a monopoly on all imports. Consequently it was the public and mixed sectors that effectively had sole access to the official rate and to associated large implicit subsidies. The private sector for the most part acquired its imports "unofficially," at a rate determined by the parallel foreign exchange market.

The volume of parallel market exchange is difficult to determine, although it was estimated at GF 2 to 3 million a day in 1960, just following independence (PICK 1979). The market was centered in Conakry, with trade also notable in neighboring Freetown and Monrovia as well as through French banks. By 1971, however, the volume of trade on the parallel market declined significantly in Conakry as the government enforced its laws against private trade and threatened heavy punishment for those caught working in the parallel market. Sporadic trade was recorded at a parallel exchange rate that in 1971 was on the order of 400 percent of the official rate (Table 3).

The difference between the parallel and official rates was to vary widely in subsequent years due to dramatic shifts in the parallel rate. This presumably reflected the thin and uncertain supply of foreign exchange in the parallel market, as well as temporal shifts in the degree of enforcement of parallel market prohibition. The fundamental implication, nevertheless, remained the same. To the extent that the parallel rate in Conakry was above the true shadow exchange rate, whether from risk or capital flight, importers and consumers purchasing imports on the parallel market faced prices in excess of world prices.[3] At the same time, those who had access to imports at the official rate had their consumption subsidized, to the detriment of domestic production. Domestic beer, for example, was three times the price of imported beer purchased from hotels (Guillaumont 1985).

TABLE 3

Guinea: Exchange Rates, 1970–1992.[a]

Year	Official Rate	Parallel Rate	Official/ Parallel Ratio
1970	246.85	404.67	0.61
1971	246.85	1,084.58	0.23
1972	22.74	—	—
1973	20.46	56.00	0.37
1974	20.46	91.25	0.22
1975	20.46	57.08	0.36
1976	20.46	60.83	0.34
1977	20.46	60.92	0.34
1978	20.46	30.58	0.67
1979	20.46	30.58	0.67
1980	20.46	41.70	0.49
1981	20.46	73.08	0.28
1982	20.46	93.33	0.21
1983	20.46	128.08	0.16
1984	20.46	283.42	0.07
1985	20.46	310.67	0.07
1986	365.00	396.25	0.92
1987	429.00	443.33	0.97
1988	475.00	521.00	0.91
1989	593.00	642.79	0.92
1990	661.67	708.75	0.93
1991	758.00	815.05	0.93
1992	911.23	990.47	0.92[b]

Sources: PICK (various years); World Bank (1984b, 1990a); BCRG (1989); BCRG unpublished data for 1990, 1991, and 1992.
a. Rates and ratios are for mid-year.
b. End of year ratio.

Likewise, the overvalued official exchange rate penalized exporters. A farmer who sold coffee to the government for GS 34 per kilogram at the official price in 1977 could have fetched the equivalent of GS 45 if he had sold the coffee at the official, heavily taxed Ivoirian price across the border and then converted the CFAF into GS at the parallel rate. As this indirect export tax became close to prohibitive, domestic production and marketing declined. The negligible amount of trade that did continue did so illegally (see chapter 4 on agriculture and food policy). Furthermore, imports also declined as a result of falling exchange earnings and strict trade restrictions. Tariffs ranged from 0 to 1,000 percent, generally exceeding 100 percent.[4] Most foreign consumables disappeared from markets in Guinea during the mid-1970s. The compression of intermediate inputs also acted to reduce national production.

The shortage of foreign exchange at the official rate and the ensuing failure of the state trading entities to market agricultural products through official channels pressured the government to take some steps toward liberalization commencing in 1977. In an attempt to promote foreign investment, an official guarantee was given that permitted nonresidents to repatriate capital and profits. A new investment code, adopted in 1980, guaranteed investors that foreign investments would not be nationalized.

In 1979, private traders were also given permission to apply for import and export licenses. The state importing company was limited to importing five essential commodities (rice, pharmaceuticals, petroleum products, sugar, and flour) and to exporting two products (coffee and palm oil products). The private sector, however, still could not import at the official exchange rate. This implied that foreign exchange had to be raised through exporting or through conversion on the parallel market. As such, this step toward liberalization had the effect of sanctioning and thus increasing the volume and decreasing the risk of trade on the parallel market for foreign exchange. Thus the transaction costs of importing declined for licenseholders, even if they accessed foreign exchange rates on the parallel market. Other traders continued to import illegally, without applying for licenses (Guillaumont 1985). These very tentative steps toward trade liberalization thus deepened the parallel market but also initially had some impact in reducing the margin between the official and parallel exchange rates. The official exchange rate was 67 percent of the parallel in 1978 and 1979, compared with an average of 35 percent in the three preceding years (Table 3).

These gains, however, did not last long. The official exchange rate remained fixed despite a deteriorating domestic economy. Meanwhile expansionist monetary policies and the rapid increase in net domestic credit put pressure on the parallel exchange rate. In 1985 the official exchange rate had maintained its value of GS 20.46 per US dollar while the parallel exchange rate rose to an average of GS 311 per US dollar. The official exchange rate was thus only 7 percent of the parallel rate, the 93 percent margin larger than recorded at any other point in the decade (Table 3).

POLICY REFORMS

In its first step toward bringing the exchange rate into line, the new government under Lansana Conte initiated a second window for foreign exchange in October

1985 that was opened to private sector transactions. At this "private sector" window the exchange rate was pegged at GS 36 = F 1 (or GS 270 = US$ 1). Effectively this corresponded to more than a seventeenfold devaluation from the prevailing official rate that continued to be available at the original public sector window. Indicative of the need for and relative success of this devaluation is that the second window rate was now 87 percent of the parallel rate, in contrast to the first (public sector) window, which was only 7 percent of the parallel rate. The secondary market, however, was limited to sales of foreign exchange to the banking system alone. Foreign exchange could not be bought from the banking system at this rate. Moreover, while open to the private sector, sales through the secondary window were restricted to foreign exchange that was derived from certain sources only: capital inflow for investment, nonmining exports, grants, expenditures for tourist and business purposes, transfers, and sales of payments instruments.

In January 1986, with the formal embarkation of the structural adjustment program, the Guinean syli was replaced by the Guinean franc at par.[5] The rate at the first window was changed dramatically from GF 24.6853 = SDR 1 to GF 300 = US$ 1. More importantly, recognizing a persisting overvaluation of the national currency, the new government instituted a flexible exchange rate system, initially for the second (private sector) window only.[6] The rate at the second window was first changed to be roughly in line with the parallel rate, as it moved to GF 370 = US$ 1 from GF 270 = US$ 1. Finally, on June 1, 1986, the first and second windows were unified at the rate prevailing at the second window.

Despite the unification of the public and private sector rates, the procedure for allocating foreign exchange to the private sector remains distinct from that of the public sector. Misleadingly referred to as *le marché aux enchères*, however, this allocative mechanism is not an auction. Rather it is simply a procedure for allocating foreign exchange to the private sector. Clients submit demands for foreign exchange at their local commercial banks, not knowing exactly what the exchange rate will be, but expecting it not to deviate more than a few percentage points from the previous week's rate. These applications are then submitted to Guinea's Central Bank (*Banque Centrale de la Republique de Guinée*, or BCRG), along with import declarations.[7] Applications that are in order are then satisfied at a rate that is fixed at the Central Bank's discretion and announced at the end of that week. Private sector applications for foreign exchange have always been satisfied. The same exchange rate applies, moreover, to the large volume of public sector transactions. Between 1986 and 1991 public sector foreign exchange receipts, largely from mining taxes and balance-of-payments support, averaged five times private sector receipts (see Table 4). Private sector "auction" transac-

TABLE 4

Guinea: Foreign Exchange Budget, 1986–1991.
(in millions of US dollars)

	1986	1987	1988	1989	1990	1991
Foreign exchange revenue	158.0	289.8	284.6	363.5	457.27	467.00
Public sector	233.2	254.6	252.1	299.5	253.39	240.09
State	—	—	—	—	234.32	231.02
Taxes and mining	—	—	—	—	209.16	172.42
Lines of foreign credit	—	—	—	—	12.80	11.68
Fishing and other	—	—	—	—	12.36	46.92
Public enterprise	—	—	—	—	0.77	—
BCRG	—	—	—	—	18.30	9.07
Private sector	24.8	35.2	32.5	64.0	203.88	226.91
Of which auction supply	—	—	—	—	100.60	170.39
Export of goods	—	—	—	—	4.00	—
Surrendering of foreign exchange	—	—	—	—	96.10	—
Sale of convertible GF	—	—	—	—	0.12	—
Retrocession	—	—	—	—	0.38	—
Off-auction	—	—	—	—	—	56.52
Foreign exchange expenditure	215.1	287.4	320.4	351.7	438.14	468.94
Public sector	134.0	172.3	155.5	187.1	162.32	161.35
State	—	—	—	—	108.18	121.38
External debt	—	—	—	—	62.54	66.81
Current expenditure	—	—	—	—	45.64	54.57
Public enterprise	—	—	—	—	28.66	32.97
BCRG	—	—	—	—	25.48	7.00
Current expenditure	—	—	—	—	4.95	—
IMF	—	—	—	—	15.32	—
Other	—	—	—	—	5.21	—
Private sector	81.1	15.1	164.9	164.6	275.82	307.59
Of which auction demand	—	—	—	—	266.43	290.79
Import of goods	—	—	—	—	218.57	—
Travel allocation	—	—	—	—	13.98	—
Air tickets	—	—	—	—	14.23	—
Purchase of convertible GF	—	—	—	—	4.93	—
Transfers	—	—	—	—	10.69	—
Accounting discrepancies	—	—	—	—	3.70	—
Off-auction	—	—	—	—	9.69	16.80

Sources: BCRG unpublished data; BCRG (1990, 1992).

tions thus constitute only a fraction of the total volume of foreign exchange traded in Guinea. Moreover, it is not the auction that determines the price of foreign exchange. No price bids are ever made. Demand and supply at the auction do not equate, demand generally being in excess of supply among the private sector. Moreover, the exchange rate is relatively unresponsive to short-term changes in relative demand and supply at the private sector (or auction) allocation. For example, throughout the last quarter of 1990 (i.e., through twelve "fixings") the official rate remained unchanged at GF 675 per US dollar while the ratio of foreign exchange supplied by the private sector to foreign exchange demanded by the private sector fluctuated weekly between 0.18 and 0.84. In 1990 the Central Bank adjusted the official rate on only six out of fifty-two weeks.[8]

Rather than a free-floating exchange rate, then, the Guinea franc is determined on the basis of a managed peg. In broad terms, the price is fixed at the discretion of the BCRG with an eye on several factors. One is that the official rate stay not more than a few percentage points below the parallel exchange rate in order to prevent large-scale leakage of foreign exchange into the parallel market. Another is that a degree of stability be guaranteed in the foreign exchange markets. In recent years the BCRG has attempted not to exceed a target average annual exchange rate it agrees upon with financing agencies. Furthermore the BCRG is required to keep sight of its foreign exchange constraint as determined by total supply at any given time. With a large fraction of total foreign exchange supplies accruing to the public sector in the form of mining tax revenue and balance-of-payments support, it has been the surplus of foreign exchange on the public sector account that has consistently permitted the government to cover the excess of demand over supply on the private sector account.[9]

Reforms of the exchange rate regime have also been accompanied by the introduction of significant reform in Guinea's trade and payments system. Whereas under the First Republic all official trade was the purview of parastatal import and export entities, the state monopoly on trade was terminated in 1984. The private sector has since been permitted to import all commodities including, most recently, petroleum products. Similarly, the private sector can now engage in export activity in all commodities but gold.

Import licensing per se was also abolished in 1986. Imports are now permitted under the purview of the Exchange Control Department of the Central Bank. Within the private sector, both off-auction and auction avenues of attaining foreign exchange for imports are permissible. The former generally entails authorization to import using one's own foreign exchange. Indeed, as a result of reforms in 1986, Guinean nationals are permitted to maintain convertible Guinea franc accounts domestically. Foreign exchange earned from remittances from abroad and from export revenues, both official and unofficial, are converted into Guinea francs and kept on deposit. Until 1992, foreign exchange revenues of exporters were retained for up to one month in accounts at commercial banks before having to be exchanged for local currency at the Central Bank. As of 1992, exporters were allowed to hold 25 percent of their export receipts in foreign exchange. Deposits are not restricted and depositors may withdraw in the form of foreign exchange, for authorized transactions.

Importers, in addition, can also use foreign exchange bought from the Central Bank (BCRG) through the auction. Until early 1989, permission to access the auction required prior approval by the BCRG of the type, quantity, and value of goods to be imported. Delays in providing such approval initially served as a continued form of rationing. A new system was adopted in 1989, abolishing the requirement of advanced verification of import declarations. Instead, the BCRG now checks after the sale that purchased foreign exchange is actually used as initially specified on the import declaration. In an additional move to liberalize the trade regime, the tariff structure was also dramatically simplified in January 1986. The basic tariff rate was set at 10 percent as opposed to the dispersed and generally higher tariffs extant during the First Republic. Certain essential goods, including agricultural inputs, faced a reduced tariff of 5 percent. Originally there were no taxes on exports.

Several adjustments have been made to the tariff schedule over the reform period. An export tax of 2 percent that was placed on all agricultural products was eliminated in January 1991 in an attempt to promote exports. Meanwhile changes in the tariff structure have resulted in higher net import tariffs since July 1986. In July 1986 the turnover tax on imports (TCA, or *taxe sur le chiffre d'affaire à l'importation*) was increased from 2 to 8 percent, and then again to 10 percent in January 1988. In March 1990, customs and fiscal taxes were raised again, increasing the net levy on imports. Taxes on food products, with the exception of rice, pharmaceuticals, and fertilizers, were raised from 15 to 18 percent (10 percent TCA + 6 percent "entry" tax + 2 percent customs duties). Subsequently all basic food items have been subject to a total duty of 30 percent. Imported rice, meanwhile, while initially subject to only a 10 percent net levy (only the TCA), now faces duties and tariffs totaling 22 percent (see chapter 4 on agriculture and food policy). In a significant attempt to restrict the importation of consumer goods, commencing in March 1990 the BCRG required the advanced deposit, in local currency, of 20 percent of the foreign exchange value of imports of all consumer goods.[10] This controversial and unpopular requirement was eliminated in early 1992. Finally, luxury items such as alcohol and tobacco have and continue to face a tariff of 25 percent plus a surtax of 20 to 130 percent, depending on the commodity.[11] These tariff adjustments appear to have been motivated more by the government's need to address low public revenues than its desire to secure greater protection on the trade front. Indeed no concerted assessment has yet been made of nominal and effective protection levels in Guinea.

ECONOMIC CONSEQUENCES OF REFORMS

Reform and the Exchange Rate

The most dramatic and significant reform undertaken by the Second Republic was the severance from a fixed exchange rate in lieu of a more adaptable exchange rate regime and the consequent large devaluation of the Guinean franc. The government devalued the franc seventeenfold from the last quarter of 1985 to the end of the first quarter of 1986. The devaluation was also pronounced in real effective terms.[12] More specifically, only about 30 percent of the (official) nominal devaluation was passed through to domestic prices. Thus, the REER was initially devalued by approximately 1,205 percent (Figure 2).[13]

Despite the impressive accomplishments in rationalizing the exchange regime, the fluctuating margin between the parallel and official exchange rates indicates the persistence of problems in the management of Guinea's exchange rate. Indeed, the convergence between the official and parallel exchange rates has been neither complete nor continuous. After the convergence of the two rates at the outset of the auction in early 1986, the spread increased to 20 percent by the latter part of that year. The reappearance of a large spread at this juncture was a result of a number of factors. First among these was the continued ban on official imports of certain goods. Second was a continuation of restrictions on most nontrade exchange, such as the purchase of airline tickets and other services. Third, pressure on the parallel market exchange rate was also enhanced by the expansion of credit (IMF 1987a). Traders were unable to borrow so as to participate in the auction. Fourth, participation in the auction required a minimum bid of US$ 10,000. Fifth, by early 1987 the government had begun requiring the advance deposit of Guinea francs to purchase foreign exchange for certain imports. Of course, the parallel market has also been a cash market, but traditionally the official market had the advantage of making credit available. Sixth, administrative procedures were made more difficult for accessing foreign ex-

FIGURE 2

Guinea: Exchange Rate Indices (1986 1st quarter = 100).

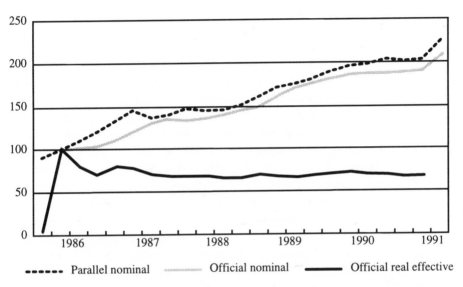

----- Parallel nominal   ░░░░░░░ Official nominal   ▬▬▬ Official real effective

Sources: Authors' calculations; GOG (1987c, 1991b); IMF (various years, 1990b); World Bank (1990a).

change for the purposes of import. Many businessmen were unaware of the required procedures. Seventh, the real effective exchange rate actually appreciated quite dramatically in early 1986 (Figure 2), as the auction rate, really a managed float, failed to capture the increase in costs of producing tradable goods that resulted from a higher price level. In contrast, the parallel rate responded more sensitively to inflation, contributing to the reappearance of a growing divergence between the two rates in late 1987.

All these factors were manifested in the low volume of exchange through the auction upon its initiation. In 1986 the BCRG sold US$ 87.9 million and bought only US$ 12.9 million through the auction (USAID 1987b). The bulk of foreign exchange sales was supplied by the influx of loans and concessional grants to the government from the donor community as well as from government revenue from the export sector (primarily bauxite and alumina).[14]

It was in the interest of drawing foreign exchange back into official channels that the government sought to restrain the spread between the two rates by undertaking a number of further reforms beginning in January 1987. First, foreign exchange trade through the auction was permitted for almost all current account transactions.[15] Second, almost all import restrictions were removed.[16] Third, all certified dividends and royalties could now be transferred through the official channel. Fourth, deposits with the banking system could now accrue interest. Fifth, in May 1987, the government dispensed with the requirement of advanced deposits for certain imports.

These factors, coupled with an increase in donor financing, were manifested in the increase in volume of transactions through the auction. In fact, the net volume of exchange transactions (purchases and sales) through the official channel increased by 71 and 77 percent in 1987 and in 1988, respectively (USAID 1987b, 1990). The growth in private sector foreign exchange demand has continued since, albeit at a slower rate, increasing by 11 percent in 1991.

The midstream adjustments of 1987 also helped to notably reduce the gap between the parallel and official exchange rates. The margin between the two rates fell from 19 percent in the first quarter of 1987 to 9 percent by the first quarter of 1988. Moreover, through 1988 and 1989 the margin was maintained at approximately 8 percent (even on a monthly basis in 1989).[17] This is in keeping with the stated government commitment, under the Second Structural Adjustment Credit of 1988, to maintain the difference between the official and parallel exchange rates at less than 10 percent and at a target level of 7 percent. The prevailing view among donors and the government is that this low margin will prevent any substantial leakage from the official to the parallel market.

The persistence of some trade on the parallel market may reflect both continued capital flight as well as problems with the auction process itself. In particular, the margin between the two exchange rates can be partly explained by certain administrative encumbrances still associated with operating in the official market. These encumbrances continue to discourage entry into the auction, encourage the use of the parallel market, and contribute to persisting distortions in the foreign exchange market. We shall consider the stumbling blocks in turn. First, many traders have been discouraged from participating in the banking system: participation has required being present in Conakry, filling out numerous forms, and paying high banking fees. Participation in the auction has required that a trader be registered with the Ministry of Commerce and have a license to participate. The trader must also have an account at a commercial bank. Second, and perhaps most important, by avoiding official channels traders also avoid filling out import declaration forms and consequently avoid customs and duty payments. Indeed most petty traders, importing from bordering Sierra Leone and Liberia, for example, would find it difficult and unattractive to deal with the commercial banks in Conakry. They invariably purchase their foreign exchange from the parallel market.[18] Third, by avoiding official channels, traders can avoid even the short negative list and use the auction to transfer interest and dividend payments overseas, for example. Fourth, circumventing the auction would allow importers to avoid the preshipment verification that is part of the official process and costs the importer a fee. Fifth, circumventing official channels also frequently means circumventing long administrative delays that are associated with the official process. Sixth, the disincentive to attain foreign exchange through official channels was significantly enhanced with the policy, effective between 1990 and 1992, that once again required advanced deposits of local currency at the BCRG by traders who want to import consumption goods.

The discussion to this point has focused on the nominal exchange rate and its behavior relative to the parallel market. Perhaps more importantly, however, policy adjustments have had a perceptible impact on the real effective exchange rate. In essence, the exchange rate adjustments of the reform period have led to a significant depreciation of the real effective exchange rate relative to its pre-1986 level. The REER (index of GF per US dollar) in early 1991 was still over eight times its level in 1985.

While the massive devaluation in the REER relative to 1986 is the biggest story here, it is also important to recognize that the REER has moved significantly since 1986 (Figure 2). In particular, the REER has, on net, appreciated since the initial large-scale devaluation of 1986. By early 1991 the official REER (GF per US dollar) had appreciated to 65 percent of its level in early 1986.

Indeed after the early gain of the initial devaluation, the real effective exchange rate appreciated by 26 percent between the second quarter of 1986 and the second quarter of 1988. Despite a continued 28 percent devaluation of the official nominal exchange rate over that period, the high rate of inflation that followed the initial dramatic devaluation and the other restrictions that persisted on the exchange markets through 1987, discussed above, contributed to this appreciation. So too did the infusion of foreign exchange, primarily in the form of loans from international financial institutions as well as bilateral aid. The midstream adjustments of 1987 (which served to decelerate inflation and accelerate the devaluation of the nominal rate to keep pace with the parallel rate) effectively helped stabilize the REER between 1988 and 1990. Then, between the first quarter of 1990 and the first quarter of 1991, the REER again experienced a 13 percent decline, with inflation picking up toward the year's end with a 57 percent increase in the price of gasoline. Partly in an attempt to reverse this real effective depreciation, the BCRG undertook a 14.5 percent nominal devaluation over the course of 1991. In 1992, the nominal rate was rapidly devalued by 20 percent from GF 803 per US dollar in January to GF 923 per dollar by April, at which level it remained through the end of the year.[19]

Finally, as alluded to in the devaluation simulation, while exchange rate policy has had a real impact on the price of foreign exchange in Guinea, it does not tell the whole story. The real effective exchange rates actually faced by both importers and exporters is affected by movements in import quotas, tariff levels, and export taxes over the adjustment period. If de facto import quotas and tariffs have been reduced over the adjustment period, the real effective exchange rate for imports (reflecting the real price of importables) will have increased less than the level attributable to the nominal devaluation (and portrayed with the REER in Figure 2). If, on the other hand, explicit or implicit de facto import tariffs have risen since 1985, the effective exchange rate for imports may have increased by more than represented with the REER in Figure 2. Similarly, to the extent that de facto export taxes and other trade restrictions have been reduced over the adjustment period, the real effective exchange rate for exports (reflecting the real price of exports) would have increased by more than the level attributable to the nominal devaluation alone.

Unfortunately, the lack of disaggregated data on sources of government revenues prior to 1986 makes it impossible to accurately estimate how pre-reform tariffs and export tax rates have changed and hence to quantify movements in the real effective exchange rate for imports or exports.[20]

Reform and the Balance of Payments

The weakness of Guinean data, especially from its years under Sekou Touré, seriously limit any analysis of trends in balance-of-payments data in the 1980s. Data from official records through 1985, for example, vary widely among sources. Also, they exclude the significant foreign exchange movements taking place through unofficial channels. Since 1986, after the establishment of the Second Republic, a concerted effort has been made to compile balance-of-payments data that are more accurate.[21]

Keeping these facts in mind, Table 5 gives the story of the evolution and state of Guinea's external sector in the face of recent reforms. In the years 1982 through 1985 Guinea ran large balance-of-payments deficits. Between 1983 through 1985 these overall deficits averaged close to US\$ 100 million per annum. Trade balances, although small, were positive, largely due to the strong performance of the mining sector in exporting bauxite and alumina.[22] On the other hand, net services and private transfers, reflecting the repatriation of mining salaries and profits, more than counterbalanced the trade surpluses, resulting

TABLE 5

Guinea: Balance of Payments, 1981–1993.
(in millions of US dollars)

	1981	1982	1983	1984	1985	1986	1987	1988	1989	1990	1991	1992	1993 (est.)
Trade balance	67.0	66.3	135.8	103.5	136.5	147.5	129.7	-6.3	135.9	66.1	19.9	-118.6	-122.9
Exports, f.o.b.	493.0	443.9	501.4	510.0	512.9	655.2	629.8	597.3	722.8	789.3	754.8	621.3	607.1
Bauxite and alumina	—	428.4	490.7	502.0	495.0	467.2	550.0	500.7	615.1	678.4	644.3	498.6	466.4
Other	—	15.5	10.7	8.0	17.9	188.0	79.8	96.6	107.7	110.9	110.5	122.7	140.7
Imports, c.i.f.	-426.0	-377.6	-365.6	-406.5	-376.5	-507.7	-500.1	-603.6	-586.9	-723.2	-734.9	-739.9	-730.0
Public sector	—	-224.1	-229.8	-264.0	-228.5	-204.3	-137.8	-159.8	-162.1	-168.0	-153.8	-152.6	-145.6
Mixed mining companies	—	-153.5	-135.8	-142.5	-145.0	-99.0	-160.9	-151.8	-140.5	-230.3	-256.4	-234.2	-217.9
Other private	—	—	—	—	-3.0	-204.4	-201.4	-292.0	-284.3	-324.9	-324.8	-353.1	-366.5
Services and private transfers, net	—	-183.2	-161.4	+165.9	-201.6	-249.8	-296.2	-309.2	-361.7	-361.1	-302.8	-284.1	-273.7
Public transfers	—	26.5	18.2	51.0	18.0	42.3	82.8	83.5	98.0	100.9	109.5	135.6	117.9
Current account deficit (–)	—	-90.4	-7.5	-11.4	-47.2	-60.1	-83.6	-232.0	-127.9	-194.1	-173.5	-267.2	-278.7
Capital movements, net	—	57.4	31.0	-24.5	-34.8	36.9	87.4	76.4	119.4	117.9	106.0	156.5	189.1
Public capital, long-term	—	6.6	25.7	-19.5	-32.0	49.8	66.2	51.9	93.0	61.0	52.0	61.8	105.1
Disbursements[a]	—	86.1	91.9	78.9	70.0	173.0	162.2	193.6	214.2	185.0	207.5	222.0	255.6
Amortization	—	-79.5	-66.3	-98.4	-102.0	-123.2	-96.4	-141.4	-121.1	-124.1	-155.4	-128.8	-97.9
Public capital, short-term	—	—	—	—	14.2	-15.2	0.0	0.0	0.0	11.3	-1.2	-1.2	-4.5
Mixed mining companies, net	—	44.2	8.6	-5.0	-17.0	-2.7	16.0	18.0	16.4	34.7	43.8	83.4	62.7
Other private, including direct investment, net	—	—	—	—	—	5.0	5.2	6.5	10.0	10.9	11.4	12.6	25.8
Errors and omissions	—	-29.9	-127.2	-59.1	-7.3	-28.9	-14.8	16.2	-28.0	11.3	-35.6	-7.5	20.3
Overall balance	—	-62.9	-103.7	-95.0	-89.3	-52.0	-56.0	-127.6	-28.0	-37.7	-67.6	-82.5	-11.4
Financing items	—	62.9	103.7	95.0	89.3	52.0	6.0	127.6	28.0	37.7	67.6	82.5	11.4
Debt rescheduling	—	—	—	—	—	—	31.8	23.2	75.8	60.5	76.5	384.4	58.9

(Table continues on the following page.)

TABLE 5 (continued)

	1981	1982	1983	1984	1985	1986	1987	1988	1989	1990	1991	1992	1993 (est.)
Change in arrears	—	—	—	—	—	—	7.5	77.5	-26.1	27.9	9.3	-329.6	79.3
Deferred payment	—	—	—	—	—	—	0.0	0.0	0.0	0.0	0.0	31.0	-77.5
Reserves	—	—	—	—	—	—	-33.3	26.9	-21.7	-50.7	-18.2	-3.3	-49.3
Of which: IMF credit (net)	—	—	—	—	—	0.0	-9.2	-19.6	-18.4	—	—	—	—
Current account balance/GDP	—	—	—	—	—	-3.3	-4.3	-10.3	-5.4	-7.1	-5.8	-9.0	-8.8
Current account balance (excluding public transfers)/GDP	—	—	—	—	—	-5.6	-8.5	-14.0	-9.5	-10.7	-9.5	-13.5	-12.5
Exports/GDP	—	—	—	—	—	35.6	32.3	26.4	30.3	28.7	25.3	20.9	19.2
Exports (excluding mining companies)/GDP	—	—	—	—	—	10.2	4.1	4.3	4.5	4.0	3.7	4.1	4.2
Imports/GDP	—	—	—	—	—	-27.6	-25.7	-26.7	-24.6	-26.3	-24.6	-24.9	-23.0
Private imports (excluding mining companies)/GDP	—	—	—	—	—	-11.1	-10.3	-12.9	-111.9	-11.8	-10.9	-11.9	-11.6
Gross official reserves (year end)[b]													
In millions of US$	—	56.0	22.5	14.7	2.2	21.0	67.6	43.1	72.6	115.7	138.7	154.9	190.8
In months of nonmining non-PIP imports	—	—	—	—	—	1.0	2.4	1.1	2.0	2.8	2.3	2.5	3.1
GDP in current prices (million US$)	—	—	—	—	—	1,839.1	1,948.5	2,259.2	2,387.5	2,751.2	2,982.0	2,974.1	3,170.2

Sources: GOG (1993b); IMF (1987, 1993); World Bank (1990a).
a. Disbursement figures include project-related loans, IDA and cofinancing, and drawings on USSR special loans.
b. Reserve figures include gold in data after 1986.

in current account deficits throughout the period prior to 1986. Interest payments, government payments for the public investment program (PIP), and large net transfers in the form of investment income payments by mixed mining companies resulted in large negative current account balances. Whereas initially this was partially offset by positive balances on the capital account in 1982 and 1983, the capital account too began to show negative balances after 1983. This trend of the capital account is explained both by movements in long-term public capital and also by the net capital flow within the mining sector. Commencing in 1984, amortization swamped disbursements of public capital. Consequently there was a net average inflow of public capital of US\$ 16 million in 1982/83, and a net average outflow of public capital of US\$ 26 million in 1984/85. Similarly, whereas there was net positive investment by mining companies in 1982/83, commencing in 1984 the mining companies too contributed to the net capital outflow.

The large negative balance-of-payments deficits between 1982 and 1985 were financed by two principal means. First, over the four-year period, Guinea experienced an average net depletion of reserves of US\$ 32.4 million per year. By 1985, end-of-period exchange reserves were down to US\$ 2.2 million, from US\$ 56 million in 1982. Second, the country accumulated large payments arrears which, by 1985, had reached US\$ 75.1 million (IMF 1987a).

It was within the context of this crisis that Guinea undertook its sweeping reforms in 1986. The effects of the trade and exchange system changes instituted starting in 1986 are revealed by balance-of-payments estimates for 1986 through 1992.[23] With the devaluation of the official exchange rate and the withdrawal of trade restrictions, private sector transactions through official channels increased. Between 1985 and 1990 official exports increased by 54 percent; between 1986 and 1990 the increase was 20 percent (Table 5). The value of exports then dropped in 1991 and again more sharply in 1992 and 1993, almost totally because of lower world prices in the mining sector. The initial growth was due largely to the dramatic increase in nonmining exports from their previously low level. The improvement in agricultural exports was seen as an early success of exchange rate adjustment and trade liberalization. However, one might question the extent to which these figures represent an important supply response rather than simply the rechanneling of previous levels of exports into official channels (see chapter 4 on agriculture and food policy).[24]

As in most Sub-Saharan African countries, the balance-of-payments problem in Guinea since the commencement of adjustment has been that, in the short term at least, exports have been unable to keep up with the large increases in imports. Indeed, the trade balance, while remaining positive, declined from US\$ 136.5

million in 1985 to US$ 129.7 million in 1987; it further declined to a deficit of US$ 6.3 million in 1988 and then, after an increase in 1989, fell again to a deficit of US$ 118.6 million in 1992. In addition to the recent difficulties in maintaining mining export revenue levels in the face of price declines, the deterioration in the trade balance is largely due to the increase in private imports that came with liberalization. According to IMF, World Bank, and GOG estimates (Table 5), imports by the private (nonmining) sector increased from US$ 3 million in 1985 to US$ 204 million in 1986 and to US$ 357 million by 1992, while public sector imports have generally declined. The trade balance deterioration in 1988 was partly due to a 20.7 percent increase in import value, which in turn was led primarily by a 45 percent increase in nonmining private imports. These imports caused a 67 percent increase in foreign exchange demand in the auction that year. Total imports have grown at an average rate of 8.6 percent annually between 1986 and 1992. Exports meanwhile increased only at an annual rate of 3.0 percent between 1986 and 1991 (before the 18 percent drop registered in 1992).

The increase in imports and consequent trade balance movements reflect a number of factors. First, the increase in imports was caused by a pent-up demand. Second, with respect to imports too there was apparently a large-scale rechanneling of extant demand that had earlier been satisfied through unofficial channels or financed through own resources. Third, balance-of-payments support permitted imports in excess of exports. To the extent that concessional financial inflows contributed to slowing a depreciation of the exchange rate, they may have additionally served to reign in exports while imports increased. The incremental eliminations of import restrictions, including the elimination of the 20 percent advance deposit requirement for importers in 1992, are also evident in the escalation of import values over time.

The decline in trade balances, finally, is also attributable to adverse movements in the terms of trade. Guinea's terms of trade began to fall sharply in 1986, dropping by 12.2 percent that year (World Bank 1986b). The terms of trade change has been a result not only of sharp increases in import prices since 1986, but also of a fall in the world prices of Guinea's major exports: bauxite, alumina, and coffee. Guinea's 1988 trade balance, the lowest on record in the decade, was partially explained by a 5.2 percent fall in export value, caused largely by a fall in BCRG's bauxite export price and by a fall in the value of agricultural exports. Adverse terms of trade movements have continued to affect Guinea. In 1990 the price of exported coffee fell due to the failure of the International Coffee Agreement and the suspension of quotas. That year Guinea was also affected by the increase in the price of imported petroleum due to the Gulf crisis.[25] Between

1990 and 1993, Guinea's export revenue fell by 23 percent, due primarily to a fall in the world price of bauxite and alumina, and the country had its first negative trade balance since the onset of reforms in 1986.

In addition to declining positive trade balances through 1987, Guinea continued to run even larger negative balances on its services and transfers accounts. Interest payments and transfer of investment income by the mining companies remained high. As a result, the current account deficits of 1986 and 1987, averaging US$ 71.9 million a year, were larger than those of the previous three years, which had averaged US$ 22.0 million per year. This is despite the large increase in public transfers that followed adjustment.[26] Excluding public transfers, the average current account deficit for 1986 through 1989 was approximately –9.5 percent of GDP. Based on GOG estimates, this deficit increased to –11.3 percent between 1991 and 1993.

The adjustment program's effect was also felt on the capital account. This was not so much due to the policy impacts of reform per se but rather to the inflow of public capital that has traditionally been associated with formal structural adjustment. It was also due to accelerated disbursements of project loans. Whereas there had been negative net flows of long-term public capital issued to Guinea in the two years preceding 1986, in 1986 alone US$ 173 million of loans were disbursed. Disbursements have continued at these high levels, with Guinea acquiring US$ 207 million of loans in 1989.[27] Despite this inflow, however, and due to continued high levels of amortization, the capital account surplus has been unable to compensate for the large current account deficit.

As a result, even after 1985, the overall balance of payments has continued to be in deficit. Nevertheless, the deficits have generally been lower in the years since 1986 than in the four years prior. With the exception of 1988, the deficit on the overall balance remained below the US$ 88 million averaged during the period 1982 through 1986, though it then rose every year between 1989 and 1992. Clearly the overall decline has been due primarily to the increased inflow of long-term capital and to the increase in public transfers that followed the adoption of the structural adjustment program.

Financing of the balance-of-payments deficit since the commencement of the formal adjustment program has been made possible by the rescheduling of debt and the extension of IMF credits. For example, total debt relief in 1986 reached close to US$ 353 million; in 1989, after another round of Paris Club rescheduling, total debt rescheduling was US$ 147 million.[28] In 1988, however, in the absence of debt relief and in the face of a large balance-of-payments deficit, Guinea had to run down its foreign exchange reserves (by US$ 42 million) and run up its arrears (by US$ 76 million) (World Bank 1990a). In 1992 once again the overall balance deficit was financed by debt rescheduling by the Paris Club (for a total of US$ 384 million) along with the sale of gold.

The importance of annual debt relief to allow Guinea to meet its balance-of-payments obligations is a matter of concern. It underlines the nation's debt crisis: Guinea's debt has been increasing at a rapid rate (Table 6). By 1992 total long-term debt (outstanding and disbursed) was almost US$ 2.5 billion, having experienced an average annual rate of growth of 10 percent over the previous decade.[29]

The 1992 debt level is high relative to the past, but it should also be noted that Guinea did not see the same acceleration in debt burdens experienced by other African countries during the 1980s. This is largely because Guinea had already reached high debt burden levels during the 1970s. The nation's total external debt to GNP ratio climbed over the initial years of reform, peaking at 99 percent in 1988, before falling to 86 percent in 1992. This compares to average debt to GNP ratios of 90 percent for other Sub-Saharan African countries in 1987 (UNDP and World Bank 1989; World Bank 1990c).

Reform and Export and Import Composition

EXPORTS. The devaluation of the exchange rate, in lowering the foreign exchange cost of Guinean exports, was a key policy tool in priming the agricultural cash crop sector. After independence agricultural exports as a percentage of total exports had fallen dramatically while, conversely, the share of mining exports had increased. In 1957, agricultural exports were 71 percent of total exports; in 1973 they were 29 percent of total exports; and in 1981 they were 0.8 percent of total exports (Figure 3). The decline in performance of the agricultural sector relative to the mining sector resulted in part from the large difference in the exchange rates faced by the two sectors prior to 1986. Adjustment, in raising the exchange rate applicable to agricultural exports, was expected to stimulate agricultural exports and their share in total exports.

Increases in agricultural exports since the commencement of adjustment, while promising at first, were slow to take off. In Figure 3 this is shown by the increase in the share of agricultural exports from 0.8 percent to 5.2 percent between 1981 and 1986, and the subsequent stall in this share's growth to 7.7 percent in 1990, and the larger increase to 12.4 percent in 1992.[30]

The large initial increase in agricultural exports was likely due, once again, to the rechanneling of existing exports to official channels. The subsequent slowdown, on the other hand, is symptomatic of more serious structural problems. The fact that exports have not responded to the realignment of the exchange rate points to a number of domestic constraints beyond the trade and exchange

TABLE 6

Guinea: Long-term Public Debt, Outstanding and Disbursed, 1970 to 1992.
(in millions of US dollars)

	1970	1975	1980	1981	1982	1983	1984	1985	1986	1987	1988	1989	1990	1991	1992
Long-term debt (outstanding and disbursed)	312	759	1,004	1,255	1,225	1,199	1,115	1,292	1,621	1,883	2,031	1,958	2,244	2,403	2,466
of which:															
Official (percent)	87.18	87.48	84.16	85.26	85.22	84.74	83.95	84.21	94.02	94.69	93.01	93.82	95.14	95.92	95.82
Multilateral (percent)	6.41	9.49	12.95	12.35	13.80	15.43	19.19	19.89	21.34	23.63	23.73	28.86	30.21	34.46	37.10
IBRD (percent)	6.41	8.96	5.48	4.14	4.00	3.75	4.30	4.26	3.76	3.45	2.31	1.89	1.25	0.62	0.00
Bilateral (percent)	80.45	78.00	71.31	72.91	71.43	69.22	64.75	64.32	72.67	71.06	69.28	64.96	64.93	61.42	58.72
Private (percent)	12.82	12.52	15.74	14.74	14.78	15.35	16.05	15.79	5.92	5.31	6.99	6.18	4.81	4.08	4.14
Long-term debt service (TDS)	15	35	98	84	78	66	108	61	53	142	117	100	148	121	80
Principal repayments	11	22	74	62	54	45	86	42	40	102	87	68	95	82	47
Interest repayments	4	13	23	22	24	21	22	19	13	41	30	32	53	39	33
of which:															
Official (percent)	60.00	88.57	85.71	84.52	80.77	80.30	87.04	90.16	96.23	95.77	80.34	83.00	83.11	90.91	90.00
Multilateral (percent)	6.67	22.86	22.45	13.10	15.38	19.70	13.89	24.59	45.28	18.31	27.35	34.00	22.30	25.62	57.50
IBRD (percent)	6.67	22.86	9.18	9.52	10.26	12.12	8.33	13.11	22.64	9.86	13.68	14.00	9.46	11.57	18.75
Bilateral (percent)	53.33	65.71	63.27	71.43	65.38	60.61	73.15	67.21	50.94	77.46	52.99	49.00	60.81	65.29	32.50
Private (percent)	40.00	11.43	13.27	14.29	19.23	19.70	12.96	9.84	3.77	4.23	19.66	17.00	16.89	9.09	10.00
Total external debt/GNP (percent)	—	—	—	86.2	87.3	76.8	68.3	80.5	93.6	95.1	99.1	85.1	89.3	88.4	86.0
Total external debt service/GNP (percent)	—	—	—	6.2	5.8	4.2	6.4	4.0	3.8	6.5	5.1	3.9	5.4	4.1	2.6
Total interest payments/GNP (percent)	—	—	—	2.0	2.1	1.6	1.6	1.6	1.0	2.2	1.5	1.5	2.1	1.5	1.2

Sources: World Bank (1989d, 1990b, 1994b).

FIGURE 3
Guinea: Composition of Exports.

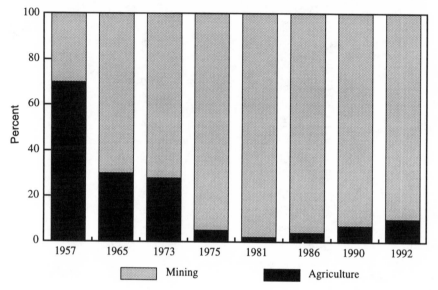

Source: IMF (1993).

system. Some of these constraints relate to trade. Impediments include, for example, problems with in-country transportation and infrastructure as well as with port facilities and management. They include the lack of a proper legal and institutional framework for traders and their difficulty in accessing credit. Some of the constraints to export response lie with agricultural production itself. For example, it is unclear to what extent exchange rate and price reform have translated into much higher producer prices, especially in the face of high transportation costs. Nor is it clear that farmers have increased yields by applying fertilizer. (These issues are discussed more extensively in chapter 4 on agriculture and food policy.)

IMPORTS. The immediate and rapid increase in imports, as discussed previously, had much to do with the negative impact of devaluation and liberalization on the trade balance from 1986 through 1989. This acceleration poses several questions relating to how liberalization in general, and the foreign exchange auction system in particular, may have affected import composition on the one hand and the sustainability of Guinea's balance-of-payments position on the other.

Indeed, in addition to determining exchange rates, the introduction of auctions has at times affected the composition and source of trade (Sahn and Alderman 1987). An examination of Guinea's auction records for 1989 and 1990 reveals the general uses of foreign exchange purchased officially in those years and gives an indication of the implications of the liberalization process to current account composition (Table 7).[31] In particular, there is a heavy consumption bias among imports through the auction. In 1989, 81 percent of all commodity imports through the auction were accounted for by consumer goods; 51 percent of all foreign exchange sold through the auction was used to import food; 21 percent was used specifically to import rice. In 1990 the BCRG's requirement of an advance deposit on imports of consumption goods accomplished the specific objective of reducing rice imports, whose nominal value decreased by 14 percent and share within the auction fell to 15 percent. Imports of consumer goods increased to constitute 80 percent of auction imports in 1992 with the removal of the requirement for advanced deposits. Intermediate goods and equipment constituted only 19 percent of total auction imports in 1989 and 20 percent in 1992. This low share of capital and intermediate good imports by the private, nonmining sector is a disheartening indicator of the prospects for early growth in the nonmining sectors.

If total national imports (auction plus off-auction) are examined, as opposed to imports of the private sector through the auction alone, a slightly different picture emerges with respect to import composition. Specifically the share of commodity imports represented by foodstuff is lower (19 percent) and the shares for capital and intermediate goods increases (see Figure 4). The larger share of capital and intermediate goods in total imports reflects the importance of purchases such as petroleum (15 percent), capital goods (20 percent), and intermediate goods (35 percent) through off-auction channels, by the government and the mining companies (GOG 1991b).

CONCLUSIONS

The above observations point to some impressive accomplishments in the reform of Guinea's exchange rate policy and management, as well as of trade policy in general. Commercial imports of consumer and other goods have increased dramatically, exports have shown some tentative signs of responding, and prices rather than quantities are beginning to clear markets. Efficiency gains have also been garnered through the removal of gross distortions, which contributed to market failures and rent-seeking. Urban consumers and traders have likely been the greatest beneficiaries of these reforms, with plentiful supplies of food (especially imported rice) and other consumer goods returning to the

TABLE 7
Guinea: Composition of Auction Imports.

	1989 US$	Share	1990 US$	Share	1991 US$	Share	1992 US$	Share
Consumer goods								
Food								
Rice	38,567,393	20.64	33,269,307	15.22	38,385,004	16.50	34,833,106	15.57
Sugar	13,368,262	7.15	15,820,617	7.24	14,787,406	6.36	15,137,175	6.77
Oil	6,986,611	3.74	8,011,340	3.67	5,695,458	2.45	8,943,655	4.00
Flour	12,991,226	6.95	17,961,367	8.22	16,226,063	6.97	16,670,819	7.45
Drinks	10,909,456	5.84	6,074,803	2.78	3,479,207	1.50	1,814,889	0.81
Other	11,964,228	6.40	28,854,999	13.20	30,189,880	12.97	32,452,191	14.50
Total	94,787,176	50.72	109,992,433	50.32	108,763,018	46.74	109,851,834	49.10
Nonfood	56,807,881	30.40	60,669,706	27.76	67,380,045	28.96	66,809,135	29.86
Total	151,595,057	81.12	170,662,139	78.08	176,143,063	75.70	176,660,969	78.96
Intermediate goods								
Construction materials	14,244,098	7.62	12,397,276	5.67	15,370,728	6.61	19,767,439	8.84
Primary materials	5,663,794	3.03	15,101,040	6.91	20,148,062	8.66	11,064,991	4.95
Total	19,907,892	10.65	27,498,316	12.58	35,518,790	15.27	30,832,425	13.78
Equipment	15,379,506	8.23	17,833,997	8.16	20,244,797	8.70	15,999,682	7.15
Other	—	—	2,571,451	—	773,236	0.33	242,884	0.11
Total	186,882,454	100.00	218,565,903	100.00	232,679,886	100.00	223,735,965	100.00

Sources: BCRG (1990, 1989); BCRG unpublished data.

FIGURE 4
Guinea: Total Import Composition, 1990.

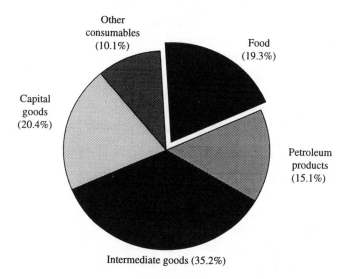

Other
consumables
(10.1%)

Food
(19.3%)

Capital
goods
(20.4%)

Petroleum
products
(15.1%)

Intermediate goods (35.2%)

Source: GOG (1991b).

markets. Furthermore, new opportunities for commercial activities have also arisen.

However, the above observations also raise some important concerns as to the extent of structural change with reform and as to the overall sustainability of the current balance-of-payment scenario. High levels of imports evident in private sector foreign exchange deficits are being counteracted not by export revenues as much as by a number of other sources. First, mining sector foreign exchange tax revenue continues to be a primary source of financing import needs (Table 4). In this respect not much has changed structurally with respect to Guinea's balance-of-payments composition. The share of nonmining exports has not grown substantially, and Guinea is critically dependent on income from one commodity (bauxite) and the companies that mine it. Recently observed and projected declines in mining tax revenues raise an alarm as to the sustainability of the balance-of-payments situation if agricultural exports do not increase.

Second, in addition to mining tax revenue, balance-of-payments assistance has also been important on the revenue side of foreign exchange accounts, especially for financing capital and intermediate good expenditures. Indeed current levels of both the parallel and official rates have been buoyed by the large supply of foreign exchange made available through balance-of-payments support in combination with mining sector tax revenue. This in turn has aided the boost in imports, especially of consumer goods. Clearly with its balance-of-payments plight in general, and its continued reliance on current levels of imports in particular, Guinea will continue to depend on high levels of donor support.

Third, Guinea's foreign exchange expenditures have also been financed through the drawing down of external reserves, the accumulation of arrears, and debt rescheduling. Indeed to the extent that the BCRG sells foreign exchange beyond its available supply (including balance-of-payments support), it not only supports the exchange rate but also runs an unsustainable current account deficit. This appears to have been the case, for example, in 1988 when the level of foreign exchange supplied to the auction was made possible only by running down reserves and running up arrears and then again in 1990 by accumulating arrears on the order of GF 31.13 billion (GOG 1991b). In fact, the IMF (1988a) noted that lack of effort by the government caused delays in the servicing of external debt. In 1988 the IMF declared that the level of sales of foreign exchange by the Central Bank was unsustainable (at US$ 57.3 million in the 2nd quarter of 1988), sustainability being defined as that level at which external debt would rise no faster than GDP (estimated at US$ 30 million).[32]

The above three factors indicate that, despite the massive trade and exchange reforms undertaken in Guinea, in the short term there has not been a heartening change in the country's fundamental balance-of-payments situation. The most important change has been the increased availability of donor financing. Indeed, as discussed below, important infrastructural and institutional constraints to short-term growth in Guinea appear to limit the immediate large-scale returns to trade and exchange reform. While trade and exchange reform is a necessary condition for growth, it does not appear to be a sufficient one.

NOTES

1. One Guinea franc equalled 0.0036 grams of gold.

2. To the extent that the parallel rate incorporates a risk premium, or the excess demand due to capital flight, it may be overvalued relative to a true shadow exchange rate.

3. A corollary to this point is that privileged importers or individuals who could access foreign exchange or goods purchased at the official, subsidized rate could have earned rents by selling these goods on the parallel market.

4. The lack of data makes it impossible to compute an average import duty rate. The extent to which the schedule of tariffs was adhered to is also unclear.

5. Some gained from this exchange at "par." The new notes issued exceeded the old notes collected by a value of GF 2.2 billion (World Bank 1990a).

6. However, the coverage of the second window was not changed.

7. In addition to the import declaration (DDI), importers must hand in four other forms, including price documentation, quality verification, and a customs declaration.

8. This does not necessarily mean that the GOG is seeking to prevent the depreciation of the official rate. As long as the government maintains the official rate within a small band of the shadow rate, it is simply choosing a managed and stable, stepwise depreciation over a fluctuating, weekly one.

9. Beginning in late 1992 the Government of Guinea also started permitting the establishment of private *bureaux de change*. Currently the role of this "formalized" parallel window is minor, in part due to a licensing requirement to establish these *bureaux*.

10. Ostensibly this measure was instituted to ensure prompt payment of customs duties upon arrival of the merchandise. However BCRG officials recognize that the policy is aimed at reducing the imports of consumer goods. The customs service does not support the policy, which has actually depressed customs revenues by depressing imports.

11. As of late 1990, the rates on nonalcoholic beverages, alcoholic beverages, and tobacco were reduced to 30, 60, and 80 percent, respectively, after increases in their respective surtax rates over the course of 1989 and early 1990. In 1991 the surtax on tobacco was also lowered to 60 percent.

12. The official real effective exchange rate (REER) takes into account not only trade shares and exchange rates of Guinea's trading partners but also Guinea's inflation rate relative to the inflation rates of trading partners. The REER is calculated here as the multilateral real rate, although only the United States and France are assumed to be trading partners. In particular, the rate at time t is calculated as:

$$REER_t = 0.4 \, \frac{(E_{Ft} * P_{Ft})}{P_{Gt}} + 0.6 \, \frac{(E_{Ut} * P_{Ut})}{P_{Gt}}$$

where E is the nominal exchange rate and P is the consumer price index (CPI). The subscripts F, G, and U represent France, Guinea, and the United States, respectively.

13. Using Guinea's GDP price deflator as a measure of annual domestic inflation, the real depreciation was only 21.0 percent between 1985 and 1987 (Sahn, Dorosh, and Younger 1994). Because the consumer price index is dominated by goods for which prices were controlled prior to the liberalization, this second measure of the real exchange rate overstates the extent of the real depreciation in the overall economy.

14. The IMF's SDR 33 million standby agreement approved in February 1986 explicitly supported the exchange system. In fact BCRG's inefficiency and delay in processing donor contributions actually prevented the government from utilizing all the funds at its disposal.

15. The transfer of salaries out of the country and the purchase of foreign exchange for tourism purposes are, however, still subject to some restrictions. Also, every capital account transaction requires prior BCRG approval.

16. The negative list on current account transactions is short. Only the import of weapons and narcotics is prohibited.

17. To some extent this may reflect the slowdown in the appreciation of the real effective exchange rate as the devaluation in the nominal exchange rate parallels the degree to which inflation is higher in Guinea than in trading partner nations.

18. The existence of a healthy parallel market even in the capital is clearly evident upon a visit to "Wall Street" in Conakry. However, no formal estimates have been made of levels of exchange on the parallel market, and, more importantly, of changes in the volume of transactions in this market over time.

19. The movement of the nominal rate in 1992 demonstrates the discretionary nature of exchange rate determination in Guinea. Given a target average annual exchange rate agreed upon with multilateral lenders, Central Bank authorities opted to quickly reach and hold at that level. One reason for devaluing earlier rather than later in the year is to maximize mining sector tax revenue, which is paid monthly in foreign exchange.

20. The reduction of quotas and simplification of tariffs since the commencement of reforms would suggest a moderating influence on the depreciation of the effective exchange rate for imports that was due to the nominal exchange rate's devaluation. However, caution should be used in making any such assumption since weighted average tariff rates may have actually increased with liberalization, as may actual tariff collection with increased fiscal discipline.

21. Table 5 presents estimates from the IMF (1987a) for the period 1982 through 1985 and from the World Bank (1990a) for the period 1986 through 1989 and from the Government of Guinea (MPF 1993a) for the period 1990 through 1992.

22. It should be noted, however, that a lot of these export receipts accruing to the private mining companies are retained and utilized outside Guinea.

23. It should be noted that the data estimates since 1986 are from different sources than the data from the previous four years. Moreover, the data since 1986 reflect adjustments and changes in data collection by the government since 1986.

24. Especially in the case of coffee, a perennial crop, the immediate export response was unlikely a production response.

25. Coffee prices dropped by 34 percent and petroleum prices rose by 31 percent in 1991 (GOG 1991b).

26. In the four years prior to 1986 public transfers averaged US$ 28 million. In the four years after 1986 public transfers averaged US$ 77 million.

27. These figures include disbursements from project-related loans, IDA and co-financing, and drawings on USSR special loans.

28. In addition to meeting the financing gap, debt relief has been used in part to replenish reserves and payoff arrears.

29. Whereas Guinea owed approximately 85 percent of this debt to official sources prior to 1986, the influx of structural adjustment related monies raised this percentage to 95 percent on average between 1987 and 1992. Similarly, the share of debt to multilateral creditors increased over this period, from 13 percent in 1980 to 37 percent in 1992 (World Bank 1994b).

30. The recent increase in this share in 1992 is due in large part to the fall in mining export revenue in addition to some increases in agricultural export revenue.

31. It is unclear to what extent over-invoicing may be used in conjunction with the auction to mask capital flight.

32. It should be noted that in 1988 balance-of-payments support was lower than in either 1987 or 1989.

4

FOOD AND AGRICULTURAL POLICY

HISTORICAL PERSPECTIVES

Overview

Guinea boasts of rich agricultural resources and potentials. Its varied agro-ecological topography favors a variety of agricultural products, from food and cash crops to livestock and fish. The agricultural diversity of the four main regions of the country is well-illustrated in Tables 8 and 9, which present data on production shares and landholding size.

While salinity and soggy terrain complicate cultivation, Lower Guinea's soil and average rainfall of 3,100 millimeters permit the widespread production of both rain-fed and swamp rice. Indeed, 63 percent of all cultivated land in this region is dedicated to the production of rice. Other principal food crops include fonio (9.5 percent of cultivated land) and cassava (4.4 percent of cultivated land). For cash crops, Lower Guinea relies heavily on groundnuts (18.7 percent of cultivated land) and a variety of fruits including bananas, pineapples, oranges, and mangos (1 percent of cultivated land) (Table 8). Farms in Lower Guinea's three rural provinces—Boké, Dubreka, and Kindia—averaged 3.41, 2.16, and

TABLE 8
Guinea: Characteristics of Agriculture, by Region.

	Lower Guinea	*Middle Guinea*	*Upper Guinea*	*Forest Guinea*	*Total Guinea*
Average rainfall (millimeters)	3,137.23	1,823.06	1,557.84	2,301.35	2,248.55
Percent of cultivated land					
Principal crops					
Rain-fed rice	55.33	22.43	31.31	47.28	39.44
Other rice	7.66	2.12	2.85	1.92	3.50
Maize	0.97	18.83	16.61	0.42	8.95
Millet	0.87	1.07	10.62	0.01	3.55
Fonio	9.49	34.69	13.00	0.75	12.99
Cassava	4.42	5.09	6.20	1.92	4.36
Yams, sweet potato	0.81	1.43	1.01	0.21	0.81
Groundnuts	18.65	12.54	13.01	0.45	10.57
Coffee	0.00	0.00	0.17	43.20	12.41
Vegetables[a]	0.00	0.51	0.01	0.08	0.13
Fruit[b]	1.07	0.74	2.80	1.42	1.62
Other	0.72	0.56	2.28	2.34	1.66
Total	100.00	100.00	99.86	100.00	100.00
Number of farms	23	35	20	22	100
Average farm size (hectares)	1.60	0.96	2.47	2.22	1.69
Percent of total holdings					
Livestock					
Cattle	20	47	23	10	100
Sheep, goats	11	51	21	17	100
Pigs	15	2	3	80	100

Sources: GOG (1989c, 1990c); UNICEF (1990a); average rainfall calculated from yearly average for major towns.
a. "Vegetables" includes beans, aubergines, tomato, lettuce, squash, and peppers.
b. "Fruits" includes bananas, mangos, avocados, and oranges.

3.60 hectares, respectively, in 1985 (Table 9). For farmers in the upland areas and flood plains of Lower Guinea, the tending of livestock is more important. Farmers in these parts of Lower Guinea raise twenty percent of the national stock of cattle.

Middle Guinea, which includes the hilly Fouta Djallon plateau, also experiences abundant rainfall. Soil quality is low, however, and erosion is extensive. Although population density compares to that of Lower Guinea without Conakry, data on holding sizes indicate a much higher share of smallholdings than elsewhere in the country. Ninety-two percent of all cultivated land in the region falls under holding sizes of less than 2 hectares (Table 9). Seventy-two percent of all

TABLE 9
Guinea: Distribution of Landholdings by Size of Holdings, 1975 and 1985.
(percent)

Region	Less than 1 Hectare		1–2 Hectares		2–5 Hectares		More than 5 Hectares		Average Hectares
	1975	1985	1975	1985	1975	1985	1975	1985	1985
Lower Guinea									
Boke	29	24	39	21	27	41	6	14	3.41
Dubreka	12	31	29	32	52	27	8	10	2.16
Kindia	22	18	35	22	38	40	5	20	3.60
Middle Guinea									
Labe	41	72	43	20	15	7	1	1	0.88
Upper Guinea									
Faranah	5	17	21	33	51	44	21	6	2.35
Kankan	4	18	9	20	35	46	52	16	3.21
Forest Guinea									
N'Zerekore	8	46	32	29	51	22	9	3	1.49

Sources: AIRD (1983) for 1975; Nellum (1980); Scetagri/Agroprogress (1986) for 1985.

cultivated land in the region falls under holding sizes of 1 hectare or less.[1] The percentage of cultivated land under holding sizes of less than 1 hectare, in contrast, was only 41 percent in 1975.

While population density relative to arable land undoubtedly contributes to these small landholding sizes, so does the primarily subsistence-oriented cropping pattern. Although fonio is the principle subsistence crop, making the region the least reliant on rice production, rice is grown on close to one-quarter of all cultivated land. Other important subsistence crops grown in this agro-ecological zone are maize (18.8 percent of cultivated land), cassava (5.1 percent of cultivated land), and yams and sweet potatoes (1.4 percent of cultivated land) (Table 8). Groundnuts are the predominant cash crop here (12.5 percent of cultivated land), while fruits and vegetables are grown on more fertile fields for sale in surrounding areas including Senegal. Middle Guinea also raises approximately 50 percent of the national stock of cattle, sheep, and goats. The average family in the Fouta Djallon raises an estimated six head of livestock (AIRD and GOG 1983). Increased intense cultivation, little reliance on inorganic fertilizer, shortening of fallow periods, and livestock grazing all contribute to the erosion problem in Middle Guinea.

Land quality in sparsely populated Upper Guinea is also relatively poor, resulting in low yields despite extensive cultivation. Upper Guinea's production is diverse, however, as evidenced by its land cultivation shares: rice is grown on 34.2 percent of cultivated land; maize on 16.6 percent; millet on 10.6 percent; fonio on 13 percent; cassava on 6.2 percent; yams and sweet potatoes on 1.0 percent. Cash crops are also diverse in Upper Guinea. Thirteen percent of this area's cultivated land is dedicated to the production of groundnuts; cotton, coffee, mangos, and oranges are also grown. Upper Guinea raises approximately one-fifth of the national stock of cattle, sheep, and goats. Holding sizes in the two Upper Guinea provinces of Faranah and Kankan averaged 2.35 and 3.21 hectares, respectively, in 1985.[2]

The Forest Region benefits from an average annual rainfall of 2,300 millimeters, which permits two harvests per year. Rice, the major crop, is grown on 49.2 percent of all cultivated land (Table 8). While cassava is grown on close to 2 percent of cultivated land, other food crops are not as important. The agro-ecological conditions prove favorable, however, for supporting the production of perennial export crops. Indeed, 43.2 percent of cultivated land in the region is dedicated to the production of coffee and 1.2 percent to that of cocoa. Some tobacco, kola, and groundnuts are also grown, as well as palm, bananas, mangos, and avocados. At 1.49 hectares in 1985, landholding sizes in the N'Zerekore province average the second smallest nationally (Table 9).[3]

Policy Failure

Despite Guinea's impressive agricultural potentials, post-independence policy has ensured that they remain largely unrealized. In per capita terms, real agricultural output actually fell from 1960 to 1985 (AIRD 1989) and stood at US$ 116 in 1987. Total agricultural GDP was approximately US$ 595 million in 1987. This level contrasts with a value-added in agriculture of US$ 2,700 million in bordering Côte d'Ivoire, a country only one-fourth larger in size, comparable in climate, and, most significant, with a comparable level of agricultural GDP when both nations attained independence.[4]

The failures of Guinea's post-independence agriculture policies were pervasive. Institutional factors such as land tenure arrangements, agricultural cooperatives, and state-managed marketing systems distorted incentive structures. The government actively discouraged private sector development in general and private trade in particular. Agricultural pricing kept down producer prices to farmers; production taxes further suppressed incentives. Concurrently, heavily subsidized consumer prices benefitted certain privileged urban consumers. These biases were reinforced by an overvalued exchange rate and by import restrictions. Equally responsible for hampering agricultural sector development was the lack of a coherent and coordinated policy framework. As a result, elements critical for a successful agricultural development strategy, such as agricultural research facilities and the rural transportation network, were neglected and allowed to fall apart. Thus, while the state subscribed to the notion that it should assume an eminent role in the development of the agricultural sector, it lacked the technical and managerial capacity and the necessary funds to effectively fulfill that role. Instead, its intervention in a variety of domains reduced incentives and created distortions, ultimately impairing the development of a robust agriculture.

For example, the state assumed the role of the legal proprietor of all land, intending to overturn the traditional land tenure system in Guinea, which entails the local assignment to families of usufructuary rights.[5,6] With independence in Guinea, the responsibility of land assignment and reassignment, although traditionally held by the village chief or elder, became the charge of the Party's PRL (village-level) council. The Party thus had a large amount of political and discretionary control, or leverage, at even the village level.[7]

Government control went beyond delineating land rights to dictating the nature and organization of agricultural production in Guinea. This was done through two mechanisms. First, the 360 FAPAs (District Agro-Pastoral Farms), large state-owned farms, were to be the technical vanguard of Guinean agriculture. Initiated in 1979, the FAPAs were to conduct adaptive research and modernize peasant farming synergistically through dissemination of technology and provision of technical support. The FAPAs were also to lead out in increasing national grain and export crop production.[8]

Their special role gave the FAPAs privileged access to inputs. While some FAPA land was appropriated from colonial plantations, other was appropriated by the PRL through its privileges in assigning land tenure rights. FAPAs also received large amounts of capital and mechanical investment from the government. In addition to initial working capital of GS 250,000 per FAPA, over 500 tractors, 450 plows, and 270 motor pumps had been made available to the FAPAs by 1984 (World Bank 1984a). The government also covered wages, the FAPAs' largest expenditure. FAPAs were staffed by civil servants, many of whom were agricultural graduates that the government was obliged to employ. In 1982 the total FAPA wage bill was approximately 6 percent of the government's budgeted recurrent expenditure. Total resources expended on the FAPAs were estimated at 27 percent of the total agricultural sector investment in the Fourth Development Plan (World Bank 1984a).

Unfortunately, the FAPAs were an unmitigated failure. FAPA yields were generally half that of smallholders' on paddy (World Bank 1984a). Furthermore, smallholders gained little from the FAPAs and instead, as 60 percent of the labor on FAPAs, were forced to volunteer time. Moreover, the mechanization of FAPAs also backfired. By 1982 only one-quarter of the FAPA factory fleet was operational (World Bank 1984a). In total, annual losses by the 360 FAPAs were estimated at GS 576 million (World Bank 1984a).

Agricultural cooperatives, called FACs (*Ferme Agricole Commune*), were the second production unit of the First Republic's agricultural policy.[9] Again, PRLs set aside communal land at the village level. This land was to be worked by mandatory labor. Revenue from production was to go toward the village budget for community services. Although not much is known about the operation of communal farms, indications are that for these farms also, output generally did not cover the investment made (Nellum and Associates 1980).

Finally, smallholders provided and continue to provide the backbone to agricultural production in Guinea, despite the intentions of failed policy and an array of obstacles to smallholder production and marketing imposed by the government. The 1975 census counted approximately 700,000 smallholder farms in Guinea, each being the domicile, on average, of six to seven people (Scetagri 1986). The national average of smallholder farms' holding size was 2.44 hectares in 1985. Important variations in holding sizes exist across provinces, of course (Table 9).

Approximately 76 percent of Guinean households actively farm (GOG 1991b) but few reliable data yet exist about their production and marketing behavior or their income and consumption patterns.[10] The majority of these households are subsistence smallholder farmers living in rural areas. These agricultural households average 6.3 members. Close to 90 percent of all farming households cultivate less than 5 hectares of land; only 7 percent cultivate between 5 and 10 hectares (GOG 1991b). Their inputs are generally only seed and family labor. Only 1 percent of subsistence farming households use fertilizer. During seasonal work peaks, such as harvest time, farmers who can afford to do so use hired help (Chemonics 1986). Several studies, however, cite labor shortages during these peak periods as a serious constraint to production for most households (Thenevin 1988; USAID 1989).[11] These households largely cultivate the subsistence crops of rice, maize, fonio, and manioc; less than 15 percent of agricultural households cultivate coffee, Guinea's major export crop (GOG 1991b). Accounting for the bulk of agricultural production, Guinea's subsistence farmers have been the group most affected by government policy regarding agricultural pricing, taxation, and marketing.

Under the First Republic, the state apparatus permeated even smallholder agriculture. A web of repressive rules and regulations affected smallholder production and marketing decisions. The central government gave regional party authorities crop and livestock production and marketing targets, which village councils were to see were attained. Each active rural household member was required to market a determined amount of agricultural output at official prices. In 1983, the obligatory sale amount of paddy was 103 kilograms per person (Thenevin 1988). Official marketing channels in Guinea were run solely by public entities, with private trade being severely restricted since independence and completely prohibited until 1981.

Local party cell (PRL) stores purchased at the official price and forwarded the produce to regional trading companies (ERCs and EPCOAs). A partial liberalization in 1981 allowed some private traders to participate in servicing this link.[12] Exports were then taken over by one of three parastatals: FRUITEX (fruit exports), PROSECO ("nonperishable" agricultural exports such as palm kernels and coffee), and PROMINEX (processed agricultural exports such as oils and leathers). They were forwarded to a holding company, SECOMEX (disbanded in 1981), and finally exported by yet another parastatal, IMPORTEX. Products for domestic consumption, on the other hand, were either sold regionally to ration card holders at official retail prices or, in the case of a regional surplus, shipped to a food deficit area, normally Conakry.

Prices increased through the marketing chain in order to incorporate marketing and handling margins. However, that these margins were often kept well below actual costs is revealed by the fact that prices changed little over time, despite high inflation rates, and by the fact that prices were equal across regions, despite varying transportation costs. Both these factors point to the heavy subsidization for consumers who purchased at official prices, an issue discussed more extensively below. Furthermore, in an effort to hold down prices for domestic consumers and to ensure that the state gained a large share of the value of exports, the First Republic depressed official producer prices. While this had negative welfare effects on farmers, it also had a disastrous impact on production, marketing, exports, and the balance of payments.

Producer Prices, Production, and Markets

Official producer prices, the only legal selling prices for farmers, were rarely changed during the First Republic. The nominal price of subsistence crops such as rice, millet, and cassava, for example, was not altered over the seven-year period from 1975 to 1982. The nominal price was also not altered for export crops such as palm kernels, plantains, pineapples, and mangos (Table 10). Coffee prices were increased only once, and the average annual rate of increase in the nominal producer price of groundnuts was only 6 percent over this period. With the limited liberalization of 1981, prices were increased more rapidly

TABLE 10

Guinea: Nominal Producer Prices of Select Crops, 1975–1992.
(Guinean Francs per kilogram)

	Export Crops								Food Crops							
Year	Coffee Robusta (net)	Coffee Arabica (net)	Ground-nuts	Palm Kernels	Palm Oil	Plant-ains	Pine-apples	Man-gos	Rice (net)	Maize	Dry Cassava	Fonio (net)	Millet	Cow-peas	On-ions	Pota-toes
1975	—	—	6	6	—	4.5	—	—	15	6	5	—	7	—	—	—
1976	—	—	7	—	—	4.5	—	—	15	6	5	—	7	—	—	—
1977	34	35	8	6	—	4.5	9	8	15	6	5	—	7	—	—	—
1978	34	35	9	6	—	4.5	9	8	15	6	5	—	7	—	—	—
1979	40	41	9	6	—	4.5	9	8	15	6	5	—	7	—	—	—
1980	40	41	9	6	—	4.5	9	8	15	6	5	—	7	—	—	—
1981	40	41	9	6	28	4.5	9	8	15	6	5	13	7	7	12	15
1982	40	41	9	6	28	4.5	9	8	15	7	5	13	7	7	12	15
1983	45	46	12	7	40	4.5	9	8	20	10	7	15	10	10	18	20
1984	55	55	12	10	40	14	15	15	20	—	7	15	10	10	18	20
1985	70	70	20	13	60	14	15	15	25	—	7	15	10	10	20	20
1986	400	400	—	60	—	14	15	15	81	—	—	—	—	—	—	—
1987	450	450	110	40	—	14	45	15	96	80	50	80	—	—	—	—
1988	500	—	—	—	—	—	—	—	105	—	—	—	—	—	—	—
1989	290	—	—	—	—	—	—	—	105	—	—	—	—	—	—	—
1990	233	—	—	—	—	—	—	—	—	—	—	—	—	—	—	—
1991	251	—	—	—	—	—	—	—	—	—	—	—	—	—	—	—
1992	—	—	366[a]	104	—	—	—	—	345	144	180	152	145	—	805	331

Sources: UNDP/World Bank (1989); MICA (unpublished data); World Bank (1984a); Weaver (1987); rice prices from Thenevin (1988); Filippi-Wilhelm (1988); Caputo (1991); and GOG (1989a, 1992a, 1992b).
a. Dry shelled.

53

between 1982 and 1985. During these years, the average annual nominal producer price of rice increased by 19 percent, that of palm oil by 21 percent, that of robusta coffee by 21 percent, and that of groundnuts by 33 percent. Even so, these increases did not keep pace with inflation. Indeed, though no price index exists for Guinea prior to 1986, the devaluation of the parallel exchange rate by an average of 54 percent annually between 1982 and 1985 reveals that in real terms producers faced a dramatic fall in their incentives to produce for official markets through the mid-1980s.

Production cost information for the period reinforces this point. In 1981/82 the production cost of traditionally cultivated rice was approximately three times the producer price; the cost by improved manual methods was still over twice the producer price (Table 11). Similarly, traditional groundnut production cost four times the producer price and traditional coffee production cost one-and-a-half times the producer price.

A more appropriate measure of the element of taxation introduced through official pricing is the nominal protection coefficient (NPC)—namely, the ratio of domestic producer prices to international prices valued at farmgate. Domestic producer prices evaluated at the official exchange rate were generally higher than border prices, less a transport and handling margin (Table 12).[13] Average NPCs for robusta coffee, groundnuts, and palm kernels between the years 1975 and 1985 were 1.24, 1.99, and 1.76, respectively. The NPCs for rice also greatly exceeded parity, using the official exchange rate. To interpret these numbers as implying that producers were subsidized, however, would be flawed. Rather, any explicit subsidy is dwarfed by the indirect tax due to the gross exchange rate distortion.[14] The large contrast between NPCs computed using the official rate and those utilizing the shadow rate (proxied by the parallel rate) gives an indication of this indirect tax.

At the parallel rate, NPCs for export crops remained well below 1.0 for the period 1975 through 1985 (Table 12). The average producer price for coffee evaluated at the parallel exchange rate was approximately one-third of the border price over this period. The average NPCs for groundnuts and palm kernels over the ten years were approximately 0.5 and 0.6, respectively. The nominal producer price increases commencing in 1982 did little to stem the decline in NPCs given the precipitous depreciation of the parallel exchange rate. In 1984, Sekou Touré's last year in power, the NPC of coffee was a low of 0.12; that of groundnuts, 0.22; and that of palm kernels, 0.11.

Production data for Guinea are even weaker than marketing and export data. Nevertheless, what data there are show production stagnating given pricing and exchange policies (Table 13). Production of groundnuts, tobacco, coffee, bananas, cassava, roots and tubers, maize, and rice increased little through the

TABLE 11

Guinea: Estimated Costs of Production, by Crop and Production Method Compared with Official and Open Market Prices, 1981–1982.
(Guinean Francs per kilogram)

| Crop | Cost of Production | | | | Prices | | |
| | Traditional (Manual) | Improved | | | Official | | Open |
		Manual	Animal Traction	Motorized	Producer	Market	Market
Rice							
Mangrove	28.7	—	—	—	9.0	20.0	40–70
Upland	30.2	21.2	—	—	—	—	—
Inland swamp	29.4	22.6	—	—	—	—	—
Flooded rice							
Uncontrolled	—	—	23.7	25.2	—	—	—
Controlled	—	—	14.8	—	—	—	—
Maize	26.6	17.3	11.3	11.9	10.0	—	—
Groundnuts	31.0	19.1	12.8	—	7.5	18.0	50–110
Tobacco	—	43.1	—	—	40.0	—	—
Coffee	62.1	58.3	—	—	45.0	—	240–280
Cocoa	75.7	46.1	—	—	—	—	—
Cotton	—	25.1	16.8	16.8	20.0	—	—
Pineapples							
Industrial	—	8.7	—	—	9.0	—	—
Village	—	8.4	—	—	9.0	—	15
Palm oil	—	—	—	—	28.0	—	—
Cassava	—	—	—	—	5.0	—	—

Source: World Bank (1984a).

55

TABLE 12
Guinea: Nominal Protection Coefficients (NPCs), 1975–1992.

Year	At Official Exchange Rate					At Parallel Exchange Rate				
	Rice	Coffee Robusta	Coffee Arabica	Ground-nuts	Palm Kernels	Rice	Coffee Robusta	Coffee Arabica	Ground-nuts	Palm Kernels
1975	1.77	—	—	1.15	2.69	0.63	—	—	0.41	0.96
1976	2.12	—	—	1.32	2.18	0.71	—	—	0.44	0.73
1977	2.68	0.77	0.62	1.15	1.48	0.90	0.26	0.21	0.39	0.50
1978	2.14	0.67	0.54	1.12	1.32	1.43	0.45	0.36	0.75	0.89
1979	1.96	1.06	0.97	1.27	0.95	1.31	0.71	0.65	0.85	0.64
1980	1.65	0.88	0.74	1.57	1.54	0.81	0.43	0.36	0.77	0.75
1981	1.47	1.10	1.26	1.21	1.75	0.41	0.31	0.35	0.34	0.49
1982	1.75	1.72	1.31	2.08	2.48	0.36	0.36	0.27	0.43	0.52
1983	3.59	1.49	2.14	2.97	1.63	0.57	0.24	0.34	0.48	0.26
1984	3.86	1.65	1.64	2.99	1.57	0.28	0.12	0.12	0.22	0.11
1985	5.03	1.86	1.85	5.02	—	0.33	0.12	0.12	0.33	—
1986	1.04	0.58	0.36	—	—	0.96	0.53	0.33	—	—
1987	1.09	0.46	0.86	—	1.00	1.05	0.44	0.83	—	0.97
1988	0.80	0.77	0.61	—	—	0.73	0.70	0.55	—	—
1989	0.57	0.42	—	—	—	0.52	0.39	—	—	—
1990	0.62	0.52	—	—	—	0.58	0.49	—	—	—
1991	—	0.58	—	—	—	—	0.55	—	—	—
1992	0.98	—	—	—	0.96	0.90	—	—	—	0.88

Sources: AIRD (1989); Caputo (1991); FAO (various years); GOG (1989b, 1992b); IMF (various years); MICA unpublished data; Nellum (1980); Thenevin (1988); UNDP and World Bank (1989); USAID (1989); Weaver (1987); World Bank (1986a, 1989b, 1990a).

TABLE 13

Guinea: Crop Production Estimates, 1970–1993.
(1,000 metric tons)

Year	Rice (Paddy)	Maize	Sorghum	Roots/Tubers	Cassava	Bananas	Pineapples	Green Coffee	Cocoa Beans	Tobacco	Sugarcane	Groundnuts	Mangos
1970	350	68	25	642	480	85	23	12	2	1	0	75	24
1971	375	68	25	663	495	80	23	13	2	1	0	76	24
1972	375	67	25	668	505	70	25	13	2	1	0	76	24
1973	413	66	25	749	598	93	18	14	2	1	0	77	24
1974	417	68	25	757	604	94	17	14	2	1	0	78	24
1975	422	68	25	765	610	95	16	14	3	1	0	79	24
1976	426	68	25	773	616	96	15	14	4	1	145	80	24
1977	418	70	25	798	622	97	15	14	4	1	145	81	24
1978	366	70	22	806	629	98	16	14	4	1	165	82	24
1979	348	80	25	654	475	99	16	14	4	1	220	82	24
1980	480	90	25	636	480	100	17	14	4	2	220	84	28
1981	485	90	25	642	485	101	17	14	4	2	220	84	28
1982	490	90	22	649	490	102	18	15	4	2	245	85	32
1983	396	90	25	654	494	103	18	15	4	2	225	77	32
1984	403	100	30	658	496	104	30	15	4	2	225	82	36
1985	437	100	32	682	520	105	40	15	4	2	225	74	36
1986	510	100	32	710	550	106	50	7	3	2	200	70	40
1987	515	90	28	730	570	107	60	7	3	2	200	60	40
1988	525	71	25	752	594	119	72	20	1	2	175	81	40
1989	560	71	27	826	642	110	76	28	1	2	175	78	50
1990	616	78	24	853	658	121	83	30	2	2	225	78	70
1991	688	85	19	887	658	113	92	30	2	2	225	78	70
1992	757	94	13	999	781	125	91	29	2	2	225	102	93
1993	833	95	10	997	781	115	87	29	2	2	225	105	77

Source: FAO (1991a, b).

57

1970s, signifying declines in per capita availability. Production costs being higher than producer prices served as an obvious disincentive to produce beyond subsistence levels for the official market. Furthermore, farmers feared that any surplus would have to be surrendered as *livraisons obligatoires*[15] (Thenevin 1988). Moreover, the lack of progress in agricultural research also contributed to low levels of technology and agricultural productivity (see Scetagri [1986] and Hirsch [1986]). Stagnant yield levels also reflect the virtual absence of any market for agricultural inputs. At approximately 0.8 MT per hectare in the mid-1970s, Guinea's mean rice yield level was extremely low compared to other countries (Hirsch 1986).

The ensuing consequence of such low official producer prices and related institution and market failures was the virtual cessation of production for official markets. Between 1977 and 1980, net rice sales to the state fell by 57 percent, fonio by 63 percent, pineapples by 46 percent, and unshelled groundnuts by 85 percent (Table 14). Consequently, rice marketed to the state was only an estimated 1.8 percent of total production. Similarly, officially-marketed fonio was only an estimated 5.5 percent of production, and officially-marketed groundnuts were approximately 0.8 percent of production. The government was able to ensure only a minimum procurement of commodities through the official window.

TABLE 14
Guinea: State Purchases of Agricultural Products, Selected Years.
(1,000 tons)

Production	1974/75	1977	1980	Percentage of Production in 1980
Rice (paddy)	28.3	32.5	7.5	1.8
Rice (net)	—	20.6	8.8	3.6
Fonio (paddy)	—	5.5	0.9	1.1
Fonio (net)	2.8	7.3	2.7	5.5
Maize	8.3	8.1	5.9	7.9
Millet	4.9	3.9	1.9	—
Dried manioc	0.7	—	1.9	0.7
Unshelled groundnuts	—	4.8	0.7	0.8
Shelled groundnuts	—	0.4	0.0	0.0
Palm kernels	—	13.2	13.7	—
Coffee	—	2.2	3.5	22.6
Bananas	0.6	0.1	0.0	0.0
Pineapples	6.5	2.4	1.3	—
Mangoes	1.3	1.5	1.0	—

Sources: AIRD (1983); GOG (1983); World Bank (1986b).

TABLE 15
Guinea: Food Import Quantities by Good, 1974–1992.
(metric tons)

Year	Cereals	Rice	Wheat Flour	Sugar	Cooking Oil
1974	63,200	30,000	11,695	12,500	3,150
1975	67,300	36,200	16,613	13,000	3,930
1976	57,800	20,000	20,000	1,200	3,000
1977	59,000	35,500	15,500	3,900	2,200
1978	89,800	50,000	22,000	4,300	3,200
1979	109,800	71,200	23,508	9,500	3,277
1980	171,400	128,000	28,000	7,300	702
1981	130,400	77,600	38,000	5,200	2,314
1982	94,000	46,500	32,000	3,900	3,030
1983	111,700	77,000	25,000	7,800	3,630
1984	161,700	80,000	55,000	19,600	3,110
1985	140,200	70,000	48,000	31,500	3,300
1986	150,800	80,000	51,000	45,700	4,100
1987	173,300	90,000	59,000	47,300	6,700
1988	178,900	85,000	67,000	25,000	5,500
1989	283,900	195,400	63,297	36,000	8,300
1990	210,400	112,200	70,510	33,000	7,100
1991	296,500	182,200	82,300	40,900	18,141
1992	338,400	246,500	66,139	48,700	13,591

Source: FAO (1991a, b).

Presumably a large part of these sales were extracted in the form of the obligatory marketing quotas (*norms de commercialization*) levied on all active household members.[16] Even after this quota system was officially abolished, local officials and the state trading companies were known to use coercion in an attempt to collect targeted amounts of produce (World Bank 1984a).

Faced with low levels of food procurement through its domestic marketing channels, the government commenced importing larger quantities of food commodities to meet domestic food needs, especially in urban areas. Between 1974 and 1977 cereal imports averaged 61,825 MT per year. The average volume of cereal imports has steadily increased since, with considerable variability from year to year (Table 15). Incorporated in this statistic is Guinea's increased reliance on imported rice over this period. In 1984, 80,000 MT of rice were imported, in contrast to approximately 30,000 MT in 1974. As a percentage of domestic production, rice imports rose from 13.4 percent in 1973-1975 to 27 percent in 1983-1985. Moreover, food aid rice imports averaged 4.5 percent of total rice imports during the former period and 41.0 percent during the latter period. This increasing reliance on imported rice has continued under trade liberalization, a contentious issue to which we shall return.

Failed agricultural policies made food imports especially vital to urban consumers. Not all Guineans, however, were reached by government imports during periods of food shortages. Consequently, many households, especially those in border regions, relied on illegal rice imports during food shortages, just as they relied on illegal export markets when a surplus was available. While such "emergency" illicit food imports came from Senegal, The Gambia, and Mali, there was a more regular demand for rice imports from Sierra Leone and Liberia (Thenevin 1988).[17]

The decline in officially marketed production increased the foreign exchange burden, not only by increasing Guinea's reliance on food imports but by dramatically reducing export earnings from cash crops (Table 16). Between 1966–1970 and 1980–1985, official pineapple exports fell by 92 percent, coffee exports by 94 percent, and palm kernel exports by 58 percent, while official banana exports virtually ceased. The share of agricultural exports in total exports fell by 71 percent to less than 1 percent between 1975 and 1981 (Figure 3). Faltering exports also resulted in part from bad management of exporting parastatals, which in turn was related to unattractive incentive structures, a lack of competition, and weak administrative capacity.[18] During these post-independence years it was agricultural pricing policy, in an environment of severe exchange rate distortions, that largely undermined Guinea's agricultural exports and, consequently, its balance-of-payments situation.

Consumer Prices, Retail Markets, and Household Welfare

The falling share of production marketed and exported through official channels was consistent with three related phenomena supported only by widespread

TABLE 16
Guinea: Volume of Agricultural Exports, 1960–1992.
(thousands of metric tons)

Year	Coffee	Palm Kernels	Pineapple	Banana
1960–65	10.38	19.73	4.12	43.00
1966–70	8.49	14.64	7.40	31.40
1971–75	4.76	12.06	8.64	9.12
1976–80	1.84	12.33	2.06	0.05
1980–85	0.58	6.08	0.62	0.00

Sources: World Bank (1984a); AIRD (1989).

anecdotal evidence. The first was an increase in the subsistence ratio, the ratio of home consumption to total household production. The terms of trade had swung so far against farmers that it no longer made sense for them to participate in the monetized economy and trade their output for imported and other consumer goods. Those who had to trade for nonstaple foods and other goods suffered increasingly costly welfare effects. In 1980, for example, it cost a farmer (selling at the official producer price and buying at the parallel price) 22.2 kilograms of paddy rice for a packet of powdered milk, 33.3 kilograms of rice for a pair of plastic shoes, and 2.8 kilograms of rice for a bar of soap (Nellum 1980). Participation in the monetized economy also became increasingly unattractive because there were fewer goods available to buy in the country's interior: many consumer goods had simply disappeared from the market as a result of Guinea's foreign exchange crisis. Moreover, farmers faced escalating domestic inflation and an unreliable and generally inaccessible financial system that frequently required currency trade-ins (see chapter 7, "Financial Sector Policies"). Under these conditions, farmers stood to lose by holding money.

A second phenomenon, related to decreased monetization in rural Guinea, was an increase in local barter trade, which became the primary means of acquiring goods not produced on the smallholder plot. By directly trading goods, farmers circumvented official prices and the handling of money. "Triangular" trade also became important. An important route, for example, was the purchase of salt in Lower Guinea which was traded for cola and palm oil in the Forest Region. These goods in turn were transported as far away as the Fouta Djallon, Senegal, and The Gambia, where they were exchanged for cloth, sheet metal, jute sacks, and other consumer goods in high demand in Guinea (Filippi-Wilhelm 1987). In the Forest Region, trade went one step beyond barter, and coffee was used as a medium of exchange. Coffee was a portable currency with a recognizable foreign currency value through informal trade (Chemonics 1987a).

The third and related phenomenon, which came to characterize rural Guinea, was an increase in unrecorded transborder trade, or smuggling. By smuggling goods, farmers could circumvent the heavy taxation imposed on them through the grossly overvalued exchange rate. In French West Africa in 1975, the producer price for coffee was CFA 175 per kilogram, in contrast to Guinea's producer price of CFA 48.75 per kilogram at the parallel exchange rate (Table 17). Similarly, rice was bought at CFA 42.50 per kilogram in neighboring countries, whereas the Guinean producer price was CFA 26.25 per kilogram. For regions in the hinterland that were closer to the borders of Liberia, Côte d'Ivoire, or Mali than to the port of Conakry, transportation margins were also lower. In the Forest Region, for example, producers concealed their coffee holdings to avoid government delivery quotas. They sold instead to illegal traders who smuggled the

TABLE 17
Guinea: Comparison of Official Guinean Prices and Neighboring Countries
Paid to the Producer for Basic Agricultural Products, 1975 (using parallel
market rate of exchange).
(CFA per kilogram)

Produce	Guinea	West Africa
Rice	26.25	42.5
Fonio	16.25	30.0
Peanuts	16.25	41.5
Maize	18.75	35.0
Manioc	16.25	55.0
Sweet potatoes	11.25	26.0
Millet	16.25	30.0
Citruses	6.25	40.0
Bananas	8.75	16.0
Coffee	48.75	175.0
Pineapples	22.50	18.0

Source: Nellum (1980).
Note: On the black market, syli 1.0 = CFA 2.5. The black market rate is used here because the farmer, once he has sold his harvest at official prices, has to turn to the parallel market for consumer goods, where prices depend on the black market foreign exchange rate.

coffee across the border (Chemonics 1987a). An estimated one-third of Guinea's coffee crop was smuggled to Sierra Leone, Liberia, and Côte d'Ivoire in 1972 contributing to the sharp decline in coffee export figures (O'Conner 1972; Johnson 1978). Border markets, additionally, gave farmers access to imported consumer goods unavailable on official markets, in addition to the foreign exchange with which to purchase them.

The growth of this large informal consumer market contrasted with the official market for consumer goods. Although clearly urban-biased and primarily providing transfers to the politically influential, this official market receives scant treatment in existing literature. Pricing and access to official markets are thus poorly understood. The lower, official market prices were accessed by urban residents, upon presentation of a ration card.[19] Monthly official entitlements of rice in Conakry were 8 kilograms per month per capita for household heads and their immediate families and 6 kilograms per month per capita for everyone else. In other urban areas, only government employees and their families were entitled to a ration of 4 kilograms at official prices (World Bank 1984a). While other commodities were on the market on a rationed basis, only rice was available consistently, with sugar available occasionally (GOG 1986).

Official retail prices effectively served as a subsidy to privileged consumers. Import parity calculated at the appropriate parallel exchange rate was close to or below the c.i.f. value of rice for all years except 1978 and 1979 (Table 18). The official margin built in for port handling charges, bagging, transportation, and marketing costs was approximately GS 9 per kilogram, or 50 percent of the c.i.f. price when evaluated at the parallel exchange rate. This implies a significant subsidy for all years except 1978 and 1979. For example, at the 1980 ratio of official retail price to c.i.f. price of 1.08, consumers would have benefitted from a subsidy of 42 percent, or of approximately GS 8 per kilogram,[20] assuming that the official marketing margins were reasonable. This subsidy policy in conjunction with a policy of increasing rice imports throughout the 1970s and the early 1980s was a huge drain on the Treasury. For example, given a rice import level of close to 62,000 MT, the government's subsidy of GS 8 per kilogram in 1980 led to a fiscal drain of GS 496 billion (or US$ 11.9 million at the parallel exchange rate).

While the uncertainties about actual c.i.f. prices and marketing costs make calculating the economic subsidy difficult, an alternative and more tangible

TABLE 18
Guinea: Official Rice Retail Prices, 1975–1985.
(US dollars per metric ton)

Year	GF/GS per Kilogram	At Official Exchange Rate		At Parallel Exchange Rate	
		US$ per Kilogram	Ratio to c.i.f.	US$ per Kilogram	Ratio to c.i.f.
1975	20	977.52	2.36	350.39	0.85
1976	20	977.52	2.82	328.79	0.95
1977	20	977.52	3.57	328.30	1.20
1978	20	977.52	2.85	654.02	1.91
1979	20	977.52	2.61	654.02	1.74
1980	20	977.52	2.20	479.62	1.08
1981	20	977.52	1.96	273.67	0.55
1982	20	977.52	2.33	203.40	0.49
1983	25	1,221.90	4.48	195.19	0.72
1984	25	1,221.90	4.82	88.21	0.35
1985	25	1,221.90	5.03	80.47	0.33

Sources: Rice c.i.f. price from import quantity and value data from AIRD (1989); producer prices and official prices from MICA unpublished data. Other sources for rice data: Chemonics (1986); Filippi-Wilhelm (1987, 1988); Hanrahan and Block (1988); Hirsch (1986); Lowdermilk (1989); Nellum (1980); Scetagri/Agroprogress (1986); Thenevin (1988); USAID (1989); World Bank (1984b).

measure of the subsidy compares the official consumer price to the parallel market retail price.[21] Although retail prices are generally unavailable for the years under the First Republic, a study performed in 1980 indicates that rice was sold on the parallel market at GS 64 per kilogram that year (Nellum 1980). The official price was 31 percent of this price, implying a subsidy of 69 percent. This measure overstates the distortion inherent in rice pricing, however, since i incorporates distortions in the parallel markets (which also are spillovers from government policy). In fact, at the parallel exchange rate the parallel market retail price for rice amounted to 3.45 times the c.i.f. import price in 1980, reflecting high transaction costs, risk premia, and scarcity in the parallel markets due to trade and other restrictions.[22] By 1984, the next year for which we have data, the parallel market price was about on par with the c.i.f. price, reflecting the loosening of controls, including the sanctioning of parallel market trade. Even so, the parallel market price of GS 70 per kilogram was about 2.8 times the official rate, indicating that the official price still conferred large benefits upon those with access.

The magnitude of the income transfer inherent in the ration program is also best measured as the difference between the official and parallel market prices (see, for example, Alderman, Sahn, and Arulpragasam [1991]). While this difference is an artifact of policy-induced distortions, the income transfer value to those with access to official markets was nevertheless real and relevant to the household's ability to purchase an adequate diet.

Survey information from 1984 provides some details about the utilization of the ration system. Due to an incomplete coverage of ration cards and shortages of rationed rice at the shops, the average per capita monthly uptake of rice at the official price was actually 6 rather than 8 kilograms.[23] In 1984, given official prices of GS 20 per kilogram early that year and parallel market prices of GS 70 per kilogram, the average income transfer through the ration would thus have been approximately GS 300 per month per person (i.e., GS [70-20] per kilogram x 6 kilograms), or, given an average household size of 11.3, GS 3,390 per household. This corresponded to approximately 11 percent of mean household expenditures in 1984.

An income transfer of this magnitude would have been especially significant if targeted to poorer families with lower incomes. In practice, however, the rations were not likely targeted to the poorest or otherwise least privileged households. In fact, a significant share of the population in Conakry did not have access to the ration system, a 1984 survey putting the proportion of have-nots at 17 percent (Table 19). Thirty-three percent of households of small-scale merchants and 22 percent of households with an unemployed head received no rations at all. In contrast, only 4 percent of the households of "officials" and 0 percent

TABLE 19
Guinea: Percent of Entitled Ration Actually Purchased, by Household
Category, 1984.
(percent)

	Unem- ployed	Low- Income Salaried Workers	Low- Level Officials	High- Level Officials	Small- Scale Merchants	Large- Scale Merchants	Total
			Household Head Categories				
100	39	21	15	53	16	36	28
100 to 75	22	32	40	23	16	36	26
75 to 50	11	25	20	8	12	18	15
50 to 25	6	11	15	12	23	9	15
25 to 0	0	0	0	0	0	0	0
Percentage without ration card	22	11	10	4	33	0	17
Total	100	100	100	100	100	100	100
Average per capita uptake of those participating (kilogram)	5.6	5.7	7.3	9	4	7.3	6

Source: GOG (1986).

of households of large merchants received no rations (Table 19). Moreover, among households with ration cards, the average monthly per capita uptake of rationed rice was variable. Uptake was highest among civil service (and some private sector) officials (9 kilograms) and among low-level civil servants and large merchants (7.3 kilograms). It was lowest among small-scale (presumably informal sector) merchants (4 kilograms), the unemployed (5.6 kilograms), and low-level (public sector) salaried workers (5.7 kilograms). Subsidized urban consumer prices thus protected the urban elite from the most harmful effects of policy-induced distortions, which were taking a heavy toll on the urban poor and rural smallholders. Effectively, the *norms de commercialization* required of farmers, coupled with the ration system, ensured an income transfer from rural areas and agrarian households to urban areas and civil servant households. To the extent that subsidized food was imported by the government, welfare gains to urban households caused foreign exchange losses to the state and income losses to the rural sector. Furthermore, the distortions inherent in such a system led to egregious rent-seeking behavior as it became common for "officially" purchased rice to be leaked out of the formal marketing channels and "unofficially" sold on the parallel market by corrupt government officials (Chemonics 1986).

The significance of the ration system for urban household welfare, however, should not be overplayed. As discussed earlier, low producer prices had dramatically reduced the level of agricultural produce entering and remaining within official marketing channels. By the early 1980s, even families entitled to rations were relying to a large extent on the parallel markets. Conakry households, on average, were getting only an estimated 25 percent of their cereals from official sources; outside the capital, ration card holders were acquiring only 5 percent of their cereal purchases from official sources (World Bank 1984a).

By the early 1980s, then, the relevant food prices for all but a handful of privileged officials and institutions (e.g., the military) had become the parallel retail prices rather than the official prices. Thus, consumers were facing extremely high prices, while at the same time official producer prices were kept artificially low at the expense of the farmer. Open market consumer prices in 1980, for example, were more than three times the import parity price, while official producer prices, at the parallel exchange rate, were substantially below world market prices. The wide gap between farmgate and consumer prices resulting from a number of distortions, including those associated with the exchange rate and forced procurement, had serious food security implications for all but the successful rent seekers and the privileged. These policies also simplified the classic food policy dilemma of how to improve producer incentives and moderate consumer prices at the same time. Reform could do both.

POLICY REFORM

It was in this context of a crippled agricultural sector and of market failures in food distribution and retailing that Guinea's Second Republic inherited power. Reforms commenced in 1984 and continued with renewed vigor after 1986 within a formal structural adjustment program. The reforms focused on the structural deficiencies inherent in production, distribution, and trade as outlined above. They emphasized dismantling the extensive state controls and establishing a policy framework conducive to the development of a market-oriented economy.

Of the several tenets associated with the government's agricultural and food sector reforms, some were implemented prior to the programs supported with funds from the World Bank, IMF, and USAID. First, in 1984 the government abolished state collective farms. In 1985, furthermore, producer prices were deregulated.

Second, the government acted in 1984 to liberalize marketing by terminating quotas that forced the marketing of agricultural products to the state and by eliminating restrictions to the internal movement of goods.[24] Commencing in 1986, private traders could participate at all levels of internal and external trade with the elimination of state marketing monopolies and parastatal monopolies on long distance transportation and storage. In 1985, for example, several parastatals lost monopoly control, including SEMAPE and AGRIMA, responsible for the marketing of fertilizers and agricultural implements respectively. FRUITEX and PROSECO, the parastatals charged, respectively, with exporting fruit and coffee, had to compete with the private sector.[25] The state cattle marketing agency was closed. Furthermore, the government promoted private trade by, for example, enacting a commercial law aimed at promoting the business sector.

Third, prices of all consumer goods were liberalized in 1986, except those of imported rice in the form of food aid and petroleum products. The ration system for officially priced goods was formally eliminated at the end of 1985. During negotiation of the second SAL a law was prepared that, when enacted, reasserted the rule of free pricing.[26] All food imports, including food aid, were subject to full cost pricing, which included the minimum 10 percent import duty. More specifically, food aid was priced at the landed c.i.f. price valued at the prevailing official (liberalized) exchange rate plus realistic margins for handling, marketing, and losses. While food aid rice was thus initially subject to administrative wholesale price setting, even these prices were increased fourfold in 1986 in step with the devaluation.

Fourth, a new national agricultural research center was established to compensate for the years of neglect in agricultural research and technological improvement in Guinean agriculture. The newly formed institute, *l'Institut de Recherche Agricole de Guinée* (IRAG), focuses on applied and adaptive agronomic research.

All of these reforms in agricultural pricing, marketing, and institutional arrangements were made more meaningful by the concurrent liberalization of the exchange rate and trade regime in 1986. In 1988 the turnover tax levied on imports and domestic production was harmonized at 10 percent. The export tax was initially set at 2 percent and then eliminated in 1991. These reforms, discussed in greater detail in chapter 3, "Trade and Exchange Rate Policy," profoundly affected the volume of trade, especially the import of foreign rice. Between 1983 and 1992 the volume of this staple imported into Guinea increased by 227 percent. The effects this increase had on household welfare, calorie consumption, and the agricultural sector will be explored thoroughly in the final section of this chapter.

In light of Guinea's history of state interventionism and discrimination against agriculture, these initial reforms dramatically indicated the government's will for quick change. Predictably these changes have also been a shock to the country's economic and institutional system. While it largely is too early to speak of the success or failure of the reforms, the following section discusses in more detail their implementation, early pitfalls, and, where possible, their initial impacts upon household welfare and poverty, and domestic production.

GENERAL ECONOMIC CONSEQUENCES OF REFORM

The reform program has entailed the liberalization of producer prices and marketing, cash crop exports, and food imports. We analyze reform and its impact first on agricultural exports and then on rice production and consumption.

Pricing, Production, and Marketing of Agricultural Exports

The liberalization of producer prices has resulted in a dramatic increase in the legal prices for the production of export crops. Although no consistent time series data have been collected either on actual prices paid to producers after adjustment, or on actual parallel market prices paid to producers before adjustment, available data provide considerable insight into the evolution of pricing policy.

In the case of coffee, indicative (i.e., targets for) official farmgate prices issued by MICA were closely adhered to from 1986 through 1989.[27] In 1986 this price, at GF 400 per kilogram, was close to six times higher than the official producer price in the preceding year (Table 10). Examining NPCs valued at the official exchange rate (Table 12) also makes it fallaciously appear that the concurrent large devaluation of the exchange resulted in producers being heavily taxed beginning in 1986. However, when prices are valued at the more appropriate parallel exchange rate, the NPC for coffee increases from 0.12 to 0.53 between 1985 and 1986. The NPC appeared to reach 0.70 in 1988 when an increase in the indicative producer price coincided with the beginning of a fall in world prices for coffee. Commencing in 1989, and then with the collapse of the International Coffee Agreement in 1990 (and the accompanying disruption of the export quota system), actual producer prices have fallen well below the stated indicative price.[28] Nevertheless, at 0.55 in 1991, the NPC for coffee continues to be higher than during the First Republic.

The effects of these improved incentives are most evident in data on official coffee production (Table 13) and exports. Official exports increased dramatically between 1980–1985 and 1986 and have increased at an average rate of close to

40 percent annually between 1986 and 1992. Whereas total official exports averaged 580 MT from 1980 to 1985, they increased to 4,600 MT by 1986 and to 29,100 MT by 1992.

This increase would appear largely to be due to the rechanneling of informal sector exports back into the formal sector because of improved incentives. As coffee is a perennial crop, the dramatic increase in exports over the course of a few years is not likely attributable to production increases alone. To the extent that coffee sales have simply been diverted from informal sales to official sales, producer welfare may not have increased as dramatically as have government export tax revenues. The continued rapid increase in exports, however, also likely signifies an increased allocation of resources to coffee production since 1985.[29]

Coffee, reportedly the crop in which Guinea holds the largest comparative advantage, is the agricultural export with apparently the most dramatic reaction to pricing and marketing changes since the liberalization of producer prices and marketing (Scetagri 1986). Although palm kernel exports also increased markedly between 1985 and 1989, they were still less than one-half their average level between 1966 and 1970 (Table 16).[30] Reliable data on other crops are difficult to find. However, the fact that an estimated 30,000 to 50,000 MT of grafted mango fruit is wasted annually in Guinea, much of it rotting on the ground for lack of entrepreneurs who have been able to get the requisite credit, indicates the difficulties of developing a marketing infrastructure, including the identification of the opportune overseas markets in which to sell the fruit (Chemonics 1987b).

The continuing lag of agricultural exports far behind levels recorded before the ruinous policies of the First Republic may be attributed to a number of factors. Beyond issues of comparative advantage and domestic resource costs, which we do not address here, institutional and policy-related factors continue to constrain exports. In particular, the major export deterrents are the high cost of internal freight, the difficulty producers have in acquiring credit, and the heavy bureaucratic costs associated with a multitude of export procedures. Exporters have been required to obtain a *demande d'autorisation*, to be renewed every six months, that indicates the quantity they will export over the next six months. Coffee exporters have to additionally register for a coffee export permit to be renewed annually on the basis of "capacity, seriousness, compliance, and actual use of the license in the previous year" (Chemonics 1987a, b).[31] A *bulletin d'expedition* and a *bulletin d'analyse* must be filed. An *ordre de transit* must be obtained. For all products, a certificate indicating the point of origin and a separate certificate from the *Service de Conditionnement* assuring export quality are required. Quality control is exercised both at the prefecture level and at Conakry. A quality control service charge, or *taxe de conditionnement*, is then charged.[32] While the tax is supposed to be 5 percent of the official reference price, a tax of 20 percent (the rate for the turnover tax) often has been incorrectly extracted and sometimes charged twice. Exporters have also had to pay a 2 percent export tax based on the f.o.b. value of the export commodity. As of 1987, exporters were required to open and maintain a foreign exchange account at the Central Bank. The minimum balance as of 1987 was GF 2.5 million equivalent. The BCRG had to approve and record each shipment by issuing a *demande d'exportation* upon checking the relevant sales contract, a measure justified as a screen for capital flight (Chemonics 1987a, b). Then, with the approval of the BCRG and the *Bureau de Conditionnement*, the exporter could apply to the Ministry of Commerce for an *ordre de transit*. With this permit, finally, the exporter could engage a freight forwarder to arrange freight and clear customs. In addition to the bill of lading, until 1990 coffee exporters also needed to secure the International Coffee Organization (ICO) documents such as the quota stamp.

In a well-functioning bureaucracy, these procedures are not likely to be debilitating. But in Conakry, where state intervention has been synonymous with rent-seeking and ineptitude, procedures should be simplified to increase exports. To this end, there has been discussion of establishing a *guichet unique*, so all procedures could be undertaken at one point at the border. In addition to consolidating processes, reducing paperwork would lower the time costs of processing exports, thereby eliminating one of the factors that also diminishes the timeliness and reliability of Guinean exporters in the eyes of international partners. Eliminating administrative hoops would also presumably lower the costs incurred in the form of rents paid to civil servants needed to get the required paperwork done. A further factor that would promote exports is the elimination of capital requirements at the Central Bank to qualify a trader as an exporter.[33] The suspension of the *taxe d'exportation* and the *taxe de conditionnement* should have a noticeable impact on the volume of exports.

A number of other policy options should also be explored with the intent of promoting exports. Inaccessibility to credit and inputs are frequently cited as primary production constraints by farmers (GOG undated [a] and [b]). Policies that address these constraints would presumably substantially improve the supply elasticities of export crops. Transport also constitutes a big bottleneck in Guinea. In addition to bad roads, trucking capacity is limited. In 1990 most of the approximately 4,000 trucks in Guinea were old, dilapidated, and small. Only a few exceeded a 10 MT capacity, and most could carry only 5 to 8 MT. The limited access would-be traders have to transport may well be a barrier to trade and a source of noncompetitive control on domestic trade. Improving the quality of roads and increasing the number of trucks should lower the cost of transport, improve the efficiency of marketing links from the interior, and lower marketing margins by improving competition. The benefits of lowering transport costs and marketing margins will be further discussed when we consider the domestic marketing of food crops.

Pricing, Production, and Marketing of Food Crops

Policy reform has also targeted the pricing, production, and marketing of food crops. These reforms have profoundly affected the production and consumption of rice, the nation's primary staple.

RICE PRODUCER PRICES AND PRODUCTION. Policy reform has effectively led to a large increase in legal producer prices for rice. In 1986 and 1987, observed producer prices (GF 81 and GF 96 per kilogram, respectively) were three to four times greater than the official producer prices of two years earlier (GF 25 per kilogram) (Table 10). NPCs calculated by employing the parallel exchange rate and excluding marketing margins thus jump from 0.33 in 1985 to 0.96 in 1986 (Table 12). The actual NPCs in 1986 and 1987 were thus very close to parity. Farmers' actual market revenues would thus have increased, due to this price effect, assuming farmers were not receiving equally high prices on unofficial markets prior to adjustment.

Given the low quality of production data, it is difficult to ascertain the extent to which production is increased by the increasing of rice producer prices.[34] Nevertheless, the little available evidence shows that rice production increased subsequent to liberalization of official producer prices. Whereas pre-reform production estimates averaged 450,000 MT between 1980 and 1984, recent production estimates generally average 500,000 MT or greater (GOG 1990c, 1992b).[35] The Filière Riz surveys in Lower Guinea (GOG undated [a]) and Upper Guinea (GOG undated [b]), which questioned farmers on land use, also indicate increases in hectarage devoted to rice between 1985 and 1987. In Upper Guinea, the mean area farmers allocated to rice increased from 2.39 hectares in 1986 to 3.23 hectares in 1987. In Lower Guinea, 61 percent of farmers claimed to have cultivated more land with rice in 1986 than in 1985, and 70 percent were going to increase their 1987 land allocation to rice beyond their 1986 levels (GOG undated [a], [b]). In Lower Guinea, the increased land planted to rice was due primarily to the clearing of new land and reduction of fallow time, rather than the reallocation of land from the production of other crops such as groundnuts and fonio (GOG undated [a]).

Despite an apparent early response to liberalization, however, several constraints are becoming evident with respect to rice production. The first relates to producer prices themselves.[36] After the rapid adjustment in 1986, producer price increases initially did not keep pace with inflation. Between 1986 and 1989 real producer prices decreased at an average annual rate of 13 percent. With a slowdown in inflation in 1992, the real producer price of rice rose approximately to the level recorded in 1988. Similarly, NPCs for rice also fell between 1987 and 1989 after initial gains with reform. Only with a general decline in the average world market price from 1989 to 1992 did NPCs for rice increase again to the levels attained immediately after producer price liberalization. At 0.90 in 1992, however, the NPC level was three times higher than that recorded in pre-adjustment years.

Other problems, beyond prices, continue to restrain domestic rice production in Guinea. There has been virtually no technological innovation during the past decade due to the years of neglect of local agricultural research and related extension efforts. Research on seed improvement, water management, and productivity-enhancing farming systems has been conspicuously lacking (AIRD 1989). Only 9 percent of farmers interviewed in Upper Guinea used "improved variety" seed (GOG undated [a]). Most farmers do not use fertilizer, pesticides, and phytosanitary products. Only 1.5 to 2.1 percent of interviewed farmers in Lower and Upper Guinea used chemical fertilizer, while this figure was less than 1 percent in Middle Guinea and the Forest Region (GOG undated [a]). Overall, only 5.6 percent of farm plots had organic fertilization, the vast majority of them being in Lower Guinea. Low utilization levels of these inputs are partially a result of the lack of credit and finance among farmers, partially a consequence of the lack of extension, and partially due to the unavailability in most rural areas of inputs such as fertilizer (USAID 1987a; GOG undated [b]). This lack of supply is itself attributable to the private sector's negligible involvement in the marketing of agricultural inputs. Moreover, anecdotal evidence suggests that the lack of demand is partly due to farmers finding it unprofitable to use unsubsidized fertilizer for rice production, even given current producer prices for rice (AIRD 1989).[37]

The limited availability of rural credit is also a potentially binding constraint to rice production in particular and agricultural production in general. While informal savings and lending institutions such as the *tontines* exist, they extend credit only in small amounts. Meanwhile the new commercial banks are reluctant to extend credit in rural areas due to high information and administration costs coupled with the absence until recently of a legal framework in which to secure formal collateral and to enforce loan recovery.

In Lower Guinea at least, farmers cite limited labor as a further constraint to production (GOG undated [a]). With the out-migration of labor to urban areas and to the mines, farm households are often short-handed for the labor intensive needs of the harvest period. Rural labor markets during this period are short in supply, and most rural households are short of cash to hire labor anyway (Thenevin 1988).

Rice Market Liberalization

DOMESTIC MARKETING. The second facet of adjustment policies with respect to local rice has been the liberalization of marketing. With the sanctioning and encouraging of private trade, marketing and distribution channels have more freely developed in rural areas, albeit slowly.[38] Rice is generally brought to market as paddy or as hand-hulled rice by farmers.[39] It is then bought either directly by a local consumer or by a local trader.[40] This trader or collector usually purchases from a number of producers, sometimes processes the rice at this stage, and then bags it in 50 kilogram sacks. The intermediary then transports the rice to an urban center (e.g., *marchés central de la prefecture*) where the rice is unloaded for sale or transported for sale to a more distant city such as Conakry. In the urban center, the 50 kilogram sacks are purchased either by wholesalers or by retailers. Finally, women sell it at market, normally in very small units, such as one-quarter kilogram cups.

The length of the marketing chain, coupled with the high costs of transportation (given bad roads and the shortage of vehicles), results in high costs of marketing and distributing local rice in Guinea (Table 20). Retail prices continue to be approximately three times the price of paddy received by producers. In 1988 and 1992, marketing and transportation costs from within Lower Guinea, the region most proximal to Conakry, were approximately 48 percent of the observed retail price of rice in Conakry.[41] It cost three times more to transport one kilogram

TABLE 20
Guinea: Conakry Local Rice Cost Structure, 1988 and 1992.
(GF per kilogram)

	1988	1992
Price to producer for paddy	70	230
Price to producer for rice	105	345
Price to collector	10	30
Price of transformation	15	60
Transport to transit points	10	30
Margin to transit trader	20	75
Transport to Conakry	20	60
Margins to wholesaler and retailer	20	80
Total (rice price to Conakry consumer)	200	680

Sources: Author's estimates based on Benz (1992); Pujo (1993) for 1992 data; Thenevin (1988) for 1987 data.

of rice from Boké to Conakry than it did to ship one kilogram from Bangkok to Conakry.[42] Consequently, despite efforts to encourage local rice production, most local rice sold in Conakry is limited to that produced nearby. Specifically, most of Conakry's local rice is brought directly into town by boat from the nearby islands of Forecariah to Boussoura port near the main market of Madina. The large majority of the total available rice in Conakry, however, continues to be imported.

As with production, the high cost structure of internal distribution indicates some enduring problems with marketing despite trade liberalization. First, the extent to which and the pace at which liberalization has proceeded raises some legitimate concerns. As of 1986, while permitting the operation of private traders, the government still required their licensing (Hanrahan and Block 1988). Effectively, licensing has barred market entry and has probably served to extract rent. It also presumably restricts the number of traders and consequently the competitiveness of trade. Second, difficulty in acquiring credit also limits the number of traders and contributes to their high cost structure (Filippi-Wilhelm 1987). Credit generally comes from the next person down the marketing chain rather than from formal lending institutions. Moreover, credit extended for domestic production and marketing requires the locking up of capital for up to an entire agricultural cycle, a further disincentive to lenders. Third, the risks involved in lending have also worked to increase marketing margins. Fourth, the shortage of trucks in Guinea, as discussed earlier, also raises marketing costs by, for one thing, rendering some degree of noncompetitive control of marketing channels to certain agents. Finally, the shortage of equipment in Guinea results in inordinately high costs of processing and dehulling rice (Hanrahan and Block 1988). Clearly addressing credit, capital, and infrastructure constraints, which raise marketing margins, should help increase the producer price offered to farmers and thus promote production itself.

IMPORTS. As already alluded to, liberalization has also affected the market for rice imports, with possible implications for food security and domestic production incentives. The increase in rice imports accompanying liberalization has been dramatic. From 1981–1983 to 1990–1992, rice imports (commercial and food aid) more than doubled (Table 21). From 1986 to 1992, imported rice accounted for more than one-third of total rice availability, far more than in any earlier period. This surge in rice imports is primarily due to the increase in commercial imports by the private sector in response to policy changes. Since the elimination of ALIMAG, the parastatal charged with rice imports during the First Republic, private traders undertook the import of food. Moreover, imports

TABLE 21

Guinea: Rice Production, Imports, and Availability.
('000 mt)

Year	Paddy Production	Commercial Imports	Food Aid Imports	Total Imports	Total National Rice Availability	Food Aid as Percent of Total Imports	Total Imports as Percent of Total Rice Availability	Per Capita Rice Availability (kilogram per year)
1973	413	30.0	0.0	30.0	234.4	0.0	12.8	57.8
1974	417	30.0	0.0	30.0	236.4	0.0	12.7	57.6
1975	422	22.7	13.5	36.2	245.1	37.3	14.8	59.1
1976	426	3.0	17.0	20.0	230.9	85.0	8.7	55.0
1977	418	30.5	5.0	35.5	242.4	14.2	14.6	57.0
1978	366	32.7	17.3	50.0	231.2	34.5	21.6	53.6
1979	348	48.4	22.8	71.2	243.5	32.0	29.2	55.5
1980	480	119.1	8.9	128.0	365.6	7.0	35.0	82.0
1981	485	55.5	22.1	77.6	317.7	28.5	24.4	69.9
1982	490	22.0	24.5	46.5	289.1	52.6	16.1	62.3
1983	396	58.5	18.5	77.0	273.0	24.0	28.2	57.5
1984	403	49.6	30.4	80.0	279.5	37.9	28.6	57.5
1985	437	27.2	42.8	70.0	286.3	61.2	24.4	57.4
1986	510	26.7	53.3	80.0	332.5	66.6	24.1	64.9
1987	515	30.7	59.3	90.0	344.9	65.9	26.1	65.5
1988	525	59.2	25.8	85.0	344.9	30.3	24.6	63.6
1989	560	160.7	34.7	195.4	472.6	17.8	41.3	84.6
1990	616	87.4	24.8	112.2	417.1	22.1	26.9	72.5
1991	688	170.0	12.2	182.2	522.8	6.7	34.9	88.1

(Table continues on the next page.)

TABLE 21 (continued)

Year	Paddy Production	Commercial Imports	Food Aid Imports	Total Imports	Total National Rice Availability	Food Aid as Percent of Total Imports	Total Imports as Percent of Total Rice Availability	Per Capita Rice Availability (kilogram per year)
1992	757	216.6	30.0	246.5	621.2	12.2	39.7	101.6
1993	833	—	29.6	—	—	—	—	—
1994	916	—	—	—	—	—	—	—

Source: FAO (1994).
Note: Local milled based on a 0.55 conversion from paddy. Losses, waste, and seed assumed to be 10 percent of paddy production.

were promoted by the fact that until 1991 only a 10 percent turnover tax was applied to rice imports. As a result, commercial imports of rice increased steadily and rapidly from the beginning of liberalization in 1986. Rice imports then fell sharply between 1989 and 1990 in part due to excessive stocks and the imposition of the requirement that importers pre-deposit 20 percent of the value of their import order with the Central Bank. The subsequent removal of this requirement explains the increase in commercial imports in 1991 and 1992.

The initial acceleration in the total volume of rice imports was also due to the increase in food aid upon adjustment.[43] Rice given as food aid doubled from 30,000 MT in 1984 to about 60,000 MT in 1987. Much of this increase was in the form of PL 480 Title I and II rice from the United States. As with commercially imported rice, the marketing and distribution of food aid rice is currently the responsibility of private traders. The procedure for transferring this rice to the private sector, however, has undergone several changes since 1985. Initially sold at a price established by the Guinean Government, in 1988 and 1989 the transfer of PL 480 rice was to take place by auction. However, problems developed with the implementation of the auction, resulting in the suspension of the PL 480 program for 1991. With the reinstatement of the PL 480 program, food aid imports of rice averaged close to 30,000 MT in 1992 and 1993. The PL 480 program's reinstatement, along with the concurrent increase in commercial imports, re-sulted in a substantial increase in total imports in 1992.

Despite the liberalization of international trade in food crops, all rice imports remain concentrated in the hands of a few importers. Ten established importers brought in all commercial rice imports in 1988/89, five of them accounting for approximately 80 percent of these imports (Lowdermilk 1989).[44] Nevertheless, the distribution and marketing channels for imported rice seem to be more streamlined and efficient than those of local rice (Thenevin 1988). There are essentially two channels. In the first case the importer sells directly to whole-saler/retailers who then sell to consumers (by the 50 kilogram sack). This is practiced only in Conakry. In the second case, importers sell to wholesalers in Conakry and the interior who then sell to retailers.[45] These then sell to micro-retailers, namely market women, who sell by the cup. Each step of these market-ing chains requires access to credit. Although the banks generally extend formal credit to Conakry wholesalers, informal credit is also crucial at various points in the marketing of imported rice. Access to the informal credit is generally easier than that for locally produced rice. This easier access reflects that the chain of events for imported rice, from import to retail sales, is much shorter than that of domestic rice, from seeding to sale. In addition, marketing costs for imported rice are much lower than those for local production, as discussed above.

RICE CONSUMER PRICES. Liberalizing prices raises the major issue of the pricing of imports, because of their effect both on consumers and on domestic producers. Discussing the evolution of rice prices is made complex because there are at least three rice markets: one for imported food aid (*riz Çaroline*), one for commercial imports (*riz Asiatique*), and one for local rice (*riz locale*). Purchased from Vietnam, Taiwan, Pakistan, and Thailand, the commercially imported *riz Asiatique* is generally of low quality (usually 35 percent broken), one-third cheaper on the Conakry retail market than locally produced rice, and not parboiled. U.S. food aid rice (*riz Caroline*) is generally well-milled, about 20 percent broken, and not parboiled. It is preferred more than the commercially imported *riz Asiatique*, but less than the local variety and is consequently priced between the two.[46] Although the quality and prices of these types of rice differ, it is not always clear how the marketing channels and regulations differ, both in terms of stated policy and implementation. Nevertheless, enough is known to give some important insight into how reforms in the last half of the 1980s have affected prices and availability.

First, with local rice, attempts to administer consumer prices were abandoned as part of the reform program, in keeping with producer price reforms discussed above. Consequently, in 1986 consumers faced an officially sanctioned free market price of GF 219 per kilogram (2.6 times c.i.f.) (Table 22) as opposed to the officially administered price of GF 25 per kilogram (0.3 times c.i.f.) the previous year (Table 18). The price change experienced by consumers was not as dramatic, however, considering the fact that even prior to price reform many consumers purchased their local rice on the parallel market at prices higher than the administered price. The parallel market retail price of GF 83 per kilogram in 1983 (Weaver 1987), for example, was 2.4 times the c.i.f. price evaluated at the parallel exchange rate that year. Since reform, the retail price-to-c.i.f. ratio has fluctuated erratically. Local rice prices, however, have remained considerably higher than c.i.f. prices valued at the parallel exchange rate, varying from 1.6 to 2.7 and averaging 2.2 times higher between 1986 and 1993. These prices reflect high costs of production, price variations due to weather, and internal marketing, as well as a quality premium (Table 22).

While the liberalization of marketing for domestically produced rice was rapid and comprehensive, this was not the case for imported rice. Despite reforms that allowed private marketing agents to play a key role in the domestic marketing of imported rice, the government was slow to stop managing the import and price of the country's most strategic food commodity. Even after liberalization in 1986, for example, the government continued to require approval (*autorisations de transit*) for moving imported rice into areas of the interior.[47] The government

TABLE 22

Guinea: Retail Rice Prices, 1985–1991.

	Local Rice Open Market Price			Imported Rice Official Price			Imported Rice Open Market Price		
Year	GF/kg	Ratio to c.i.f.[a]	Ratio to c.i.f.[b]	GF/kg	Ratio to c.i.f.[a]	Ratio to c.i.f.[b]	GF/kg	Ratio to c.i.f.[a]	Ratio to c.i.f.[b]
1985	149.62	30.11	1.98	100	—	—	—	100.20	20.17
1986	219.09	2.82	2.60	100	1.29	1.19	129.53	1.67	1.54
1987	194.42	2.20	2.13	173	1.13	1.10	119.25	1.35	1.31
1988	319.64	2.44	2.22	210	1.32	1.20	212.64	1.62	1.48
1989	319.00	1.72	1.59	210	1.13	1.05	230.00	1.24	1.15
1990	406.87	2.41	2.25	—	1.24	1.16	277.05	1.64	1.53
1991	422.27	2.18	2.02	—	—	—	327.23	1.69	1.57
1992	639.70	2.89	2.66	—	—	—	373.10	1.68	1.55
1993[c]	555.00	2.43	2.31	—	—	—	368.00	1.61	1.53

Sources: Rice c.i.f. price from import quantity and value data from AIRD (1989). Figures from 1988 and 1989 are calculated using 0.85 BKK f.o.b. plus freight. Retail price data: 1989 data are derived from early 1990 based on ENCOMEC survey results. 1990 and 1991 (first quarter) prices from unpublished MCPI data. Other sources for rice data: Chemonics (1986); Caputo (1991); Filippi-Wilhelm (1988); Hirsch (1986); Hanrahan and Block (1988); Lowdermilk (1989); Nellum (1980); PNAFR (1992); Scetagri/Agroprogress (1986); Thenevin (1988); USAID (1989); World Bank (1984b).

a. Prices evaluated at official exchange rate.
b. Prices evaluated at parallel exchange rate.
c. Figures for 1993 based on first quarter (March) data.

also continued to maintain an official price for imported rice. The official price did evolve, however, decreasing in significance during the transition to free market pricing. Ostensibly, prices for commercial and food aid imports were to be determined by a formula based on c.i.f. plus a reasonable fee for handling and distributing the commodity. In 1986 the counterpart payment for food aid imports was thus set at GF 73 per kilogram, with an official price of GF 93 per kilogram at the wholesale level. Given a fixed legal retail margin, this translated into an official retail price of GF 100 per kilogram for imported rice in Conakry.[48] By 1989 this official price, although largely disregarded, had been raised to GF 210 per kilogram. Indeed while earlier studies discuss the actual distribution of food aid rice at an official price since 1986, by 1989 this price appears to have been largely irrelevant.

The 1986 price of GF 100 per kilogram represented a subsidy to consumers, albeit a small one. Based on a 30 percent marketing margin, subsidy levels were approximately 10 to 25 percent between 1986 and 1990, when evaluated at the parallel exchange rate.[49] The existence of an official, subsidized price for imported rice below that observed in retail markets raises questions as to how this rice was distributed and who was able to access it. According to Thenevin (1988), despite the formal abandonment of the ration system that existed before structural adjustment (distributing domestic and imported rice), imported rice continued to be sold at the official price of GF 100 per kilogram at the boutiques or *commerçants de quartier* in 1986 and early 1987. It is unclear exactly how the distribution occurred during the transition and, if rationed, in what quantities.[50] Currently, however, all rice is sold at a free market price.

The actual free market retail prices for imported rice have fluctuated relative to import parity between 1986 and 1993 (Table 22).[51,52] After initially declining from 1.54 in 1986 to 1.15 in 1989, the ratio between the retail price of imported rice and the c.i.f. price rose to 1.57 in 1991. This was primarily a consequence of increased restrictions on imports, such as the imposition in 1990 of the requirement of a 20 percent deposit by importers for consumer imports, in conjunction with falling world rice prices.[53] Effectively the increased cost to importing faced by traders was passed on to consumers, who were subjected to an increase in the level of implicit taxation and consequently did not observe the fall in the world price of rice. Since 1991, however, continued declines in the real c.i.f. price of rice, along with the elimination in 1992 of the advance deposit requirement on consumer imports, resulted not only in a fall in the ratio of retail prices relative to the c.i.f. price, but in real declines in the consumer retail price of imported rice itself. After a 6.6 percent increase in the real price of imported rice between 1989 and 1990, the real retail price of imported rice fell by 1.2 percent in 1991 and by 2.2 percent in 1992.[54]

Rice Consumption, Price Policy, and Food Security

Rice marketing and pricing are of particular concern in considering household consumption and food security, especially given the importance of rice as a staple in Guinea. In the short term, therefore, food policy can most affect household welfare, both in urban and most rural areas, when mediated through rice price policy.

In the absence of good data, inferences about changes in national rice consumption must be based on estimates of the actual quantity of rice produced and imported (net) into the country. While the precise level of changes ought to be treated cautiously, these estimates (presented in Table 21) nevertheless tell the basic story.

Rice availability has dramatically increased since 1986 primarily because of the large increase in rice imports.[55] Whereas per capita rice availability nationally averaged close to 68 kilograms per year between 1980 and 1984, it had risen to average about 87 kilograms per capita per year between 1988 and 1992 (Table 21).[56] The exact extent of the increase in rice availability is, however, clearly sensitive to the estimate of domestic production used.[57]

Rice consumption levels are generally higher in Conakry, where large quantities of imported rice are readily available. Several estimates have placed the consumption of rice in Conakry at 18 to 20 percent of the rice available nationally (Chemonics 1986; Filippi-Wilhelm 1987). Recent empirical evidence gathered by the CFNPP/ENCOMEC household survey shows consumption levels in Conakry to be even higher. At an annual per capita rice consumption of 91.2 kilograms in 1990/91, Conakry residents eat more rice than the Guinean population in general. Moreover, Conakry residents primarily consume imported rice: 84 percent of all rice was imported. Conakry residents consumed an estimated 60 percent of total rice imports in 1990/91 (Arulpragasam 1994).[58]

The 1989/90 CFNPP/ENCOMEC survey greatly enhances our understanding of food consumption patterns in urban areas. Indeed, data from the survey indicate that for consumers in Conakry, rice is a critical commodity and is more important in their diet and expenditure bundles than any other commodity, including bread, fish, and oil (Table 23). It comprises 14.9 percent of food expenditures and 8.5 percent of total expenditures. In those households in the bottom 30 percent of the per capita expenditure distribution, rice constitutes even higher percentages of food and total expenditures: 22.9 and 13.1 percent, respectively.

The importance of rice in the consumption bundle of the poor is further reinforced by an examination of demand parameters estimated from the survey data utilizing an Almost Ideal Demand System (AIDS). Income elasticities in this study reveal that imported rice has the lowest income elasticity of all foods

TABLE 23

Guinea: Expenditure Budget Shares by Per Capita Expenditure Quintile.
(percent)

	Quintiles					All	Bottom 30th Percentile
	1	2	3	4	5		
Local rice	1.69	1.36	1.93	1.42	0.97	1.48	1.57
Imported rice	12.33	9.11	6.76	4.70	2.35	7.05	11.51
Other coarse grains, roots, tubers	1.86	2.17	2.31	2.13	1.74	2.04	1.97
Bread	5.41	4.85	4.40	3.47	2.41	4.11	5.25
Meat	4.12	6.15	6.83	7.25	6.05	6.08	4.69
Fish	9.13	7.64	7.14	5.93	3.44	6.65	8.76
Milk and dairy products	1.28	2.25	2.53	2.68	2.48	2.24	1.59
Vegetables	8.69	7.96	7.59	6.14	3.82	6.84	8.59
Fruits	1.93	2.62	3.04	3.65	3.36	2.92	2.19
Butter and oil	3.40	3.31	2.84	2.39	1.62	2.71	3.33
Spices	3.36	2.72	2.45	2.02	1.13	2.34	3.15
Sugar	1.85	1.71	1.56	1.19	0.88	1.44	1.89
Beverages	0.96	1.57	1.45	2.06	2.89	1.79	1.11
Food away from home	1.54	1.50	2.07	4.19	5.14	2.89	1.52
Fuel	6.81	6.19	5.27	4.18	3.00	5.09	6.70
Domestic consumables	3.26	3.02	2.95	2.90	2.41	2.91	3.18
Clothes and shoes	2.52	4.44	4.80	5.24	6.18	4.64	2.97
Housing, household durables, utilities, taxes	15.45	13.77	13.90	14.32	15.92	14.67	14.88
Personal, discretionary, recreation	5.31	6.86	8.72	10.09	16.69	9.53	5.52
Transport	5.92	7.37	7.93	10.64	14.33	9.24	6.31

Education	1.40	1.47	1.41	1.04	0.85	1.23	1.47
Health	1.79	1.95	2.11	2.35	2.33	2.11	1.85
Total	100.00	100.00	100.00	100.00	100.00	100.00	100.00
Food Share	57.55	54.92	52.91	49.23	38.28	50.58	57.12
Total Expenditure (GNF)	11,961	18,643	25,400	36,040	82,418	34,892	13,699
Number of households	345	345	345	345	345	1,725	518

Source: Arulpragasam and del Ninno (1993).

among the sample (Table 24).[59] Interestingly, imported rice has a negative income
elasticity among the nonpoor households, indicating that it is an inferior good
among this group.[60] Furthermore, the low absolute value of the own-price
elasticity computed from demand estimation also reflects that rice is basic to diets
in Conakry and thus least responsive to price changes.[61]

Economic liberalization has contributed to two countervailing effects of rice
policy on the poor: the formal abandonment of the ration system and the increased
supply of rice imports. The welfare implications of rice policy changes thus
varied according to consumers' relative reliance on the parallel market in fulfill-
ing their rice needs prior to adjustment. As shown in Table 19, those who lost
were mainly large-scale merchants and higher level *functionnaires* who had
access to the ration system. Those who gained from policy reform, by contrast,
were mainly the smaller merchants, part-time workers, and unemployed, who had
always had difficulty accessing the official market (GOG 1986). These groups
benefit from cheap and abundant imported rice on the free market (rather than
rationed and subsidized rice on the official market), which, as shown in Figure
5, was 34 percent cheaper, and more stable, than domestic rice for the period
1985–1992.

While the urban poor thus directly benefit from cheap and plentiful imported
rice, liberalization policies that encourage imports have more complex effects on

TABLE 24
Guinea: Estimated Elasticities of Food Commodities.

	Income Elasticities			Own-Price Elasticities		
	Poor	Non-poor	All	Poor	Non-poor	All
Local rice	0.644	0.596	0.625	−1.893	−2.020	−1.874
Imported rice	0.338	−0.531	0.069	−0.592	−0.151	−0.455
Other grains, root, tubers	1.069	1.068	1.062	−0.857	−0.859	−0.872
Bread	0.510	0.265	0.397	−0.673	−0.523	−0.604
Meat and dairy	1.317	1.230	1.239	−0.930	−0.955	−0.952
Fish	0.408	0.048	0.314	−0.727	−0.610	−0.692
Vegetables	0.515	0.308	0.460	−0.644	−0.510	−0.608
Fruits	1.152	1.102	1.114	−0.968	−0.980	−0.977
Butter and oil	0.467	0.227	0.396	−0.823	−0.751	−0.801
Spices	0.325	−0.092	0.193	−0.697	−0.522	−0.642
Sugar	0.381	0.070	0.248	−0.543	−0.319	−0.447
Beverages	0.584	1.323	1.420	−1.304	−1.171	−1.221
Nonfoods	1.473	1.374	1.437	−1.207	−1.066	−1.041

Source: Arulpragasam (1994).

FIGURE 5
Monthly Retail Rice Prices in Conakry, Imported vs. Domestic Rice.

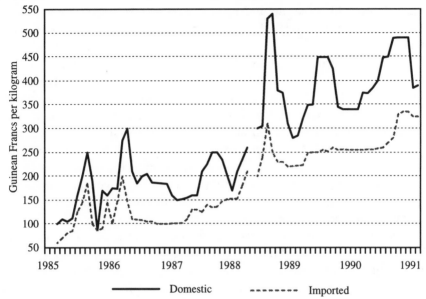

Domestic ──────── Imported ────────

Source: GOG (undated [e]).

rural food security. It is difficult to address the issue of consumption and food security in Guinea's rural areas, however. There is a dearth of information on consumption patterns in rural areas, and production data, as discussed earlier, are weak. Moreover, production and consumption patterns vary across the country. The importance of rice for food security is not as critical in the Fouta Djallon, for example, as it is in Conakry. It is impossible to get good disaggregated region-specific information in production and consumption, though more information is available for Lower Guinea.

Nevertheless, rice is indeed the most important food crop produced and consumed in rural Guinea, which hosts 74 percent of the nation's population. Rice, in fact, is grown on approximately 43 percent of all cultivated land throughout the country, though there is considerable geographic diversity.[62] Changes in producer and consumer prices of rice, therefore, have certainly affected food security in the interior. Moreover, adjustment policies have raised the important question of the impact of rice import liberalization, specifically on domestic production, farmer incomes, rural consumption patterns, and rural food security.[63]

With respect to food security in rural areas, households must be distinguished according to their purchasing and selling patterns with regard to rice. Two general types of households exist: net purchasers and net sellers. The former includes subsistence farm households, which live primarily off own-production and make market purchases on occasion, especially during the *soudure*, or pre-harvest season. This type also includes farm households more actively selling and buying back rice throughout the year, with the largest sales being at harvest, typically in order to repay debt.[64] The latter consists of a smaller number of households who are net sellers of rice. In addition to production for own-consumption, these commercial farmers sell their surplus rice at harvest as well as for a higher price during the *soudure*.[65] A high percentage of net sellers, like net purchasers, however, buy rice from the market at some time in the year. In Lower Guinea this was an estimated 87 percent in 1986 (GOG undated [a]). Consequently, the welfare of rural households, including rice farmers, depends not only on producer price but on consumer price in rural areas.

Several brief but important observations can be made regarding consumer price of rice in rural areas. First, the price of local rice varies across regions in Guinea (Table 25). Consumer prices for local rice are generally highest in low production areas, such as the Fouta Djallon region of Middle Guinea (GF 250 per kilogram in 1987) and Upper Guinea (GF 195 to 250 per kilogram in 1987), and lower in high production areas, such as the Forest Region (GF 170 to 175 per kilogram in 1987) and Lower Guinea (GF 180 to 200 per kilogram in 1987). Second, the price of imported rice also varies greatly across regions, tending to

TABLE 25
Guinea: Regional Variations in Consumer Prices of Local and Imported Rice, 1986, 1987, 1992.

	Local Rice			Imported Rice		
	1986	*1987*	*1992*	*1986*	*1987*	*1992*
Lower Guinea	120–140	180–200	524–800[a]	115–120	130–150	371–392[a]
Middle Guinea						
Fouta Djallon	160–190	250	160–175	200–250	200–250	—
North-West	150–180	175–200	140–180	160–180	—	—
Upper Guinea	200–220	195–250	452–675	155–160	175–200	425–535
Forest Region	125–135	170–175	250–650	115–125	160	320–415

Sources: Filippi-Wilhelm (1988); Lower and Middle Guinea 1992 data from PNAFR (1992); Forest Region 1992 data from Pujo (1993).
a. Conakry.

be higher the more distant the market is from Conakry, reflecting the costs of internal transportation. Thus the price of imported rice in 1987 was approximately GF 130 to 150 per kilogram in Lower Guinea, GF 200 to 250 per kilogram in the Fouta Djallon region, and GF 175 to 200 per kilogram in Upper Guinea. (In 1992, however, imported rice prices in the Forest Region were even comparable with those in Conakry largely because of the abundance of donated food aid rice, intended for Liberian refugees, that was diverted and sold on the market.) Third, the price of imported rice is almost always lower than that of local rice, although the discount for imported rice is lower in producing regions. This observation lends some credit to the argument that there is a quality premium paid for local rice. The narrower price margin in the Forest Region is also consistent with the fact that it is a high production area that is distant from Conakry.

The fact that as a consequence of liberalization the price of imported rice is lower than local rice, even in rural areas, highlights the benefits accrued by the majority of rural households that are net rice purchasers, as a consequence of economic reform.[66] This is especially true given that many net rice-purchasing households tend to buy their rice predominantly during the *soudure* period when the margin between the prices of cheaper imported rice and more expensive local rice is the greatest. In most parts of Guinea, therefore, imported rice potentially plays an important food security role for consumers.

The availability of cheaper imported rice on rural retail markets has also raised the argument that rice import liberalization constitutes a longer-term food security threat to the nation by transmitting a production disincentive to domestic rice farmers (Hirsch 1986; Filippi-Wilhelm 1987; and Thenevin 1988). The doubling of the volume of rice imports from 1984 to 1989, coupled with the rice crisis in 1988, heightened concerns regarding the heavy dependence on imports and has effectively instigated a reversal of rice policy.

Particularly in 1989, the government commenced aiming to reduce rice imports. Although rice was exempt from all customs and tariffs between 1985 and 1988, it became subject to the 10 percent tax on consumer good imports in 1988 and 1989. In late 1989, however, the addition of a 2 percent customs duty and an 8 percent entry tax raised the levy to 20 percent of c.i.f. value. This increase raised the tariff on rice to even more than the 18 percent imposed on other important food imports such as wheat flour and sugar. Furthermore, as noted previously, in March 1990 the government imposed the requirement that 20 percent of the c.i.f. value of imports of consumption goods on order had to be deposited in advance at the BCRG in order to access foreign exchange. This requirement severely restricted supply, given the working capital constraints of smaller importers. The procedure for accessing foreign exchange further limited rice imports in that it required importers to lock in to the exchange rate that prevailed at the time of import declaration. Especially in an environment of frequent devaluations, this requirement exposed importers to substantial exchange rate risk.[67]

The debate regarding the appropriateness of protectionist rice policies became particularly relevant as new proposals emerged that restricted the import of rice even further. Policies suggested have ranged from the establishment of a quota and licensing system to a return to the government's contracting of imports, leaving only domestic distribution and marketing in the hands of the private sector (Kande 1991). Of particular importance has been the consideration to raising the import levy on rice (Caputo 1990). This variable levy would aim to raise the price of imported rice closer to the level of domestic rice so as to make the latter more competitive. It would also aim to stabilize the price of imported rice. The tariff proposal has furthermore been raised in the context of helping to alleviate the government's fiscal revenue crisis.

To address this controversy, we rely on analysis, reported in Arulpragasam (1994) and Arulpragasam and del Ninno (forthcoming), which uses a multimarket modeling framework.[68] The model allows us to consider the welfare effects of the government's historic 10 percent increase in tariffs on all imported commodities, a 30 percent tariff increase on imported rice alone, a 30 percent rice tariff with improved production, and a 10 percent tariff decrease on imported rice. Finally, we examine the impact of reducing the marketing margin on rice through investing in domestic infrastructure.

The Multimarket Model

Analyzing the impact of policy on agricultural commodities and household outcomes involves consideration of supply, demand, trade, and incomes. The multimarket model used here captures important interactions between commodities on both the supply and demand side. The model is also intended to capture the critical interactions across commodity markets, thus supplying an appropriate framework for analyzing the trade policies discussed below.

The model is calibrated with data from Lower Guinea which makes it regional in focus. The model contains thirteen commodity groups, eight of which are produced domestically, and three household groups: urban (Conakry) poor, urban nonpoor, and rural (Lower Guinea). The commodities and households are listed below.

Commodities		*Households*
Domestic Nontraded	*Traded Internationally*	*Groups*
Local rice	Imported rice	Conakry poor
Cereals, roots, and tubers	Wheat	Conakry nonpoor
Spices	Sugar	Rural Lower Guinea
Meat, dairy	Butter, oil	
Fish	Beverages	
Vegetables	Nonfood	
Fruit		

The model works as follows (the equations are outlined in the Appendix, and the baseline supply and demand parameters are shown in Appendix Table 1). In consumer markets, excess demand for traded goods is met through import quantity adjustment, whereas in domestic nontraded markets domestic prices adjust to clear markets. Production of nonagricultural goods in urban and rural areas is fixed exogenously, whereas the supply of domestic food commodities is determined endogenously at equilibrium rural prices. Rural producers are assumed to select a production pattern that will maximize their agricultural profits based on prices and then relate rural producer prices to urban consumer prices by a fixed transformation and marketing margin.

Consumption levels are based on household income levels and household response (elasticities) to consumer prices. Urban households are assumed to derive all income from nonagricultural sources, whereas rural households derive income from both agricultural and nonagricultural production. With the level of nonfood output fixed, nonfood output and income varies only with its price.

Demand and supply parameter estimates are essential to the model's application. On the demand side, own- and cross-price and income elasticities are estimated from a complete system of demand based upon Conakry household survey data (the 1989/90 CFNPP/ENCOMEC dataset). Also, expenditure budget shares are estimated for rural and urban households in Lower Guinea. Owing to the lack of production survey data available, supply parameters are based on less firm foundations. Supply parameter estimates are derived from studies in other countries, discussions with policymakers, and theoretical restrictions such as symmetry of cross-price elasticities of supply and zero-homogeneity in all prices. Other data on production, trade and price levels by commodity, and consumption by household group were taken from government sectoral and import statistics and agricultural survey data.

Finally, a poverty line is used to delineate the urban poor and nonpoor and to evaluate the welfare effects of various policies. The poverty line is normatively set based on the level of per capita expenditure, given a vector of prices required to reach a threshold level of food energy intake of 2,000 calories per capita. Using estimated demand parameters, one can calculate a new poverty line when policies, such as tariffs, result in a new price vector. To do so, the demand parameters are used to determine the new level of per capita expenditures that would be associated with the consumption of the 2,000 calorie threshold, given the new vector of prices, where the prices are endogenously determined in the multimarket models based on the simulated policy change. A poverty line, calculated with a full demand system in this way, reflects actual behavioral choices and will itself adjust as prices or income change. That is, a new poverty line can be computed for a new equilibrium vector of prices and real incomes generated in the multimarket model for any given simulated policy change. The new poverty line accounts not only for changed prices but also for the altered consumption behavior that results from the change in real prices and incomes.[69]

SIMULATION RESULTS. The first simulation, a 10 percent increase in tariffs on all food commodities, parallels the government's actual policy between 1990 and 1993. As noted earlier, this increase raises the price of imported rice by 9.09 percent and the prices of all other imported commodities by 8.33 percent. As a result, urban poor households reduce their consumption of imported rice by 4.87 percent, bread by 5.95 percent, cooking oil by 4.46 percent, and sugar by 5.52 percent (Table 26). The urban poor increase consumption of local rice by 9.57 percent, as do the urban nonpoor by 11.13 percent. Though rural households reduce their demand for local rice, the total demand for local rice increases, stimulating an increase in the producer and consumer prices by 3.86 percent each and in production by 1.12 percent. The local production of oil, fish, spices, fruits, and vegetables also increases. Goods, such as domestic meat and dairy, and cereals other than rice, roots, and tubers, have negative uncompensated cross-price elasticities of demand with the imported foods and decline in demand and therefore in production.

Important to household welfare is the effect of the 10 percent food tariff increase on household incomes. Urban incomes fall in nominal terms because the demand and subsequent price of nonagricultural goods produced in urban areas fall. Moreover, the rise in import prices causes urban real incomes to fall further, by 2.18 percent among the reference group of urban poor and by 1.18 percent among the urban nonpoor. Expenditure and calorie shares and poverty measures are also affected, as seen in Table 27. Daily per capita calorie consumption among the reference group of poor households falls 4.2 percent, from 1,720 to 1,647.

TABLE 26

Guinea: Simulated Sectoral Effects of Tariff Increases.
(percent change from base case)

	Increase All Food Tariffs by 10 Percent			Increase Tariff on Rice by 30 Percent			Increase Tariff on Rice by 30 Percent with Increased Rice Production			Decrease Tariff on Rice by 10 Percent		
	Urban Poor	Urban Non-poor	Rural	Urban Poor	Urban Non-poor	Rural	Urban Poor	Urban Non-poor	Rural	Urban Poor	Urban Non-poor	Rural
Consumption												
Local rice	9.57	11.13	-0.24	13.27	15.47	0.39	44.02	48.18	23.45	-4.45	-5.18	-0.13
Imported rice	-4.87	-0.30	-4.23	-15.04	-0.93	-14.58	-17.13	-6.57	-23.31	5.02	0.31	4.87
Cereals, roots, tubers	-1.97	-1.88	0.06	-2.30	-2.15	0.20	-1.49	-1.36	1.33	0.76	0.71	-0.06
Bread	-5.95	-5.26	-4.89	-1.00	-2.55	-0.41	-1.26	-3.28	-1.63	0.34	0.86	0.15
Meat and dairy	-1.15	-0.19	0.09	-1.99	-0.44	0.20	-2.18	-1.08	1.94	0.66	0.14	-0.05
Fish	0.04	-0.13	0.66	0.17	-0.66	1.04	0.60	-0.01	0.53	-0.06	0.22	-0.34
Vegetables	-0.15	-0.62	0.41	-0.17	-0.92	0.80	0.21	-0.31	0.90	0.06	0.31	-0.26
Fruit	-0.39	-0.40	0.68	-0.26	-0.64	1.44	0.02	-0.77	2.59	0.08	0.21	-0.47
Butter, oil	-4.46	-3.27	-3.89	3.06	3.27	3.97	-0.19	-1.70	0.19	-1.02	-1.09	-1.31
Spices	-0.07	0.57	0.23	-0.03	0.58	0.47	0.42	1.01	0.20	0.01	-0.19	-0.15
Sugar	-5.52	-4.79	-5.33	-2.11	-4.59	-1.21	-4.98	-9.19	-4.24	0.71	1.54	0.42
Beverages	-14.32	-11.48	-12.98	-5.59	-2.79	-2.67	-6.15	-2.76	-0.91	1.88	0.94	0.93
Nonfood	-2.26	-1.43	-0.98	-4.41	-2.74	-2.00	-3.87	-2.39	0.83	1.47	0.91	0.69
					National							
Production												
Local rice		1.12			2.19			-2.79			-0.73	
Cereals, roots, tubers		-0.31			-0.25			0.82			0.09	
Meat and dairy		-0.39			-0.56			-0.04			0.19	
Fish		0.23			0.21			0.34			-0.07	
Vegetables		0.04			0.18			0.49			-0.06	
Fruit		0.12			0.39			0.92			-0.13	

(Table continues on the following page.)

TABLE 26 (continued)

	Increase All Food Tariffs by 10 Percent	Increase Tariff on Rice by 30 Percent	Increase Tariff on Rice by 30 Percent with Increased Rice Production	Decrease Tariff on Rice by 10 Percent
Butter, oil	1.89	−0.41	0.35	0.13
Spices	0.47	0.73	0.75	−0.24
Consumer prices				
Local rice	3.86	7.36	−9.12	−2.44
Imported rice	9.09	27.27	27.27	−9.09
Cereals, roots, tubers	−0.09	0.65	1.91	−0.20
Bread	8.33	0.00	0.00	0.00
Meat and dairy	−1.96	−2.78	−0.18	0.94
Fish	0.91	0.84	1.38	−0.27
Vegetables	0.20	0.74	1.52	−0.24
Fruit	0.40	1.31	3.08	−0.42
Butter, oil	8.33	0.00	0.00	0.00
Spices	2.40	3.68	3.79	−1.22
Sugar	8.33	0.00	0.00	0.00
Beverages	8.33	0.00	0.00	0.00
Nonfood	−0.34	−0.78	0.13	0.27
Imports				
Imported rice	−2.30	−7.54	−11.89	2.52
Wheat	−3.11	−0.82	−1.29	0.28
Butter, oil	−4.89	4.32	−0.73	−1.43
Sugar	−1.73	−0.85	−2.02	0.29
Beverages	−12.24	−3.13	−2.73	1.06
Nonfood	−1.86	−3.61	−2.14	1.21
Real incomes				
Urban poor	−2.18	−3.45	−3.03	1.19
Urban-nonpoor	−1.18	−1.15	−1.35	0.52
Rural	−1.19	−1.55	1.24	0.55
Tariff revenue	57.46	72.44	66.73	−26.85

Source: Arulpragasam and del Ninno (forthcoming).

TABLE 27

Guinea: Welfare Effects on the Poor of Tariff Changes, Conakry.

	Base Run		Increase All Food Tariffs by 10 Percent		Increase Tariff on Rice by 30 Percent		Increase Tariff on Rice by 30 Percent with Increased Rice Production		Decrease Tariffs on Rice by 10 Percent	
	Expenditure Shares	Calorie Shares	Expenditure Shares	Calorie Shares	Expenditure Shares	Calorie Shares	Expenditure Shares	Calorie Shares	Expenditure Shares	Calorie Shares
Local rice	1.67	5.48	1.89	6.10	1.98	6.31	2.20	8.26	1.54	5.10
Imported rice	11.76	46.92	12.38	46.24	13.24	43.29	12.95	42.21	11.20	48.33
Other grains, roots, tubers	2.16	2.16	2.12	2.17	2.14	2.22	2.16	2.21	2.17	2.14
Bread	5.22	8.57	5.41	8.37	5.29	9.04	5.24	8.94	5.21	8.40
Meat and dairy	7.37	2.03	7.15	2.05	7.07	2.09	7.16	2.06	7.48	2.01
Fish	9.71	9.44	9.91	9.75	9.98	10.04	10.01	9.99	9.61	9.21
Vegetables	9.36	5.30	9.47	5.46	9.58	5.61	9.62	5.57	9.28	5.18
Fruits	2.64	2.07	2.64	2.11	2.66	2.16	2.69	2.13	2.63	2.04
Butter and oil	3.74	11.85	3.91	11.68	3.91	12.91	3.77	12.44	3.68	11.46
Spices	3.54	0.25	3.65	0.25	3.72	0.26	3.72	0.26	3.47	0.24
Sugar	1.98	3.51	2.06	3.44	1.99	3.69	1.93	3.56	1.98	3.45
Beverages	1.17	0.21	1.09	0.18	1.10	0.21	1.08	0.20	1.20	0.21
Nonfood (including food away from home)	39.69	2.21	38.32	2.19	37.34	2.19	37.48	2.17	40.57	2.22
Total real expenditure and total calories per capita	14,799	1,720	14,477	1,647	14,289	1,593	14,350	1,603	14,976	1,769

(Table continues on the following page.)

TABLE 27 (continued)

	Base Run		Increase All Food Tariffs by 10 Percent		Increase Tariff on Rice by 30 Percent		Increase Tariff on Rice by 30 Percent with Increased Rice Production		Decrease Tariffs on Rice by 10 Percent	
	Expenditure Shares	Calorie Shares	Expenditure Shares	Calorie Shares	Expenditure Shares	Calorie Shares	Expenditure Shares	Calorie Shares	Expenditure Shares	Calorie Shares
Poverty line (post-simulation)	20,250	2,000	21,300	2,000	22,100	2,000	21,930	2,000	19,500	2,000
Poverty measures										
Head count (P_0)	35.594		38.841		40.580		40.290		32.985	
Poverty gap (P_1)	9.938		11.276		12.309		12.091		9.009	
Severity (P_2)	3.906		4.551		5.066		4.955		3.470	

Source: Arulpragasam and del Ninno (forthcoming).

94

Calorie shares are reallocated toward domestic foods that are more expensive sources of calories. The (expenditure) poverty line increases, raising the poverty headcount from 35.6 to 38.8 percent. The poverty gap rises from 9.94 to 11.28 percent. Among rural households, nominal incomes do increase marginally because of the increase in domestic production, but rising consumer prices negate the benefit, causing rural real incomes to *fall* by 1.19 percent.

Model simulations indicate that raising the tariff on imported rice alone by 30 percent raises its consumer price by 27.27 percent (Table 26). This tariff successfully reduces total consumption of imported rice by 10.21 percent and increases local rice production and consumption by 2.19 percent. This large tariff hike also increases demand and the subsequent consumer prices of almost all nontraded domestic crops, most notably effecting a 7.36 percent rise in the price of local rice. Consumption outcomes differ dramatically by group. Urban poor and rural households reduce their consumption of imported rice by roughly 15 percent each, while urban nonpoor households show little response. Once again, this tariff successfully increases demand for local rice, by 13.27 percent among the urban poor and by 15.47 percent among the urban nonpoor. The income effects of the tariff are such, however, that urban households decrease their consumption of almost all other commodities. Their nominal incomes fall as the demand for nonagricultural goods falls. Rural households, in contrast, enjoy marginal increases in consumption of many domestic foods, though they too reduce consumption of imports. Rural households increase their production of local rice by 2.19 percent and see their nominal incomes rise 1.16 percent.

At the same time, however, the inflationary effect of a 30 percent tariff on imported rice lowers the real incomes of all consumers. This only worsens the nominal income loss of urban households, resulting in a 3.45 drop in the real income of the urban poor. Inflation also completely erodes the nominal gains of rural households, such that their real incomes fall by 1.55 percent. This tariff is thus unable to improve real rural incomes despite promoting a 2 percent increase in demand and production of local rice and smaller increases in the production of other domestic foods. Concerning public revenues, the government would experience a clear increase in real income, with food tariff revenues increasing by 72.44 percent. This is a 7.2 percent increase in nonmining tax revenue, or a 2.1 percent increase in total government revenues and grants. The cost in poverty aggravation, however, is substantial; the reference poor population must substitute away from what was the cheapest source of calories, and reduce total per capita intake by 7.4 percent, to 1,593 calories per day (Table 27). The expenditure poverty line increases by 9.1 percent, raising the headcount of poverty from 35.59 percent to 40.58 percent.

Arulpragasam (1994) notes that the negative effect of a tariff increase upon rural real income is a consequence in part of already high levels of rural consumption of imported rice. He thus considers a more optimistic scenario, not implausible in the near future, where the production and consumption of local rice increases by 30 percent before the imposition of the 30 percent tariff increase on imported rice.

When the tariff is added after a production increase, the level of net consumption of local rice is higher than without the production increase (Table 27). The tariff lowers urban households' real incomes by slightly less when preceded by a production increase, though the urban poor still experience a 3.03 percent real income fall relative to the base case. Rural households, on the other hand, see their real incomes rise by 1.24 percent with the production increase and tariff, where they saw a decrease of 1.55 percent with the tariff alone. This result, however, is due to increased levels of initial production and not to the tariff. Rural real incomes would rise by 2.65 percent with the production increase alone. Thus, relative to having only the production increase, the additional 30 percent tariff causes a decrease in the real incomes of both urban and rural households. The effect on urban poverty of a 30 percent tariff increase is not much altered by the increase in domestic rice production. Intake among the reference urban poor rises by only 10 calories per day relative to the tariff imposition at the lower production level, and the headcount of poverty is only marginally lower, remaining above 40 percent (Table 27). In short, imported rice continues to be an important staple among all households. Tariffs that increase the price of imported rice drive up the average price of all staple foods, eroding any nominal income gains to rural (or urban) households.

Given these results, Arulpragasam simulates the effects of a 10 percent tariff *reduction* on imported rice. All household groups increase their consumption of imported rice, the urban poor by 5.02 percent (Table 26). Consumption of local rice falls among all household groups, by 4.45 percent among the urban poor, but by only 0.13 percent among rural households. The lower demand for local rice results in a 2.44 percent reduction in its price and less than a 1 percent fall in its production. On the other hand, households paying a lower price for imported rice marginally increase their demand for other imports, such as wheat (for bread) and sugar, and other domestic foods, such as meat and dairy, and cooking oil. The demand for nonagricultural goods also increase raising urban nominal incomes. Rural households, on the other hand, experience a drop in nominal income. However, the reduced price of imported rice and of many domestic crops leads to a fall in the consumer price index. The nominal income decrease among rural households thus translates into a .55 percent real income gain. The increase in nominal income among the urban poor is augmented at the real level, rising by 1.19 percent.

The 10 percent tariff reduction also helps reduce poverty. Imported rice would account for 48.33 percent of the calorie intake among the reference population of the urban poor (Table 27). This group would increase the average daily per capita caloric intake by 2.85 percent and lower the expenditure poverty line by 3.7 percent relative to the base. In contrast, the headcount of poverty changes insignificantly with a fall from 35.59 to 32.99 percent of the total population.

While these simulations do not directly address the issue of Guinean reliance on foreign rice, they do suggest that the government would increase the real incomes of both rural and urban households and alleviate poverty by lowering the tariff on rice, not by raising it. If the government desires to increase tariffs to secure revenue, other commodities could be targeted. Arulpragasam (1994) estimates the effects of a 10 percent tariff increase on rice, wheat, oil and sugar in turn, considering the effects upon welfare and government revenue. The tariff on rice has the largest negative effects upon average real per capita expenditure and calorie intake (Table 28). A 10 percent tariff increase on imported sugar would raise total nonmining tax revenue by 2.4 percent, almost equivalent to the 2.5 percent increase from an additional 10 percent rice tariff. In contrast, the headcount index of poverty would change insignificantly with the sugar tariff, rising from a base of 35.59 to 35.94, as opposed to rising to a level of 37.33 with the tariff on rice.

While the simulation results above help point out the less obvious costs of protectionism, they, along with all other analyses carried out on Guinea to date, are based on weak supply-side information. Estimates of the extent to which domestic producers of crops would or could respond to demand increases for domestic rice have had to be taken from regional studies, other African countries, and discussions with policymakers. Farm-level production surveys are needed to more accurately determine the price elasticity of supply for rice and to enhance our understanding of the binding constraints to crop production. It is not yet clear whether the high cost of domestic rice on the Conakry market is currently due to cost of production factors or to other impediments ranging from a shortage of trucks to labor technology and credit constraints. These latter high costs would likely be better addressed by technological innovation and road improvements, for example, than by the imposition of a tariff. Moreover, if markets are indeed so fragmented by marketing and transport costs, by implication there already exists built-in protection for domestic rice in rural markets.[70]

In short, the success of local farms in capturing a larger share of the domestic rice market, especially in Conakry, does hinge in important ways on government

TABLE 28

Guinea: Summary Effects of a 10 Percent Tariff on Alternative Food Commodities, Conakry.

| | Base Run | Tariff Increase of 10 Percent on: | | | | |
		Rice	Oil	Wheat	Sugar
Total per capita monthly					
expenditure (real GNF)	14,799	14,626	14,724	14,667	14,754
Total per capita daily calories	1,720	1,674	1,700	1,699	1,713
Poverty line (real GNF)	20,250	20,925	20,575	20,525	20,325
Poverty measures					
Head count (P_0)	35.594	37.333	36.464	36.464	35.941
Poverty gap (P_1)	9.938	10.795	10.352	10.288	10.033
Severity (P_2)	3.906	4.317	4.102	4.072	3.951
Government tariff revenue					
(percentage chase)					
Food tariff revenue	0.00	25.50	9.45	20.45	24.09
Nonmining tax revenue	0.00	2.54	0.94	2.04	2.40
Total revenue and grants	0.00	0.73	0.27	0.58	0.69

Source: Arulpragasam and del Ninno (forthcoming).

policy. Actions that can further technological efficiency in domestic production and reduce marketing and transport costs could help increase consumption of domestic rice and other domestically produced crops. As revealed by a final simulation, a 30 percent reduction in marketing and transformation margins has striking results (Table 29). Urban consumer prices fall sufficiently to increase the urban poor's consumption of local rice by 18.48 percent and of other cereals,

TABLE 29
Guinea: Simulated Sectoral Effects of Reduced Marketing Margins.

	Decrease in Marketing Margins by 30 Percent		
	Urban Poor	*Urban Nonpoor*	*Rural*
Consumption			
Local rice	18.48	19.92	−2.14
Imported rice	−1.91	−4.80	6.10
Cereals, roots, tubers	13.47	13.50	−1.72
Bread	−0.16	−0.38	5.16
Meat and dairy	3.80	3.59	−2.51
Fish	−0.65	−0.96	1.40
Vegetables	4.06	2.84	−0.47
Fruit	5.63	5.68	−2.57
Butter, oil	0.26	0.29	0.48
Spices	4.73	3.33	−1.75
Sugar	−1.91	−2.97	6.15
Beverages	−1.59	−0.71	15.00
Nonfood	−1.50	1.12	4.82
		National	
Production			
Local rice		0.56	
Cereals, roots, tubers		1.12	
Meat and dairy		1.74	
Fish		0.06	
Vegetables		1.22	
Fruit		1.73	
Butter, oil		−0.47	
Spices		0.81	
Consumer prices			
Local rice		−8.32	
Imported rice		0.00	
Cereals, roots, tubers		−15.91	

(Table continues on the following page.)

Table 29 (continued)

	Decrease in Marketing Margins by 30 Percent
	National
Consumer prices (continued)	
Bread	0.00
Meat and dairy	-2.71
Fish	0.25
Vegetables	-6.71
Fruit	-5.32
Butter, oil	0.00
Spices	-6.79
Sugar	0.00
Beverages	0.00
Nonfood	0.52
Imports	
Imported rice	0.30
Wheat	1.03
Butter, oil	0.53
Sugar	0.48
Beverages	3.24
Nonfood	3.00
Real incomes	
Urban poor	1.83
Urban nonpoor	1.61
Rural	2.27
Food tariff revenue	0.87

Source: Arulpragasam (1994).

roots, and tubers by 13.47 percent. Though the production of local rice and other cereals, roots, and tubers rises only marginally by .56 and 1.12 percent respectively, the increased urban demand is still met as rural households switch consumption to more imported foods such as rice and bread. The net effect of the 30 percent reduction in marketing margins is an increase in real incomes for all three household groups: 1.83 percent for the urban poor, 1.61 percent for the urban nonpoor, and 2.27 percent for rural households. As for the effect on poverty, simulation results indicate that a 30 percent reduction in marketing margins lowers the headcount ratio of urban households below the poverty line from 35.59 to 33.97 percent (Table 30).

TABLE 30

Guinea: Welfare Effects on the Poor of Reduced Marketing Margins, Conakry.

	Base Run		*Decrease in Marketing Margins by 30 Percent*	
	Expenditure Shares	*Calorie Shares*	*Expenditure Shares*	*Calorie Shares*
Local rice	1.67	5.48	1.82	6.53
Imported rice	11.76	46.92	11.39	45.52
Other grains, roots, tubers	2.16	2.16	2.10	2.50
Bread	5.22	8.57	5.15	8.47
Meat and dairy	7.37	2.03	7.44	2.11
Fish	9.71	9.44	9.56	9.29
Vegetables	9.36	5.30	9.03	5.48
Fruits	2.64	2.07	2.64	2.19
Butter and oil	3.74	11.85	3.71	11.76
Spices	3.54	0.25	3.43	0.26
Sugar	1.98	3.51	1.92	3.41
Beverages	1.17	0.21	1.15	0.21
Nonfood (including food away from home)	39.69	2.21	40.67	2.26
Total expenditure and total calories	14,799	1,720	15,070	1,748
Poverty line (post-simulation)	20,250	2,000	19,900	2,000
Poverty measures				
Head count (P_0)	35.594		33.971	
Poverty gap (P_1)	9.938		9.501	
Severity (P_2)	3.906		3.760	

Source: Arulpragasam (1994).

APPENDIX.   GUINEA MULTI-MARKET MODEL EQUATIONS[71]

Supply, Demand, and Incomes

Domestic production of commodity i (X_i) is modeled as a function of the base level of production (XO_i) and domestic producer prices (PP_j):

(1)
$$X_i = XO_i * \left[1 + \sum \varepsilon_{i,j}^s * (PP_j / PPO_j - 1) \right]$$

The elasticities of supply ($\varepsilon_{i,j}^s$) determine the price-responsiveness of production to changes in the prices of the output and competing activities.

Household consumption of commodity i is a function of prices faced by the household and household income (Y_h). For urban households, consumption is determined by consumer prices (equation 2). Rural household consumption is determined by producer prices for agricultural commodities produced in rural areas (equation 3).

(2)
$$UC_i = UCO_i * \left[1 + \sum \varepsilon_{i,j,h}^D * (PC_j / PCO_j - 1) + \eta_{i,h} * (Y_h / YO_h - 1) \right]$$

(3)
$$RC_i = RCO_i * \left[1 + \sum \varepsilon_{i,j,h}^D * (PP_j / PPO_j - 1) + \eta_{i,h} * (Y_h / YO_h - 1) \right]$$

Total consumption of each commodity (CD_i) is simply the sum of the demands by all households:

(4)
$$CD_i = \sum UC_i + RC_i$$

Production of nonagricultural goods is fixed (exogenous) in the model. Nonagricultural incomes for each household ($YNAG_h$) are assumed to change only according to a change in the consumer price of nonagricultural goods.

(5)
$$YNAG_h = YNAGO_h * PC_{NA} / PCO_{NA}$$

Agricultural income for household h is simply the sum of the gross value of production of each crop times the share of production by household h (w_{ih}). In this model, w_{ih} for urban households is zero for all crops.

(6)
$$YAG_h = \sum PP_i X_i * W_{ih}$$

Prices

For tradable goods, the border price is determined as the world price in dollars converted to Guinean francs by the exchange rate and adjusted for tariffs and taxes. For the model simulations in this paper, world prices are exogenous.

$$(7) \qquad PM_i = PW_i * ER * (1 + tm_i)$$

The consumer price for tradable goods is then determined by the border price and marketing costs ($trmarg_i$). Marketing cost margins are fixed at their base levels for each commodity.

$$(8) \qquad PC_{it} = PM_{it} * (1 + trmarg_i)$$

Producer prices are related to consumer prices by a marketing margin ($marg_i$). This margin too is fixed at the base level for each commodity.

$$(9) \qquad PC_i = PP_i * (1 + marg_i)$$

Market Clearing

Given the base levels of consumption, production, incomes, and prices, the model solves for new values of all endogenous variables so that total supply equals total demand for each commodity.

$$(10) \qquad X_i = C_i - (M_i + DM_i)$$

For tradable goods, domestic prices are determined by world prices and the exchange rate (equations 7 and 8), and net international imports (M_i) are endogenous. Interregional domestic trade (DM_i) is fixed exogenously at base levels for all commodities.[72] For "non-tradable goods," net international imports are very small relative to total supply and are fixed exogenously. Domestic prices of non-tradables adjust to clear the markets.

Model Closure and the Real Exchange Rate

The above equations determine a complete partial equilibrium system of equations. In this system, the exogenous exchange rate determines the price level of the economy. An increase in the exchange rate will result only in an increase of equal magnitude in all domestic prices.

In order to simulate changes in the real exchange rate, some other price or nominal value must be held fixed. Two equations are added to define price index for non-tradables (*PNT*). First, an index of the price of non-agricultural non-tradables (PNT_{NA}) is defined as part of a weighted average making up the domestic price of non-agricultural goods (PC_{NA}).

(11) $$PC_{NA} = PNT_{NA}^{\alpha^{NA}} * \Big[ER * (1 + TM_{NA}) * PWM_{NA} \Big]^{(1 - \alpha^{NA})}$$

TM_{NA} is the tariff on non-agricultural tradables; PWM_{NA} is the world price of non-agricultural tradables; and α_{NA} is the share of non-tradables in total non-agricultural expenditures.

The price index of non-tradables (*PNT*) is then defined as a weighted average of the price index of non-traded non-agricultural commodities (PNT_{NA}) and of the price index of non-traded agricultural commodities (PNT_{AG}).

(12) $$PNT = PNT_{NA}^{\beta^{NT}} * PNT_{AG}^{(1 - \beta^{NT})}$$

Then the price index of non-traded agricultural commodities (PNT_{AG}), is computed as:

(13) $$PNT_{AG} = \Pi \left(\frac{PC_k}{PCO_k} \right)^{\phi_k} + \Pi \left(\frac{PP_k}{PPO_k} \right)^{\xi_k}$$

where k is the set of non-traded agricultural goods, ϕ_k is the value share of non-traded agricultural commodity k in total urban consumption of non-traded agriculture, and ξ_k is the value share of non-traded agricultural commodity k in total rural consumption of non-traded agriculture. By fixing the domestic price of non-tradables (*PNT*), a change in the nominal exchange rate results in a change in the real exchange rate of the same proportion.

Finally, an equation is added that determines the level of the real exchange rate given a change in foreign savings and a fixed price of nontradables. The real exchange rate is computed as:

(14) $$ER = ERO * \Big[1 - CHFSAV * (1 - \beta) / (P_x X * \varepsilon_x - P_m M * \eta_m) \Big]$$

where the change in foreign savings (*CHFSAV*) is equal to the change in the trade balance ($P_m M - P_x X$). β is the income elasticity of demand for imports, ε_x is the export supply elasticity, and η_m is the import price elasticity of demand.

APPENDIX TABLE 1
Multimarket Baseline Supply and Demand, 1990/91.

	Demand (MT)					Supply (MT)			
	Conakry Poor	Conakry Nonpoor	Conakry Total	Rural (G.M.) Total	Total Demand	Rural (G.M.) Production	Domestic Trade	Imports	Total Supply
Imported rice	33,247	39,344	72,591	49,542	122,133	0	-44,867	167,000	122,133
Local rice	4,291	9,721	14,012	98,450	112,462	112,462	0	0	112,462
Other grains, roots, tubers	3,222	10,084	13,305	58,081	71,386	71,386	0	0	71,386
Bread[a]	7,838	13,051	20,889	12,469	33,358	0	-23,050	56,408	33,358
Meat and dairy	4,032	15,246	19,278	12,610	31,888	22,087	9,800	0	31,888
Fish	8,391	14,519	22,910	15,569	38,479	38,479	0	0	38,479
Vegetables	13,579	25,570	39,149	51,610	90,760	84,617	6,143	0	90,760
Fruits	6,865	26,660	33,525	30,686	64,211	64,211	0	0	64,211
Oils	2,879	5,248	8,128	6,671	14,798	2,422	0	12,376	14,798
Condiments	3,279	5,414	8,693	13,325	22,018	12,690	9,328	0	22,018
Sugar	2,062	3,417	5,480	4,634	10,113	0	-20,201	30,314	10,113
Beverages	157	717	874	305	1,179	0	0	1,179	1,179
Nonfoods	1.78	6.64	8.42	7.30	15.72	5.69	0.00	1.00	6.69

Sources: CFNPP (1990); GOG (1991a, b); PNAFR (1992).
a. A 0.8 transformation factor is applied to imported wheat in producing bread.

NOTES

1. A 1975 census suggested that only 41 percent of the holdings were less than 1 hectare in size. The unlikeliness of this extreme change occurring during the ten-year period suggests some caution in interpreting both sets of figures.

2. While mean holding sizes are larger than in Middle Guinea, the distribution is shifting toward smaller holding sizes, as evidenced by comparisons between the 1975 and 1985 data.

3. Once again the impact of population pressure is evident in shrinking holding sizes over time. Holding sizes of 2 to 5 hectares fell between 1975 and 1985 from 51 percent to 22 percent of all cultivated land, while holding sizes of less than 1 hectare comprised only 8 percent of the total in 1975.

4. In 1960 Guinea's agricultural GDP was approximately US$ 200 million and Côte d'Ivoire's was US$ 245 million (World Bank 1981a, 1990a).

5. This is generally true for all of Guinea except the Fouta Djallon region, which had a history of slavery. In the Fouta Djallon region, former serfs have traditionally gained access to land through their former masters. In the remainder of Guinea, these rights could be passed down within the family as inheritance, but the family did not have the right to sell.

6. In practice, there is almost no free cultivatable land in Guinea: almost every plot has an assigned "user" (Scetagri 1986).

7. Beyond political considerations, traditionally an outsider wanting land can get short-term access to land (with restrictions on the plantation of perennial crops) by presentation of a gift to the village council or chief. Longer-term use of the land invariably has required some form of "rent" payment (Scetagri 1986).

8. While average cultivated area per farmer was between 50 and 100 hectares in 1979, it had decreased by 23 percent by 1982. Rice was the main crop grown on this land, followed by cassava. In some areas fruits and vegetables were also grown. Perennial crops such as coffee, oil, palm, and cocoa, however, were rarely produced.

9. The FACs were established in 1979 to consolidate the preexisting production brigade collectives.

10. A planned national household survey has yet to be completed. What little data exist as of 1993 were results from the pilot survey preceding the national survey and from an independent agricultural survey by the Ministry of Agriculture.

11. Labor demands are high in Guinea given the variety of crops produced and the labor intensity of the cultivation of each, especially rice. In Lower Guinea the problem is particularly compounded by the exodus of young laborers from the rural areas to the cities and mines. Detailed studies (cited by Thenevin 1988) show that these labor shortages are truly binding and are not easily relaxed by changing farming systems and crop portfolios.

12. The marginal liberalization of trade was largely ineffective and its impact minimal for several reasons. First, the reforms focused on addressing short-term balance-of-payments problems rather than the long-term development of private trade. Second, private trade of "priority goods" was still prohibited. These goods included most important agricultural commodities, such as rice, sugar, coffee, palm kernels, and

pineapples. Third, whereas policy changed, legal texts permitting free trade did not exist, implying only ad hoc implementation of liberalization and risk to the trader. Fourth, liberalization did not address the exchange rate distortion. Fifth, in defiance of free trade, the government continued its commitment to move food to Conakry. Sixth, private traders faced barriers due to difficulties in accessing spare parts and gasoline, for example, and a variety of ad hoc administrative controls (Hirsch 1986).

13. This margin was estimated at 35 percent of the f.o.b. cost of the commodity. The handling and port cost estimate of 15 percent was based on data presented in Chemonics (1987a), and the 20 percent internal transportation margin was based on information in USAID (1989).

14. Producers were not paid in foreign exchange; moreover, if they wanted to convert their producer revenue into foreign exchange, their only access was to the parallel exchange rate, not the official one.

15. Although required sales were per person, those with a surplus were evidently forced to sell more than those without one. It is unclear, furthermore, to what degree powerful village-level party officials coerced farmers to sell to them at prices below the official price or quantities beyond the legal *norms*.

16. While in 1983 the obligatory sale amount of paddy was 103 kilograms per person (Thenevin 1988), some marketing quotas were evidently eliminated in 1981 and replaced by a "development tax" of GS 600 per worker (World Bank 1984a). The details of this policy change and the extent to which it was actually implemented are unclear.

17. Presumably, this demand was primarily in the south central parts of the country where rice production may have been less economic and transport costs lower from Sierra Leone and Liberia than from Conakry.

18. FRUITEX, for example, made only one purchasing agreement with pineapple producers in 1984. The parastatal failed to follow through, however, and the entire expected shipment was wasted (AIRD 1989).

19. The one ration card per household enumerated all the household members. In practice there was not a one-to-one correspondence between the number of people on the card and the number in each household (GOG 1986).

20. The official price was supposedly based on the c.i.f. price valued at the official rate. The valuation of the official price at 2.2 times the c.i.f. price would thus imply that these margins may have been as high as GS 9 per kilogram. Evaluated at the parallel exchange rate, this same margin would have represented 50 percent of the c.i.f. price. If this were indeed the true marketing margin, the fact that the actual official price evaluated at the parallel rate was only 8 percent of the c.i.f. price would thus imply a 42 percent subsidy.

21. Yet another measure of the subsidy would be a calculation based on the deficit that the government incurred on its rice import account. Such information, however, is unavailable.

22. Given the restrictions on domestic marketing, Guinean producers did not take advantage of these high prices.

23. Evidence that these families could draw on rations for only part of their food needs (World Bank 1984a) strongly indicates that the rations were generally inframarginal.

24. Police barricades on all roads were removed, except for one at the 36 kilometer mark (PK36) on the road out of Conakry.

25. As a result, in 1988 PROSECO was exporting only 500 MT of coffee, two to five times less than it was exporting before losing its monopoly control.

26. While such a law was to eliminate any need for prior approval of most prices, it also listed "strategic" goods whose prices and marketing were to be monitored.

27. PROSECO, for example, purchased at the indicative price through 1989.

28. Whereas the indicative price for coffee was GF 500 per kilogram in 1990 and 1991, actual producer prices paid to farmers were GF 233 and GF 251 per kilogram, respectively.

29. While coffee hectarage and production estimates do not tell this story very clearly, the 1989 Agriculture Census data indicate actual hectarage in 1989 to be almost double that estimated in 1985, and 1989 coffee production, at 24,000 MT, to be over one-and-a-half times greater than estimated production in 1985. By 1992 coffee production was estimated at close to 100,000 MT (Table 13). Of course, the magnitude of the apparent change could also be due to underestimation of actual coffee production destined to the parallel market before liberalization. The excess of estimated production over formal exports is likely informally exported to Côte d'Ivoire, Sierra Leone, and Liberia, domestic consumption being low.

30. Palm kernels were also assigned an indicative producer price by which PROSECO abided. In 1987 that price implied an increase in the NPC, evaluated at the parallel exchange rate, from 0.11 in 1984 to 0.97 in 1987. The increase, however, was due primarily to a fall in world prices rather than to the producer price increase. Moreover, given its cost structure, PROSECO considered the indicative producer price too close to the world price and thus elected not to buy at all. (This would indicate that our estimates of transport, processing, and marketing margins may underestimate the actual margin.) As a result, traders were left with large stocks of kernels that year. This example highlights the dangers of rigid adherence to reference prices.

31. The rationale for this record keeping was to more closely track coffee marketing so as to prevent illegal exports. This measure was intended to increase government revenues through taxes and assure that exports were going to official quota countries, thus protecting and possibly enlarging Guinea's coffee quota (Chemonics 1987a, b).

32. Two significant disincentives to exporters were eliminated with the suspension of the export tax in 1989 and of the *taxe de conditionnement* in 1991.

33. As of 1991 there were only six formal exporters of coffee.

34. The production data problem is exacerbated by farmers' continued reluctance to reveal actual amounts produced, presumably continuing to fear government extraction of *norms de production*. As a result, more recent studies continue to estimate production from data on hectarage (GOG undated [a], [b]).

35. The 1989 Agriculture Census (GOG 1990c) estimated a rice (paddy) production level of 596,000 MT for 1989; the Permanent Agricultural Survey (GOG 1992b) reported an estimate of 501,440 MT for 1991.

36. No systematic collection of producer prices has taken place in Guinea since the liberalization of fixed prices. Even when producer prices are recorded at the local level,

there is no system whereby this data is transmitted, recorded, and made available for the central government in Conakry. Consequently the producer price estimates used here are drawn from a number of available studies and from different parts of the country.

37. Potentially a result of inappropriate or inadequate application, some rice farmers have indicated that their increase in yields due to the use of fertilizer is negligible (GOG undated [b]). Without further empirical support, such as the calculation of value cost ratios, however, such an assertion must be treated with care.

38. Hirsch (1986) wrote of an "institutional void" when 34 government EPCOAS (*Enterprises Preféctorales de Commercialisation Agricole*) were liquidated in December 1985. Some market "voids" probably still persist.

39. Few farmers have direct access to machine hullers, although at larger markets rice can be machine hulled for a fee. According to the Filière Riz survey in Lower Guinea, only 8 percent of all paddy was actually machine hulled by farmers prior to sale. In both Upper and Lower Guinea, 60 to 90 percent of farmers usually sold their rice in the form of paddy, the gain in value due to rice processing thus not accruing to producers.

40. In the Filière Riz survey in Upper Guinea, as many as 72 percent of farmers claimed to sell directly to other peasants and only 31 percent sold to traders. Traders appear to be more prevalent in Lower Guinea (GOG undated [a]).

41. This margin did not change between 1987 and 1992, with both producer prices and retail prices rising at a slightly lower rate than the rate of inflation.

42. In 1987, domestic marketing and distribution costs (net wholesale and retail margins in Conakry) were approximately US$ 170 per MT, whereas estimated freight, insurance, transit, and port charges for importing rice from Bangkok were approximately US$ 55 per MT at the parallel exchange rate.

43. To the extent that this increased food aid was in response to Guinea's adoption of a structural adjustment program, it too, like the increase in commercial rice imports, is an indirect outcome of adjustment.

44. These large importers generally import a variety of food commodities such as sugar, vegetable oil, and flour, hedging their risk by limiting their investment in rice to 20 to 60 percent of their total operating capital (Bremer-Fox et al. 1990). Some smaller traders (generally wholesalers themselves) import intermittently during times of shortage. In 1990 the number of rice wholesalers in Conakry was estimated at over 100 and retailers at over 300 (Bremer-Fox et al. 1990).

45. The wholesalers at Madina market in Conakry are essential to both circuits for imported rice. It is they who have direct business relations with importers and with commercial banks. The wholesalers also possess the only real storage capability in the city (1,000 to 2,000 MT among the bigger players) (Filippi-Wilhelm 1987). Meanwhile, it is with the wholesalers in the interior that imported goods such as rice and sugar are exchanged for high value domestic agricultural crops such as palm oil and groundnuts. On occasion this trade continues to be in the form of barter (Filippi-Wilhelm 1987).

46. It is unclear whether the preference is for local rice per se, or for lightly milled, parboiled rice. Parboiling (cooking briefly with a small amount of water), followed by air drying, partially cooks the rice, making it more resistant to pests. It also loosens the hulls around each kernel, easing the dehulling step prior to cooking. AIRD (1989) noted

that some parboiled Thai rice has sold on the market with the same premium as the local variety, indicating that the premium may be more a function of the processing method than the source. In either case, some reasons given for the preference of the local over the imported variety include that the texture of the local variety is better and that the imported variety induces constipation.

47. Upper and Middle Guinea got approximately 90 percent of the approved *autorisations de transit* in 1987 (Filippi-Wilhelm 1988).

48. The official retail price was GF 120 per kilogram in Lower Guinea, GF 125 per kilogram in Middle Guinea, and GF 130 per kilogram in Upper Guinea and the Forest Region (Filippi-Wilhelm 1987).

49. The ratio of the official consumer price (at the parallel exchange rate) to the c.i.f. price (excluding port charges, handling margins, and taxes) ranged between 1.20 and 1.05 between 1986 and 1990 (Table 22). Given the fact that actual cost margins between c.i.f. and retail prices were closer to 30 percent (AIRD 1989; unpublished MICA data), the subsidy rate would have been approximately 10 to 25 percent.

50. According to certain studies, the official market was supplied specifically with food aid rice (Thenevin 1988; Filippi-Wilhelm 1988). The market at this official price was estimated at close to 15,000 MT in 1986 and between 15,000 and 20,000 MT in 1987—namely, between one-half and one-third of total food aid (Thenevin 1988; Filippi-Wilhelm 1988).

51. Presumably the recorded price for imported rice captures an average of both imported rice types—namely, the PL 480 *riz Caroline* and the *riz Asiatique*.

52. Given the period's average tariff rates on rice of approximately 20 percent, the average retail markup over the c.i.f. price of close to 50 percent during the eight-year period reflects an estimated internal marketing margin of approximately 30 percent.

53. In fact the real c.i.f. price of rice declined at an average rate of 17.3 percent per year between 1989 and 1992.

54. Compared to 1992, in early 1993 even the nominal price of imported rice had fallen by 1.4 percent.

55. The estimations in Table 21 allow for a 0.55 transformation coefficient in processing paddy into rice and account for a 0.10 loss/waste/seed coefficient. These coefficients are based on information from a variety of sources (Table 21). Table 21 is constructed assuming no carry-over stocks and no re-exports. Re-exports are likely to vary greatly from year to year. Estimates of the volume of re-exports range from 5 to 20 percent of total imports. Overestimation of rice availability by not accounting for re-exports will be compensated to some extent by the likely underreporting of official imports as reflected in customs data.

56. The latter figure implies a caloric intake of approximately 715 per day. While this is well below the benchmark minimum daily requirement of 2,200 calories, Guineans do rely on a number of food staples other than rice (e.g., cassava, fonio, sorghum, millet, and tubers).

57. Estimates of annual domestic rice production at any point in time since reform have varied widely, from 425,000 MT to 715,000 MT of rice paddy (AGRER 1991). The Agricultural Census (GOG 1990c) estimated rice production at 596,000 MT in 1988/89. Many consider this estimate to be based on unrealistically high yields. More recently,

a national production survey (GOG 1992b) estimated rice production in 1991/92 at 501,440 MT. In the absence of accurate information regarding the changes in production over time since the commencement of reform, Table 21 assumes constant production at a level of 500,000 MT. The story in Table 21 thus focuses primarily on the effect of food imports on food security, given a base level of domestic production.

58. The increased importance of imported rice in Conakry is evident in some estimations. Estimated annual per capita consumption of imported rice in Conakry for 1990 is 76 kilograms as compared to an estimated 58 kilograms in 1975 (based on the assumption that 90 percent of all imported rice stayed in Conakry in 1975 and that the capital accounted for 15 percent of the national population in 1975).

59. The sample used for estimation consisted of 1,557 households that cooked at home.

60. The distinction between poor and nonpoor is described in the Appendix.

61. Other foods in order of increasing (absolute value) own-price elasticities are bread, vegetables, spices, and fish—all basic components of the Conakry diet.

62. Saline marsh rice is grown extensively in the mangrove swamp lands of the estuaries and coastal areas of Lower Guinea. Flooded rice production is practiced in the alluvial plains and river basins of the Niger tributaries in Upper Guinea. Rain-fed rice grown in shifting cultivation is the most common production technique, and one used extensively in the Forest Region, where rainfall is abundant and reliable. Farmers produce rice on 63 percent of all cultivated land in Lower Guinea, 49 percent of cultivated land in the Forest Region, 34 percent of cultivated land in Upper Guinea, and 24.5 percent of cultivated land in Middle Guinea (Table 8).

63. In discussing the general picture, we look in particular at Lower Guinea, the site of a rice-related survey. The policy issues of interest are of particular relevance in this economically and politically strategic region of the country. This coastal region in effect supplies Conakry with domestic rice. In 1986 rice was the principal crop produced by approximately 96 percent of farmers in the region (GOG undated [a]). Moreover, Lower Guinea's production of rice cannot cover its total consumption needs, including its rural areas, urban centers, and mines (Filippi-Wilhelm 1988). In addition, since Lower Guinea is the region most proximate to the port of Conakry, it is the market where the competition between local and domestic rice is most acutely played out.

64. While debt may have been incurred to purchase inputs, an observed phenomenon is the purchasing of rice on credit during the *soudure*, with repayment, plus interest, at the next harvest.

65. For 1987, Thenevin (1988) quotes producer prices of approximately GF 50 to GF 70 per kilogram at harvest, depending on the region. During the *soudure* period, however, rice earned prices in excess of GF 100 per kilogram. This seasonal price increase is consistent with expectations and reasonably competitive markets (Sahn and Delgado 1989).

66. Of the 87 percent of Lower Guinea farm households that purchase rice, 32 percent consumed both imported and local rice, 32 percent consumed only local rice, and 36 percent consumed only imported rice (GOG undated [a]).

67. Importers innovated several new procedures designed to circumvent these regulations. First, to restrict the exposure to exchange risk, importers attempted to limit the

time between ordering an import and its receipt (when full payment is due). The practice of contracting to buy rice at short notice from ships off the coast (*bateaux flottants*) limits this risk and sometimes permits purchases at lower prices. Second, some importers devised a system that addresses the working capital constraint born of the rule requiring the advanced deposit of funds at the BCRG. This system of *tiers detention* involves the provision of rice by the supplier to a third party on the basis of a commercial bank guarantee. The rice is then purchased by the importer from the third party piece meal on the basis of the agreement made with the commercial bank.

68. This multimarket model builds upon the previous work of Dorosh, del Ninno, and Sahn (forthcoming), Braverman, Hammer, and Ahn (1987), and Braverman and Hammer (1986).

69. For a more detailed discussion of this approach, see Ravallion and Bidani (1994), Greer and Thorbecke (1986), and Paul (1989).

70. Indeed the argument that imported rice has hurt domestic production is contradicted by some estimates that indicate a production increase of 15 to 20 percent over the past 10 years, despite the doubling of imports.

71. This appendix is taken from Dorosh and Bernier (1994).

72. For local rice, other grains, roots, and tubers, fish, fruits, oil, and beverages, DMi is fixed exogenously at zero in the model.

5

URBAN LABOR MARKETS

In this chapter, we explore the characteristics and functioning of urban labor markets. We give specific attention to understanding how the urban poor will be affected by economic reforms through changes in their earnings potential. The discussion is based largely on the CFNPP household survey discussed previously.

We divide our analysis of the Conakry labor market into three sections. The first section provides a general description of the labor force in Conakry, emphasizing participation rates and labor segmentation while distinguishing between the public and private wage sectors and the nonwage sector. The second section examines civil service reform under the Second Republic and, more specifically, the effects of the program to reduce the size of the public sector on workers who are retrenched. Small-scale enterprises and the role of the nonwage sector in providing employment is the focus of the third section. Throughout the discussion of urban labor markets, gender differentiation is emphasized in light of women's special roles in nonmarket work, coupled with the prospect of the rigidities and discrimination that limit women's labor market mobility and earnings.

LABOR FORCE PARTICIPATION AND SEGMENTATION[1]

The CFNPP random sample survey of nearly two thousand households in Conakry recorded labor force participation and wage data from 3,566 men and 3,306 women. From this data we can provide an overview of the Conakry labor market, focusing upon participation rates and labor segmentation and sorting between the public and private wage and self-employment sectors.

Overall, 56 percent of men and 71 percent of women in the potential labor force are currently not working (Table 31). Participation rates are very low for those under 30 years of age; only slightly more than 25 percent of men and women between 21 and 30 are working.[2] Participation rates rise dramatically after age 30, though the rate for women rises to a level only half that of men. Participation rates are close to employment rates, because most individuals who do not have work indicate that they are not seeking work, and thus are counted as outside the labor force. Seventy-three percent of men aged 21 to 30 are not working and only 15 percent report that they are looking for work. Men aged 31 to 50 are the only group for whom searchers outnumber nonsearchers. For women, the share of

TABLE 31

Guinea: Participation Rates and Job Search Behavior, by Age and Gender.
(percent)

| | | | | Nonparticipants | | |
| | | | | | Not | |
Gender and Age Group	Partici- pants	Nonparti- cipants	All	Searching	Searching	All
Men						
15 to 20	4.08	95.92	100	2.51	97.49	100
21 to 30	27.29	72.71	100	14.66	85.34	100
31 to 50	80.85	19.15	100	73.58	26.42	100
51 to 65	64.80	35.20	100	35.42	64.58	100
Over 65	30.30	69.70	100	3.08	96.92	100
All	43.83	56.17	100	15.15	84.85	100
Women						
15 to 20	9.45	90.55	100	1.19	98.81	100
21 to 30	28.08	71.92	100	8.31	91.69	100
31 to 50	47.04	52.96	100	7.27	92.73	100
51 to 65	31.84	68.16	100	0.70	99.30	100
Over 65	10.39	89.61	100	0.00	100.00	100
All	29.34	70.66	100	4.90	95.10	100

Source: Glick and Sahn (1993).

nonworkers not searching remains above 90 percent for all age cohorts (Glick and Sahn 1993).

For adults under 31, the most frequent reason given for not searching is that they are still in school or are engaged as apprentices (Table 32). For the most part, these young men remain in the homes of their parents and do not enter the labor force until they marry, which, as noted earlier, is usually not until after age 30. Among the older cohorts, the primary reason given for not working differs by gender. Eighty-eight percent of women between 31 and 50 report nonparticipation because they are homemakers. For men aged 51 to 65, the modal explanation for not searching for work is that they are too old or retired, whereas for women of this age, being a homemaker remains the main reason.

Of those adults who are working, men are dispersed relatively equally across the three sectors of private wage, public wage, and self-employment. Women, in contrast, are engaged predominantly in self-employment activities. As Table 33 shows, only 7.2 percent of working women work in the private wage sector, and only 14.5 percent work in the public wage sector. Women comprise more than

TABLE 32
Guinea: Nonparticipants Not Searching for Work—Reasons, by Age and Gender.
(percent)

Gender and Age Group	Appren-tice	Student	Too Old	Too Young	Retired	Home-maker	Other	All
			Reason Not Searching					
Men								
15 to 20	28.96	55.34	0.00	1.80	0.00	0.77	13.00	100
21 to 30	43.50	40.25	0.00	0.00	0.00	1.55	14.71	100
31 to 50	26.19	14.29	0.00	0.00	7.14	0.00	52.38	100
51 to 65	0.00	1.61	12.90	0.00	59.68	0.00	25.81	100
Over 65	0.00	1.59	61.90	0.00	34.92	0.00	1.59	100
All	32.52	43.90	3.02	0.88	3.90	1.01	14.78	100
Women								
15 to 20	9.37	30.12	0.13	1.20	0.00	33.47	25.70	100
21 to 30	10.55	13.52	0.45	0.89	0.00	64.04	10.55	100
31 to 50	0.82	0.41	0.62	0.41	0.62	88.25	8.87	100
51 to 65	0.00	0.00	28.17	0.00	4.23	54.23	13.38	100
Over 65	0.00	0.00	88.24	0.00	0.00	2.94	8.82	100
All	6.86	15.04	5.06	0.80	0.43	56.17	15.65	100

Source: Glick and Sahn (1993).

TABLE 33

Guinea: Labor Market Participants—Sector of Employment, by Gender.

Sector	Men	Women	All
Private wage			
Number	544	70	614
Row percent	88.8	11.40	100.00
Column percent	34.80	7.22	24.24
Public wage			
Number	472	141	613
Row percent	77.00	23.0	100.00
Column percent	30.20	14.54	24.20
Self-employment			
Number	547	759	1,306
Row percent	41.88	58.12	100.00
Column percent	35.00	78.25	51.56
All			
Number	1,563	970	2,533
Row percent	61.71	38.29	100.00
Column percent	100.00	100.00	100.00

Source: Glick and Sahn (1993).

half of all self-employed workers in Conakry, in contrast to comprising 11.4 percent of private wage and 23.0 percent of public wage employees.

A particular cause for concern is the source of income of poor households. The examination by Glick and Sahn (1993) of the distribution of persons in the labor market by sector across the expenditure quintiles of the households in which they live highlights three points. Women who work in the public wage sector tend to reside in households that are heavily concentrated in the upper end of the income distribution. For example, 58.9 percent of women engaged in the public sector live in households that are in the top 40th percentile of the income distribution. Secondly, women engaged in self-employment activities tend to be poor; 59.3 percent live in households in the bottom 40th percentile of the income distribution. Finally, no strong associations appear for men between sector of employment and household income.

When examining the relationship between the number of household income earners, sector of employment, and household income, several other patterns also emerge (see Table 34). Over half of all households have only one income earner, and only 13 percent have three or more. Households with more workers are

TABLE 34
Guinea: Sector of Employment for Single and Multiple Earner Households,
by Per Capita Expenditure Quintile.
(percent)

| | | | *Quintile* | | | | |
Household Type and Sector	*1*	*2*	*3*	*4*	*5*	*All*	*N*
One earner							
Private wage	14.18	18.91	19.27	22.55	25.09	100.00	275
Public wage	14.72	15.58	16.88	21.65	31.17	100.00	231
Self-employment	21.60	21.07	18.67	19.73	18.93	100.00	375
All	17.48	18.96	18.39	21.11	24.06	100.00	881
Two earners							
Both wage	10.66	19.67	14.75	22.95	31.97	100.00	122
Wage/self	17.99	24.87	26.46	19.05	11.64	100.00	189
Both self	26.49	28.48	19.87	13.91	11.26	100.00	151
All	18.83	24.68	21.21	18.40	16.88	100.00	462
More than two earners							
All	34.33	20.40	22.39	15.42	7.46	100.00	201

Source: Glick and Sahn (1993).

disproportionately in the bottom end of the income distribution. For example, 55 percent of households with three or more income earners are in the bottom 40th percentile. Among two-earner households, those with both workers in the private or public wage sector tend to be considerably better off than the general population. Among single-earner households, 53 percent of public wage earners have households in the top 40th percent of the income distribution.

The predominance of women in the nonwage sector raises the issue of differential access to employment in various sectors. Are jobs in what may be described as the formal sector (public and private wage jobs) subject to rationing as suggested in the segmented or dual labor market literature? The existence of labor market segmentation, defined as the presence of barriers to entry into one or more sectors of the labor market, cannot be assessed unambiguously here. A common source of ambiguity in interpretation for both male and female behavior arises from the difficulty in distinguishing the presence of actual institutional barriers to entry from the effects of unobserved preferences for one type of employment over another. With regard to gender-based differentials in sector of employment, differences in the backgrounds of men and women, especially in schooling, partly explain the relatively low representation of women in the public sector. Schooling differences do not, however, explain the small number of women in the private sector.

By comparing the predicted entry probabilities for each sector for men and women while controlling for educational achievement, Glick and Sahn (1993) showed that differences in educational attainment alone do not completely explain the low presence of women in the public sector workforce. As seen in Table 35,[3] the chances that a woman with a primary, secondary, or university education enters the civil service are 2.4, 7.1, and 25.1 percent, respectively. For men with identical characteristics, the corresponding predicted probabilities are 7.6, 19.6 and 24.2 percent respectively. Except for university graduates, therefore, men are far more likely than women to be in the civil service. Participation in the labor force in general is lower for women for all levels of schooling other than university, so it is not surprising that it is also lower in the public sector. Even among employed men and women, however, women are less likely to be in the public sector, and more likely to be self-employed, than men of similar backgrounds.

Whether these disparities reflect gender-based discrimination in public sector hiring or differences in the preferences of men and women is impossible to say given the nature of the data. Women in Guinean culture may have lower career aspirations and less desire to seek work in any sector of the labor market, and

TABLE 35
Guinea: Predicted Sector Entry Probabilities, by Gender and Level of Education.

Gender and Level of Education Completed	Not Working	Self- Employment	Private Wage	Public Wage
Men				
None	0.532	0.250	0.180	0.039
Primary	0.628	0.133	0.164	0.076
Secondary	0.571	0.079	0.155	0.196
University	0.626	0.028	0.104	0.242
Women				
None	0.772	0.221	0.006	0.014
Primary	0.809	0.132	0.036	0.024
Secondary	0.767	0.097	0.063	0.071
University	0.541	0.043	0.166	0.251

Source: Glick and Sahn (1993).
Note: Probabilities are evaluated at data means for the total sample using multinomial logit parameter estimates.

they may prefer self-employment if they do participate. As Appleton et al. (1990) point out in their study of Côte d'Ivoire, however, the policy implications are the same in either case. Increasing the enrollment rate of girls, in secondary school and university in the case of Guinea, will lead to greater female participation in the public sector, even if it will not be entirely sufficient to close the gender gap.

As will be discussed subsequently, ongoing reforms in Guinea are aimed at reducing the role of government and expanding the private sector. Possible barriers to women's employment opportunities in the private sector may prevent such adjustment from being complete or equitable. Unfortunately, there is evidence of possible gender discrimination in hiring in the private wage sector, at least for women with low skills. The negative effect of schooling on men's probability of entering private sector work suggests that many, if not most, of the positions held by men in this sector are characterized by low education or skill requirements. For women, in contrast, the positive effect of schooling on entry indicates that it is primarily educated women who have access to employment in the private wage sector. Evaluated at sample means in Table 35, men with no schooling or primary schooling have 18.0 and 16.4 percent probabilities of being in the private wage sector, respectively, compared with just 0.6 percent and 3.6 percent, respectively, for women. Policy lessons are much the same here as they are for the public sector: raising the school enrollment of girls will lead to a greater representation of women in private sector employment. In the short or medium term, however, the benefits to less educated women of reforms that encourage private sector expansion are likely to be limited to changes in opportunities and incentives in small-scale self-employment activities. In contrast, for men of all educational backgrounds, private sector expansion can be expected to create employment opportunities in the wage sector and improve incentives for microenterprise development.

In their examination of the urban labor market by sectors, Glick and Sahn (1993) also examined the predicted wages of men and women across sectors and educational groups. Based on wage equations corrected for sample selectivity using the Mill's ratio derived from the participation models discussed above,[4] Table 36 presents predicted earnings for men and women. To make accurate comparisons of the earnings of men and women, it is necessary to control for characteristics beyond schooling, such as duration at the current job, age, ethnicity, and so on. Table 36 thus presents wage predictions for men and women at each level of education based on an identical set of characteristics, namely the means of independent variables calculated from the entire labor force. Clearly in most cases men can expect to earn a good deal more than women with similar amounts of human capital. The largest gap is in self-employment, where male

TABLE 36

Guinea: Male-Female Comparisons of Predicted Hourly Earnings, by Sector and Level of Education.

	Public Wage (GF)		Private Wage (GF)		Self-employment (GF)	
	Men	Women	Men	Women[a]	Men	Women
Education level completed						
None	258	104	244	259	461	203
Primary school	349	192	315	292	573	273
Secondary school	371	242	436	361	887	263
University	499	387	612	558	1,665	1,273
All	303	146	298	295	581	260

Source: Glick and Sahn (1993).
Note: Calculations for both men and women are based on means for all (male and female) labor force participants.
a. Uses OLS parameter estimates.

earnings are more than double female earnings at the "None" through "Secondary school" completed levels.

This can be explained partly by the tendency of enterprises run by men to be much larger than those run by women; hourly profits are highly correlated with the scale of the enterprise. As will be discussed in greater detail below, the majority of self-employed women are engaged in very small retailing activities and are shut out of more lucrative or larger ventures either by custom or through lack of access to credit from formal institutions or informal sources.

The results of Glick and Sahn (1993) also indicate that the gender gap in earnings is also large in the public sector, though it narrows substantially as education levels rise. Men in the public sector have, relative to women, a flat schooling-wage profile. Only in private wage employment are representative wages fairly close for men and women at a given level of education. Unfortunately, our women's earning function in the private sector is based upon a small sample and is not reliable. We therefore urge caution in inferring a similarity of returns in the private sector. Overall, the comparisons in the table point to a substantial gap in earnings between men and women controlling for differences in human capital. Such a large gender earnings differential is of major policy concern and is clearly an area for more research.

As we stated previously, one factor for the concern over the barriers to women's entry to the private sector is the Guinean government's attempts to reduce the size of the public sector. We also offered indirect evidence of rationing of civil service employment that is consistent with Guinea's recent public sector retrenchment. We turn our attention now to the retrenchment and reform program and examine its direct effects upon Conakry's public sector workers.

CIVIL SERVICE REFORM

The civil service under Guinea's First Republic was inflated, underpaid, and unmotivated.[5] The bloated bureaucracy, with its corresponding low pay and low productivity, had its genesis in the misperception during the First Republic that the state sector was an important engine of growth, able to address the social and economic problems of the country. This confidence in state-led growth in turn led to the policy of guaranteeing employment for all graduates. Other motivations for the state to guarantee employment included promoting education, as well as ensuring a means of political patronage, especially for the urban elite who exerted considerable influence over the survival of the self-appointed political heads of state. Thus, by 1979 there were an estimated 140,830 government employees in Guinea (World Bank 1981b). In other words, about 35 percent of the country's labor force that was not engaged in rural self-employment had a job in the public sector (World Bank 1981b). A more recent public sector census in 1986 indicated that, excluding military personnel, there were 90,000 public servants, of whom 72,000 worked in administration and 18,000 worked in public enterprises (World Bank 1990a).

The inflated employment levels had a number of important implications. First, the macroeconomic effects of unsustainable wage payments included budget deficits and inflation. These effects in turn contributed to other deleterious consequences, including a decline in investment and the appreciation of the real exchange rate. In addition, institutional inefficiencies that arose in the public sector had deleterious spillover effects on the rest of the economy. For example, the government's weak financial state contributed to a rapid erosion in the salaries of civil servants: by 1985, Guinean civil servants earned on average GF 5,500 per month, or about US$ 18 per month at the parallel exchange rate. In contrast, civil servants in neighboring Mali, where per capita GDP was comparable to Guinea's, earned about three times as much (IMF 1987a).[6] These low wages in turn contributed to a pattern of public sector rent-seeking, which significantly increased the costs of economic transactions. Thus, instead of receiving adequate on-budget payments, civil servants benefited through their positions from a number of additional allowances and in-kind transfers, especially access to ration shops that sold goods at substantially below open market prices. In addition, public sector workers ventured into other avenues of work to make ends meet. In fact some estimates put the official wage at only one-quarter of total income among civil servants, the rest coming from other jobs, income in kind, remittances, etc. (IMF 1987a).

Working at multiple jobs (*pluriactivité*), now a well-established labor market phenomenon in Guinea as well as in other African countries, also contributed to widespread absenteeism within the civil service and an extraordinary low level of maturation and productivity. "Ghost workers" appeared on the government payroll. A staff verification committee (CORAGEPE) established in 1987, for example, found that over a thousand people in Conakry should not have been on the state payroll at all (World Bank 1990a).

Thus, with the beginning of economic reforms in Guinea, the need to address the problems of the massive human resources devoted to the public sector became overt. In particular, reformers were concerned not only with the imbalances in the internal accounts, but with the large deadweight losses in the economy through rent seeking and the related imposition of arbitrary and opportunistic regulations on market activities imposed by the state bureaucracy. Coupled with the inability of the public sector to deliver the most basic social and economic services ranging from primary health and education to essential infrastructure such as roads, communications, and market information, these factors compelled the Second Republic to reform the civil service, while privatizating and liquidating numerous parastatals.

The reform program initially focused on cutting down the ranks of the civil service with the added objective of increasing the pay and incentive structure to those who would remain on the government payroll. The public sector employment level was targeted at 60,000 (Larfeuil 1990). The public sector staff was reduced in several ways. First, all staff members above the legal retirement age of 55 were obliged to retire; those with 30 or more years of service were obliged to take early retirement. Second, employees of liquidated parastatals and state banks were laid off. Third, workers at the joint-venture mining companies were transferred onto the payroll of those companies. Fourth, civil servants working at the ministries were laid off if they lacked required skills, which were determined through examinations.[7] Of the 25,000 tested, 53 percent were retained, 26 percent were temporarily placed in a reserve with a possibility of being rehired upon successful completion of training, and 21 percent were placed on administrative reserve status, which entitled them to severance pay (see below) (World Bank 1990a). Fifth, the government instituted a "voluntary departure" program, which entitled resigning employees a bonus payment of approximately 5 years' salary.[8]

From both the political and poverty perspectives, the government has been sensitive to the potentially harmful effects of public sector retrenchment and has taken a number of steps to moderate its impact. First, from the political standpoint, special personnel (*effectifs spéciaux*), including the paramilitary corps (presidential guard, police, and customs), were exempt from discharge.[9] Second, the administrative reserve status (*disponibilité spéciale*) entitled laid-off public sector workers to receive severance pay for six months at their base salary, plus a cost-of-living allowance, before they were completely cut from the payroll. Third, a self-employment advisory service, BARAF (*Bureau d'aide à la reconversion des agents de la fonction publique*), was created to facilitate the transition of public sector workers into the private sector. These workers were entitled to use their severance pay as down-payment to secure loans of up to five times that amount, or twenty-five years' worth of salary, in order to start self-employment schemes of their own.[10] As of early 1989, about 2,000 project proposals were filed with BARAF, 800 submitted to banks, and 370 actually financed.[11] The BARAF scheme, however, has experienced a number of technical and administrative difficulties with implementation.[12]

Although the process has been slower than planned, the government has nevertheless been fairly effective in taking people off its payroll. Civil service staff was reduced to 71,000 by the end of 1989, down from its level of 104,000 at the end of 1985 (Table 37).[13] Of the more than 35,000 employees who left the

TABLE 37
Guinea: Civil Service Reform—Net Staff Reduction.

	Mining Compa- nies	State Banks	Public Enter- prise	Ministry Staff	Military	Indeter- minate	Total
Staff at end of 1985	6,517	4,394	6,200	70,989	12,700	2,000	103,800
Retirements	—	–610	—	–4,090	—	—	–4,700
Early retirements	—	–380	—	–6,146	—	—	–6,526
Voluntary departures	—	–2,391	–5,985	–1,744	—	—	–10,120
Administrative reserve[a]	—	—	—	–4,245	—	—	–4,245
Défonctionnairisés[b]	–5,617	—	—	—	—	—	–5,617
Staff to be trained	—	—	—	–4,061	—	—	–4,061
Recruitments	—	—	—	1,330	2,300	—	1,330
Staff at end of 1989	900	1,012	215	52,033	15,000	2,000	71,161

Sources: Mills and Sahn (1995); World Bank (1990a).
a. Change of status from being on administrative reserve (leave) to being redeployed.
b. *Défonctionnairisés* means removed from established posts and reemployed on a contractual basis.

TABLE 38

Guinea: Government Expenditure and Wage Statistics for 1986 to 1992.

Year	Wage/Total Public Expenditures (percent)	Real Government Wage (GF) (1986=100)
1986	15.6	100
1987	10.4	93
1988	16.5	172
1989	17.5	212
1990	17.1	252
1991	19.9	—[a]
1992	23.1	—
1993 (estimated)	24.1	—

Sources: Mills and Sahn (1995); IMF (1991) for 1987-1990; ROG (1991) for 1991-1992 (proj.); World Bank (1983) for 1980-1986; World Bank (1990a) for real government wage figures; IMF (1994).
a. Not available, but nominal base salaries increased 145 percent.

public sector over the four-year period, approximately 11,000 retired or took early retirement and about 10,000 took a voluntary departure.

Nevertheless, even though civil service employment has been cut back, the public sector continues to be an important employer in Conakry. Results from the CFNPP household survey show that, even in 1990, 24 percent of all workers in Conakry still had jobs in the public sector. The figure was 30 percent for men and only 15 percent for women (Glick, del Ninno, and Sahn 1993).

The redeployment of public sector employees has been offset, however, by the concurrent increases in real wages. Thus, the government budget deficit has been only marginally affected. The data in Table 38 show that in conjunction with the reductions in the size of bureaucracy, wages were increased dramatically during the course of the economic reform program to boost the morale and productivity of the remaining workers. Large wage increases were initially granted in 1985 and 1986, following a decline in real salaries during the pre-reform years of the early 1980s.[14] Salary bases were again increased by over 80 percent in 1988, and allowances and premia also increased (Table 38). Then in April 1989, a new compensation plan was instituted under which the base salary was determined by an index calculated on the basis of an individual's education and experience levels. Previous allowances for cost of living and transportation were abolished, and a comprehensive set of new allowances was defined. These changes resulted in an average increase in real remuneration of 23 percent. More importantly, they represented a first attempt to explicitly link promotions and pay increases to performance. The trend of yearly salary increases, however, was not altered by the new payroll framework as real compensation was increased again in 1990. Then, in 1991, under pressure from a national strike of government workers, the nominal base salary was increased 145 percent, far exceeding the rise in consumer prices.[15]

The international lending community opposed the latter two rounds of increases, considering them unnecessary for achieving the purported objectives of rationalizing the civil service and raising incentives and worker productivity. From the government's point of view, however, political considerations mandated such continued increases. This perceived need, in fact, finds some support in the figures that can be derived from the CFNPP survey, which indicates that even in 1990, the average monthly household expenditure was approximately twice the average monthly public sector wage. Similarly, if a household had five or more persons, the average civil servant's wage in 1990 would have placed that household below the poverty line.

Thus, the impact of the public sector retrenchment program on the government budget deficit was limited by the concurrent increases in real wages. Nonetheless, results in Table 38 indicate that, at least initially, efforts to reduce the size of the public sector have had some impact on total government expenditures. Wage payments were estimated to comprise more than one-third of total government expenditures in 1980. By 1987 this share had fallen to only 10.4 percent. However, as civil service real wages increased, so did the wage bill, and between 1987 and 1991 both the real wage bill and wages as a percentage of total public expenditure more than doubled.

While the overall budgetary picture from 1987 to 1993 suggests that the fiscal benefits of the early efforts of public reform have been eroded, some positive outcomes remain. Of greatest note is the government's relative success in decreasing recurrent expenses and re-allocating overall government expenditure into investment. This improvement is partially attributed to large inflows of foreign capital from international donors and to redeployment programs that were crucial in obtaining and continuing the flow of this assistance. Thus, from a budgetary standpoint, perhaps the greatest impact of the redeployment programs has been to help secure foreign assistance by sending a strong signal to the international donor community of the government's commitment to economic reform.

Notwithstanding these rather modest short-term fiscal gains, other institutional objectives to improve the functioning of the civil service were not achieved. For example, the Ministry of Reform and Civil Service (MRAFP) was created in 1988 to institutionalize the reform process. Their mandate included improving institutional organization, enhancing financial management, and furthering the development of skills among workers. Progress in these areas, in contrast to the efforts to reduce the civil service employment roles, has been slow. A key activity of MRAFP was to institute a testing program as the basis for dismissals and reclassification. The efforts, however, stalled and were subverted in some cases. For example, more than 26,000 civil servants, mostly from the Ministries of Education and Health, were not tested at all. And many of those who failed the tests were never officially notified, and they continued working as usual.

But perhaps of greater importance than the short-term budgetary implications of the redeployment program and its effect on the efficiency of workers who remain employed is the concern over the welfare of those who left the government service. In that regard, a recent study of former civil servants provides considerable insight into the plight of the redeployed. Mills and Sahn (1995) explore the fate of those who left the public sector, distinguishing between redeployees, retirees, and those who left because they found other positions. The first category includes those forced to leave because of the closure of public sector enterprise, cutbacks in staff, and failure to pass skills tests, as well as those participating in the voluntary departure program. The latter two categories include those who were motivated to retire early and seek alternative employment because of the redeployment program, as well as those who would have made such transitions regardless of the circumstances. Results indicate that by 1992, 71 percent of those who left the public sector as redeployees between 1979 and 1990 had found other jobs, compared with only 46 percent of the retirees. However, among the retirees, those not searching for a job comprised 84 percent of those not working, in contrast to only 40 percent of the redeployees who were not working. From these results we calculate the unemployment rate among those leaving the public sector to be 17 percent, higher than the overall unemployment rate for Conakry of 12 percent.

Of greater concern is the finding that among those redeployed between 1985 and 1988, nearly two-thirds did not find a job within two years of leaving their public sector positions, and nearly half had not re-entered the labor force four years after being redeployed (Table 39). A multinomial logit model reported by Mills and Sahn (1995) examines the effects of various individual characteristics on employment status after redeployment. Overall, the results indicate that the household heads that were retrenched are more likely to find employment than other household members. Likewise, the model supports the hypothesis that older persons, as well as those who left the civil service as retirees, are more likely to be nonparticipants. Furthermore, the model results indicate that the severance payments that were provided to public servants for up to 30 months after leaving their jobs may have created some job search disincentive effects. Furthermore,

TABLE 39

Guinea: Duration of Spell without Work upon Leaving the Public Sector, by Reason and Period of Departure.
(percent)

	Period of Departure							
	1979–1984				1985–1988			
	Retirees	Re-deployees	Found Other Work	All	Retirees	Re-deployees	Found Other Work	All
Duration without work								
Less than 1 month (i.e., no spell)	8.0	31.6	100.0	22.0	11.4	15.9	100.0	18.3
More than 1 month to 1 year	4.0	10.5	0.0	6.0	8.6	8.7	0.0	8.3
1 to 2 years	12.0	5.3	0.0	8.0	17.1	11.6	0.0	12.8
2 to 4 years	4.0	10.5	0.0	8.0	11.4	15.9	0.0	13.8
4 to 6 years	8.0	10.5	0.0	10.0	0.0	13.0	0.0	8.3
6 to 8 years	4.0	10.5	0.0	8.0	2.9	0.0	0.0	0.9
More than 8 years[a]	0.0	10.5	0.0	4.0	—	—	—	—
Percent not re-entering work force by 1992[a,b]	60.0	10.5	0.0	34.0	48.6	34.8	0.0	37.6
Total	100	100	100	100	100	100	100	100
Number of individuals[b]	N = 25	N = 19	N = 2	N = 50	N = 35	N = 69	N = 5	N = 109

Source: Mills and Sahn (1995).

a. Figures are biased by the truncation of the sample period in 1992; "—" means not applicable.

b. In 1979–1984, four individuals listing "other reasons" for leaving the public sector are included in the "All" sample.

while none of the education level variables are statistically significant, the parameter estimate for university education is positive and large.

It is also noteworthy that among those who found another job, 64.5 percent of the public sector departees between 1985 and 1988 found another position in the wage sector (Table 40), even though only 49.5 percent of overall employment in Conakry is in the wage sector. This fact, in combination with the long duration of unemployment discussed above, suggests that former public sector workers have been willing to queue for wage sector opportunities. Among redeployees who re-entered the labor market, nearly two-thirds of wage workers and just under one-half of the self-employed earned more in their new positions than in the public sector (Table 40). This result suggests that expected earnings alone would not motivate redeployees to remain unemployed while waiting for rationed wage sector positions. However, several factors may make the wage sector a preferred sector, even though expected earnings are lower. Particularly important factors may be the lower risk and associated lower variability in earnings associated with wage sector employment. Also, as the results indicate, capital constraints may seriously limit the earnings opportunities available in the non-wage sector for some groups, including redeployees (Mills and Sahn 1995).

While our earnings estimates indicate that redeployees who re-enter the labor market fare relatively well, the overriding concern about the overall welfare of households of redeployees is not addressed by such models. In analyzing this issue, Mills and Sahn (1995) first compare consumption levels of individuals leaving the public sector with the household per capita consumption levels by quintile for the general population.[16] Table 41 indicates that in 1990, 51.6 percent

TABLE 40
Guinea: A Comparison of 1990 Private Sector Earnings with the Most Recent Public Sector Earnings in 1990 Terms.

	Sector	
	Wage	*Self-employment*
Percent of re-entrants in sector	64.5	35.5
Percent of individuals with increased earnings	63.0	48.0
Average percent change in salary	118.0	102.0

Source: Mills and Sahn (1995).
Notes: Wages from 1985–1986 deflated using GOG (1987e); 1987–1991 wages deflated using CPI from IMF (1992).

TABLE 41

Guinea: Ranking in Per Capita Expenditure Distribution in 1990, by Reason for Leaving the Public Sector and 1990 Employment Status.

| | Ranking in Per Capita Expenditure Distribution | | | | | | | |
| | Bottom 30 Percent | Quintile | | | | | Total | Number of Individuals |
		Lowest	2nd	Middle	4th	Highest		
Total 1990 public sector	23.5	14.7	18.4	17.9	25.8	25.8	100	694
Total leaving public sector between 1979 and 1990	37.1	25.7	23.4	17.7	16.0	17.1	100	175
By reason								
Redeployment	35.1	25.5	23.4	17.0	16.0	18.1	100	94
Not working	38.3	34.0	21.3	14.9	14.9	14.9	100	47
Working	31.9	17.0	25.5	19.2	17.0	29.3	100	47
Retirement	43.9	28.8	25.8	19.7	13.6	12.0	100	66
Not working	50.0	37.5	22.5	20.0	12.5	7.5	100	40
Working	34.6	15.4	30.8	19.2	15.4	19.2	100	26
Found other work	9.1	9.1	9.1	18.2	27.3	36.4	100	11

Source: Mills and Sahn (1995).

of the individuals working in the public sector were from households that fell in the upper two quintiles, while only 23.5 percent of individuals resided in households in the lower 30 percent of the per capita consumption distribution. Of the individuals who departed from public sector positions between 1979 and 1990, in contrast, 37.1 percent were in the lower 30 percent of the per capita consumption distribution. Individuals leaving the public sector due to redeployment and retirement were particularly vulnerable, with 35.1 percent and 43.9 percent, respectively, falling into the lower 30 percent of the distribution.

More important than the reason for leaving is the subsequent transition path. Among redeployees who successfully transitioned from public sector jobs into the private sector before the 1990 survey, 31.4 percent resided in households in the lower 30 percent, compared with 38.3 percent for redeployees who were not working in 1990. Similarly, among retirees who found other positions in the private sector, 34.6 percent were from households in the lower 30 percent versus 50 percent of retirees who remained without work.

Mills and Sahn (1995) recommend caution in interpreting the above numbers. The numbers do not support the conclusion that the households of public sector workers who were laid off and remained unemployed in 1990 were worse off than they were when they were working for the state. For example, it is possible that loss of employment income among former state employees caused lower household consumption. Another interpretation is that given the lower educational levels we have observed among these workers, public sector job losers were poor when they were still working for the government.

Mills and Sahn (1995) specified a reduced form household welfare model for the general population to test whether the welfare of former public sector workers' households is lower than that of the general population, after controlling for human capital and other social variables important in determining household welfare. They find that the most important factor in determining household welfare after redeployment was the subsequent ability to find another job. In fact, the results clearly show that while education was paramount in determining the incomes of households, whether a worker was redeployed had no independent effect on overall household welfare.

A final issue regarding the redeployment program was its effectiveness in targeting compensation. In practice, the government appears to have done a good job, with 88 percent of retirees receiving pensions and 63 percent of redeployees receiving severance (with an additional 6 percent of redeployees receiving a pension). This, however, left 34 percent of redeployees without compensation. In exploring whether any systematic discrimination occurred in the provision of benefits, Mills and Sahn (1995) found that females were less likely to receive retirement benefits, even after controlling for age and duration of service; similar gender bias was found in the provision of severance benefits.

In sum, the government was reasonably successful in certain aspects of the redeployment program, particularly in reducing the size of the public sector work force. This success has not brought about any major improvement in the budgetary crisis, owing to the concurrent increase in wages to remaining workers. While those able to find jobs after departing the state have not witnessed a decline in their earnings, the transition has been costly for many who lost their jobs and have remained unemployed or faced a long duration of unemployment. These unemployment transitions have been less difficult for younger workers, males, and persons with a university education.

Part of the hardship associated with redeployment has been mitigated by reasonably well-targeted compensation programs. However, the evidence indicates that the compensation has not spurred the types of investment in self-employment activities that were hoped for. This suggests that policymakers need to focus on identifying and removing barriers to self-employment in order to reduce the transition costs associated with a reduction in the size of the civil service. With the importance of the self-employment sector in mind, we turn now to an examination of small enterprises and their proprietors in Conakry.

SMALL-SCALE ENTERPRISES AND PROPRIETORS[17]

One of the most challenging issues facing policymakers in Guinea and throughout sub-Saharan Africa is the need to create small-enterprise jobs. In Conakry as elsewhere, this need is especially acute in the urban centers of countries that are undergoing economic reforms. In part, high fertility rates and rural-to-urban migration have led to a rapid growth of the labor force in cities over the past several decades. This in turn has placed demands on governments to ensure adequate economic opportunities. Compounding this, as we have seen in Conakry, the role of the state as an employer has diminished under economic reform. Former state-run or state-protected enterprises, the largest employers of formal sector workers in many cases, are closing. Concomitantly, the liberalization of markets that is integral to economic reform is expected to provide a framework under which small enterprises can become an engine of economic growth.

Inevitably, a large share of employment creation will be in the nonwage sector. At the same time, the state has an important role in stimulating small-enterprise growth and employment, both by setting the correct legal and regulatory framework for market activities and by ameliorating key constraints to growth such as credit. Yet in Guinea at least, we know very little about the nature of small enterprises, their constraints, or their contribution to economic growth since the beginning of economic reform. This lack of knowledge is apparent in Conakry, a city where 86 percent of household heads are migrants and where 51 percent of total employment is in the nonwage sector.

We provide here some baseline information on the characteristics of the firms that comprise the nonwage sector. In doing so we hope to broaden the reader's appreciation of the small-enterprise sector's position in the economy and its potential as an engine of growth. Because small enterprises pay little or no tax, are not formally registered, and are of such small size, their importance in the economy is easily ignored or unrecognized.

In Conakry more than half of all households have an enterprise in which one or more members participate. In addition, nearly one-fifth of households that have an enterprise actually have two or more (see Table 42). The average share of household revenue from enterprises for such households is 76.3 percent. Conversely, in these households wage employment contributes only 21.1 percent of household revenue, and agriculture and fisheries contribute 2.6 percent. In examining the relationship between the share of a household's income from enterprises and its wealth, we find that on average, households with lower per capita consumption receive a higher share of their revenue from independent enterprises (see Figure 6). Thus, not only are small enterprises important in general, but they are important sources of income for the poor in particular.

We consider next the nature of enterprises. As Table 43 shows, around 72 percent involve commercial activities at the retail level. The next largest category, comprising one-tenth of enterprises, is small industry. Interestingly, the nature of enterprises changes according to date of inception. Newer enterprises are more likely to be engaged in retail commerce. Conversely, while only 5 percent of the currently existing enterprises that were started between 1988 and 1990 were categorized as small industry, 13 percent of enterprises started before

TABLE 42
Guinea: Number of Independent Enterprises in All Households.

Number of Enterprises	Percent of Households
0	47
1	36
2	13
More than 3	4

Source: Mills and Sahn (1993b).

FIGURE 6

Guinea: Average Share of Household Revenue from the Small Enterprise Sector, by Expenditure Quintile.

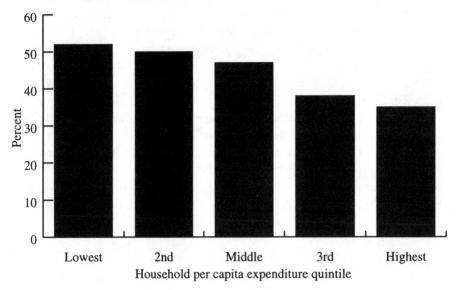

Source: Mills and Sahn (1993b).

TABLE 43

Guinea: Enterprise Type by Period of Inception.

	Period of Inception			
Enterprise Type	*Before 1985*	*1985–1987*	*1988–1990*	*All*
Retail commerce	66	78	83	72
Wholesale commerce	4	2	2	3
Small industry	13	8	5	10
Transportation	3	1	2	2
Construction, utilities, etc.	8	6	5	7
Services, miscellaneous	6	5	3	6

Source: Mills and Sahn (1993b).

1985 were so categorized. Two factors may be involved in this change in sectoral composition. First, the failure rate of retail enterprises may be higher than that of other industries. Second, trade may have expanded rapidly under the economic reform program, thus fueling rapid expansion for retail commerce. However, our findings also suggest that manufacturing jobs, which must form the basis of sustained enterprise growth in the postreform period, have been slow to develop in the nonwage sector.

Most enterprises are extremely small, having a median net revenue per month of only GF 28,667 (Table 44). This is equivalent to approximately $44 per month in 1990. For comparison, the average compensation for civil servants in 1990 was GF 93,000 per month. However, the most profitable enterprises pull the *average* net revenue of these businesses up to GF 106,907, corresponding approximately to the 90th percentile of the distribution of enterprise net revenue. Most enterprises also entail few expenses outside of material costs, the median of which is GF 40,000 per month. In fact, the median expenditures on salary

TABLE 44
Guinea: Characteristics of Enterprises.

	Mean	*Median*
Monthly expenses (GF)		
Total	220,010	52,500
Capital	22,677	0
Salaries	3,632	0
Materials	181,192	40,000
Taxes	1,967	1,250
Other	10,542	0
Monthly revenue (GF)		
Value of production	380,917	98,400
Sold	366,463	88,400
Consumed by household	9,713	233
Donations	4,454	0
Monthly new revenues (GF)		
(Percentile distributions)	160,907	28,667
90 percent	—	169,620
75 percent	—	72,333
50 percent	—	28,667
25 percent	—	11,200
10 percent	—	–4,167

Source: Mills and Sahn (1993b).

payments and capital expenditures is zero. On the gross revenue side, small enterprises provide an important secondary benefit of, on average, GF 9,713 of goods for home consumption per month.

Enterprise revenues and expenses are highest amongst those enterprises that came into being prior to 1985, as Figure 7 demonstrates. These may be the "proven survivors." More surprisingly, however, those enterprises formed most recently, between 1988 and 1990, have higher revenues and expenses than those formed in the years immediately following the start of the economic recovery program.

Most small enterprises are individually owned and managed. Ninety-one percent of enterprise profits are retained by a sole proprietor, and only 11 percent of enterprises employ wage labor. However, labor contributions by other family members, especially children, are often significant. For the purpose of the following analysis, we define the main proprietor as the individual who receives the largest share of revenue from an enterprise.

Table 45 shows that most small-enterprise owners are female and that a significant minority are household heads. Proprietors are, on average, less edu-

FIGURE 7
Guinea: Enterprise Budgets by Period of Establishment.

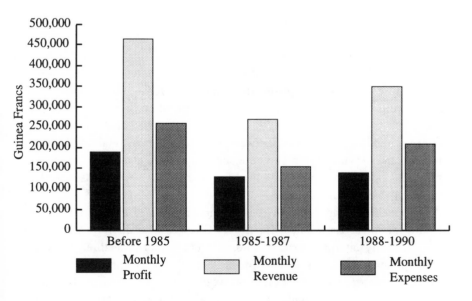

Source: Mills and Sahn (1993b).

TABLE 45
Guinea: Personal Characteristics of Main Proprietor.

Percent female	57.1
Average age (years)	37.2
Position in household (percent of total)	
Head	40.9
Spouse of head	45.2
Other family member	10.3
Non-family member	3.6
Level of education (percent of total)	
None	77.9
Primary	16.5
Secondary	4.5
University	1.0
Distribution of proprietors by household per capita consumption quintiles (percent)	
Lowest	27.6
2nd	23.9
Middle	19.5
4th	16.5
Highest	12.5

Source: Mills and Sahn (1993b).

cated than the general labor force, and they are more likely to be members of households in the bottom two quintiles of per capita household consumption.

The nature of small enterprises also tends to differ by the proprietors' sex. Most striking is the difference in sectoral composition. Female-headed small enterprises are almost exclusively in the retail commerce subsector, while male enterprises tend to be disbursed between retail commerce, small industry, construction, and service enterprises. Female proprietors also have, on average, slightly less education and are far more likely to reside in households in the lower per capita consumption quintile.

Correspondingly, as shown in Table 46, mean and median monthly net revenues are far lower for women. Enterprise finances also differ in structure by gender. Monthly enterprise expenses are, on average, more than three times larger for enterprises headed by men than for those headed by women. Yet capital and salary expenses are an average of ten and six times greater, respectively. Monthly gross revenues are also roughly three and a half times greater for males than for females. Despite the small size of their enterprises, however, females actually

TABLE 46
Guinea: Characteristics of Enterprise by Gender of Proprietor.

	Male		Female	
Monthly net revenue (GF)				
Distribution (percentiles)				
10 percent	−12,267		−17	
25 percent	15,167		8,825	
50 percent	44,800		20,817	
75 percent	128,100		44,775	
90 percent	374,188		99,770	
Mean	275,743		74,859	
	Mean	*Median*	*Mean*	*Median*
Monthly expenses (GF)				
Total	368,611	80,000	108,662	42,010
Capital	46,751	1,250	4,638	0
Salaries	6,819	0	1,244	0
Materials	293,772	50,000	96,835	35,000
Taxes	3,267	1,500	993	758
Other	18,002	0	4,952	0
Monthly Revenues (GF)				
Value of production	644,354	150,000	183,521	70,300
Sold	628,014	140,000	170,480	60,000
Consumed by household	8,496	0	10,625	2,000
Donations	7,658	0	2,054	0

Source: Mills and Sahn (1993b).

donate more, on average, of their gross revenues to their households through transfers of goods.

Interestingly, the ratio of female-to-male-headed enterprises changes by the age of the enterprise. The proprietorship of enterprises started before 1985 is almost equally divided between men and women. However, amongst enterprises begun between 1988 and 1990, 73 percent are female. This change in the gender of the owner is probably due to the higher survival rate of large enterprises, which as we have seen, are predominantly male.

Other factors, such as the age and education of enterprise proprietors, also appear to be related to enterprise earnings. Table 47 shows that proprietors over 35 have substantially higher net monthly revenues, both at the mean and median, than those 35 and under. This difference is primarily due to the larger size of enterprises in the older age groups, since the gross revenue-to-cost ratio for the

TABLE 47
Guinea: Characteristics of Enterprise by Age of Proprietor and Education.

	Mean	*Median*
Monthly net revenue (GF)		
Age		
Less than 35	91,085	22,700
More than 35	228,017	34,842
Education		
None	101,081	27,858
Primary	118,003	33,000
Secondary	918,440	30,833
University	2,057,467	22,500
Monthly expenses (GF)		
Age		
Less than 35	133,823	39,167
More than 35	302,852	74,880
Education		
None	179,868	50,633
Primary	258,461	59,583
Secondary	663,229	68,750
University	696,897	275,000
Monthly gross revenue (GF)		
Age		
Less than 35	224,908	74,000
More than 35	530,869	125,500
Education		
None	280,950	92,000
Primary	376,464	112,000
Secondary	1,581,669	140,000
University	2,754,364	297,500

Source: Mills and Sahn (1993b).

two groups is almost identical. Average net revenues also increase with the education of the proprietor, though not evenly within education categories. But more important than these correlations are the figures presented at the beginning of this chapter showing that, particularly for men, there are high rates of return to education and experience. These econometric results, in fact, provide the compelling evidence in support of investing more in human capital, particularly for the small-scale entrepreneurs engaged in the microenterprise sector.

In summary, we have seen that revenue from the small-enterprise sector is an extremely important component of household income in Conakry, particularly among poorer households. At the same time, median monthly net revenues are very low and are derived overwhelmingly from small retail trade. It is disturbing to note that small-scale manufacturing, an important engine for growth in the small-enterprise sector, does not appear to have responded to the economic reforms introduced between 1985 and 1987 and represents only 5 percent of all small enterprises started between 1988 and 1990.

We also see several clear stratifications in the enterprise sector. Keeping in mind our earlier discussion of private wage sector barriers for women and civil service redeployees, these stratifications have important implications for targeting development assistance. Female proprietors, who tend to have similar returns on costs, have much smaller enterprises, are concentrated in the retail trade sector and usually come from among the poorest households. Programs to nourish the diversification of the sector, particularly through the development of manufacturing, would have strong multiplier effects throughout the rest of the sector. Finally, low education levels, especially lack of math and literacy skills, appear to be a major constraint to enterprise profitability. Entrepreneur skill development programs should play a part in any major initiative to assist small-enterprise development.

NOTES

1. This entire section draws heavily upon Glick and Sahn (1993).

2. In part, this low participation rate for men under 30 may reflect a shortcoming in the ability to capture some of the irregular and intermittent menial self-employment activities in which young men and women are engaged. It is nonetheless of note that this very low level of participation for under 30-year-olds, in contrast to those over 30, exists alongside the unusual demographic situation where the vast majority of the men under 30 are unmarried.

3. The entry probabilities in Table 35 are derived by applying multinomial logit model parameters for men and women to identical values for all explanatory variables. See Glick and Sahn (1993) for details.

4. For a discussion of the method for dealing with selectivity implied in the conditional regression equation used for calculating wages, see Lee (1983).

5. By civil service here we refer to all public sector employment, namely employment with the civil service administration, as well as with public and parapublic enterprises.

6. Furthermore, in 1987 it was estimated that the average annual public sector wage in Guinea was twice the nation's per capita GDP. In the same year civil servants in Côte d'Ivoire and Togo were earning average annual wages that were about eight and nine times their respective per capita GDPs (World Bank 1990a).

7. Technical staff from the Ministries of Health and Education, however, were not laid off in recognition of the policy priority of strengthening these two service sectors.

8. Thirty percent of this bonus was to be paid as a lump sum, with the remaining 70 percent to be paid in monthly installments over a twenty-month period.

9. The number of employees exempt from discharge, including both the *effectifs spéciaux* and technical staff at the Ministries of Health and Education, was almost 26,000 (World Bank 1990a).

10. The loans were to be guaranteed in part (80 percent) by an externally financed fund and in part (20 percent) by the government. Foreign exchange components of approved projects are financed by donor funds.

11. The number submitting proposals represented 20 percent of all voluntary departures, with close to 4 percent actually procuring funding. As of February 1989, the total amount extended as loans was GF 3 billion, of which GF 2.2 billion was in foreign exchange. For a more detailed discussion of the procedures for acquiring funds through the BARAF, see Larfeuil (1990).

12. Banks have been incapable of evaluating project proposals, which they have received by BARAF at a rate of 60 per month; arbitrary bank regulations and procedures have discouraged applicants from pursuing proposals; and the government's shouldering of risk and slack enforcement of overdue loans have led to a high default rate. As of March 1989, 55 percent of payments due on these bank loans remained unpaid. For more on these issues, refer to Larfeuil (1990).

13. The ambitious, initial Structural Adjustment Credit document had actually targeted a reduction of public service employment by 20,000 people by the end of 1986.

14. Because of the unreliability of deflators during this period, the actual real wage declines prior to the initiation of the reform program are not shown in Table 38. They were estimated, however, at more than half those that existed prior to the beginning of the economic crisis.

15. Table 38 does not include data on real wages for 1991 because we have information only on the base salary, exclusive of other payments and bonuses that are included in the real wage figures for the earlier years.

16. The distribution of household per capita consumption by quintile for the general population is, by definition, 20 percent for each quintile group.

17. This section draws heavily upon Mills and Sahn (1993b).

6

MINING SECTOR POLICIES

HISTORICAL PERSPECTIVES

If the sole criteria for assessing a country's wealth were its endowment of nonrenewable resources, then Guinea would be wealthy indeed. It has approximately one-third of the world's bauxite reserves; it has an extraction potential of ten to fifteen tons of gold a year; and its diamond production is currently at a level of 250,000 carats annually. The largely untapped Mount Nimba deposits consist of over 300 million tons of premium iron ore reserves. Furthermore, Guinea can also potentially produce granite, lead, platinum, silver, zinc, nickel, cobalt, and uranium.

The mining sector has become the backbone of the Guinean economy, however, for reasons that go beyond natural resource endowment alone. Postindependence policy has had much to do with the relative growth in importance of mining in general and of bauxite and aluminum exports in particular. An enclave sector, mining has been nurtured under different rules from those faced by the rest of Guinea's formal sector. Its success, in the face of an otherwise failing formal economy, is a large part of the story of Guinea's economic evolution leading to adjustment.

After independence the government formulated different policies for this sector than those that regulate the rest of the Guinean economy. Most mines, for example, are jointly-owned and run by the private sector. This differs dramatically with the government's policy toward agricultural markets where private trading was considered "anti-social" (see chapter 4). All the large private mine operators in Guinea are foreign.

This description is particularly true of the bauxite mines in Guinea. The large Compagnie des Bauxites de Guinée (CBG) is owned jointly by Halco, Inc. (51 percent), a private U.S. holdings group comprising seven international aluminum companies, and by the government (49 percent). It is managed solely by the foreign partners and currently produces approximately ten million tons of ore annually. This ore is exported to CBG's shareholders. FRIGUIA is another mixed bauxite mining company, owned 49 percent by the government and 51 percent by the holdings group of five international aluminum companies. FRIGUIA processes bauxite into alumina before exporting it, currently producing an average 600,000 MT annually. Another, somewhat different bauxite mining company is the Société des Bauxites de Kindia, SBK, previously OBK, owned entirely by the government and managed by technicians from the former Soviet Union. This company formerly sent all bauxite exports to the Soviet Union at slightly above world prices. Production has fallen at SBK from an average of roughly three million tons of bauxite annually following the termination of a bilateral trade arrangement with the former Soviet Union in 1992. With respect to gold, the Compagnie Aurifére de Guinée (AUG) is owned jointly by a private company (50 percent) and the government (50 percent). The main diamond mining firm, AREDOR-Guinea, is similarly split, with the government having joint ownership (50 percent) with an Australian holding company (50 percent). AREDOR produces high quality stones, 85 percent of which are gem quality and carry high prices per carat. Its production has also steadily declined since 1981, its output in 1991 nearly matched by only recently legalized artisanal mining (IMF 1993).

Mining enterprises have operated according to rules that have set them apart and protected them from the numerous infrastructural weaknesses and economic distortions that have come to plague Guinea. Indeed, the mining sector's third major distinction has been its reliance primarily on its own infrastructure, rather than on public infrastructure. Private mining companies have been largely responsible for their own services, in areas of the country where the public provision and maintenance of roads, rail, bridges, water, and electricity, for example, would otherwise be scant and subject to the vagaries of a debt-ridden government's public finance. While this has represented a large cost burden to these firms, it has also assured them of a reliable infrastructure necessary for timely production and export.

Fourth, the government allows the mining companies to bypass some import taxes and trade restrictions, thus sheltering them from some of the inefficiencies inherent in the trade regime. For example, these companies are permitted to import their own petroleum and avoid the specific tax on petroleum products. Not having been subject to most quotas, they have been free to import their intermediate and capital good input requirements and are thus not subject to the same production bottlenecks that have affected other enterprises operating in Guinea.

Fifth, and most important, the government not only allows the mining companies to retain much of their foreign exchange earnings, but allows them to hold it in foreign accounts. Firms are granted free use of foreign exchange earnings after the deduction of profits and taxes payable to the government and of counterpart funds for the payment of local expenses such as wages. Thus, rather than purchasing limited foreign exchange from the Central Bank, mining companies use the international financial markets to save and use their own funds as well as to raise new funds. As such these firms have been able to avoid the severe distortions associated with the exchange regime.

In return for the above arrangements permitting the mining sector to operate as an efficient enclave economy, the government has received foreign exchange in the form of tax revenues. Mining firms have been subject to both export taxes and profit taxes. Clearly the implicit tax on minerals is largely a function of the price established for the mineral. This is especially relevant in the case of bauxite, which, for all practical purposes, has no world price since it is rarely traded on world markets. Prices thus vary between companies, subject to the agreements between governments, producers, and customers.[1]

The history of a classic enclave economy ensconced within a distorted, protectionist economy has, in Guinea's case, been one of success juxtaposed against failure. In general the mining sector has flourished, in both absolute and relative terms, in contrast to the floundering agricultural sector. Table 48 reveals the dramatic increase in mining exports between 1975 and 1985. In nominal terms, the value of bauxite exports increased from US$ 103.8 million to US$ 389.9 million, or by 276 percent, over this ten-year period. Between 1975 and 1985 the value of alumina exports also increased, from US$ 59.2 million to US$ 106 million, or by 79 percent. As a result, the share of mining product in GDP was approximately 14 percent in 1980 (World Bank 1990a). This contrasts to a share on the order of 7 to 10 percent between 1960 and 1975.

The mining sector now dominates total exports. It has jumped from 29 percent of total exports at the time of independence to comprising the vast majority of exports in the 1980s and 1990s.

It must be noted, however, that profits from exports did not all accrue to Guinea since the foreign holding companies rationed their earnings in foreign

TABLE 48

Guinea: Exports of Minerals.
(US$ million)

	1975	1985	1986	1987	1988	1989	1990	1991	1992
Bauxite	103.8	389.9	382.2	399.3	361.2	400.1	445.80	418.80	358.10
CBG	80.6	309.4	305.7	317.0	277.8	324.1	364.20	355.70	335.00
OBK	23.2	80.5	76.5	89.3	83.4	76.0	81.60	63.10	23.10
Alumina	59.2	106.0	85.0	87.4	93.2	130.5	166.00	153.50	102.50
FRIGUIA	59.2	106.0	85.0	87.4	93.2	130.5	166.00	153.50	102.50
Gold	—	—	94.7	105.5	90.5	93.1	44.60	30.30	19.80
AUG	—	—	—	—	3.7	13.5	19.60	15.40	12.00
Artisans	—	—	94.7	105.5	86.8	79.6	25.00	14.90	7.80
Diamonds	—	—	59.1	73.4	60.8	77.8	63.70	54.80	55.40
AREDOR	—	—	46.7	59.3	45.6	56.2	45.20	35.30	26.50
Artisans	—	—	12.4	14.1	15.2	21.6	18.50	19.50	28.90
Total mineral exports	163.0	495.9	621.0	665.6	605.7	701.5	720.16	657.45	535.8
Formal mineral exports	—	—	513.9	546.0	503.7	600.3	376.60	623.00	499.10
Informal mineral exports	—	—	107.1	119.6	102.0	101.2	43.50	34.40	36.70
(Total formal mineral exports in 1985, US$)	(248.8)	(495.9)	(437.8)	(424.1)	(364.8)	(436.3)	—	—	—
Total exports	—	—	655.2	687.1	650.9	761.5	810.90	758.80	651.80
Share of formal mineral exports in total exports (percent)	—	—	78.4	79.2	77.4	78.8	83.44	82.10	76.57
Share of informal mineral exports in total exports (percent)	—	—	16.4	18.1	17.2	14.7	5.36	4.53	5.63

Sources: World Bank (1990a) for 1975–1988; GOG (1993a) for 1989–1992.

accounts. The government, nonetheless,through taxation on domestic companies has certainly benefited from the mining as well. Indeed it is the success of the enclave mining sector that has to a large extent helped sustain a hemorrhaging public sector and a distorted trade regime for over two decades. More accurate accounting of Guinea's fiscal and foreign exchange budgets are available since 1986. In 1986, the mining sector's contribution totaled 88 percent of the total tax revenue and 69 percent of total government revenues and grants (Table 49). Consequently, Guinea relies heavily on the mining sector for its foreign exchange. In 1988, 68 percent of all public sector foreign exchange revenue came from mining taxes (World Bank 1994a).

Although mining has contributed greatly to government coffers, it has not been very successful in creating jobs for Guinean citizens. In fact, there are several hundred expatriates among the relatively small number of approximately 9,000 workers employed by the mining companies (World Bank 1990a). Thus mining companies employed only approximately 0.4 percent of the domestic labor force in 1986.[2]

As a result, though the mining sector contributed close to 25 percent of GDP as recently as 1986, its role in poverty alleviation and income enhancement among Guineans has been negligible. With few forward or backward linkages with the rest of the economy and with little generation of domestic employment within the sector, the mining sector's contribution to domestic income and

TABLE 49
Guinea: Tax Revenues from Mining, 1986–1992.
(US$ million)

	1986	*1987*	*1988*	*1989*	*1990*	*1991*	*1992*[a]
Total tax revenues	238.5	251.7	244.4	297.4	323.2	339.6	339.6
Tax revenues from mining[a]	210.4	198.7	167.1	201.5	217.4	195.6	162.7
Share of mining (percent)	88.2	79.0	68.4	67.8	67.3	57.6	47.9
Tax revenues from CBG	195.2	176.4	140.2	171.5	186.9	165.9	—
Share of CBG in total tax revenues (percent)	81.8	70.1	57.4	57.7	57.8	48.9	—
Tax revenues from mining in constant 1985 prices[b]	186.3	154.3	121.0	146.4	150.6	—	—
Tax revenues from CBG in constant 1985 prices[b]	166.3	137.0	101.5	124.5	129.4	—	—

Sources: IMF (1993); GOG (1993a) for 1991 and 1992 (footnote "a" does not apply to these data).
a. 1992 estimates.
b. Deflated by the manufacturing unit value (MUV) index.

welfare enhancement has been limited. The contributions to the fiscal budget may have been rechanneled to households in the form of public transfers and public sector employment creation.

POLICY REFORMS

In light of the successful production performance of the mining sector, the government has seen no need for radical reform. The formal adjustment program has not targeted change in the mining sector as it has in other sectors. Nevertheless, there have been some discernible policy priorities originating in the mid-1980s (some even before the formal adjustment program began) that represent important current policy concerns within the mining sector. Some of these are laid out in the mining code introduced in 1986 under the Second Republic.

First among these policy directions is that of increasing mining production through further diversification into minerals other than bauxite.[3] As a step in that direction the diamond company AREDOR, established in 1981, commenced exporting in 1986. Efforts have also been underway to begin mining iron ore at Mount Nimba, with a new initiative currently underway to resuscitate the Mifergui iron ore project.[4] Furthermore, in 1986, Niandan mining, a three-way venture between the government and a French and a Saudi Arabian company, was set up to develop a gold vein deposit in Karoussa.

A second, though less consistent sectoral policy focus has been the promotion of artisanal mining. Both the mining of gold and diamonds lend themselves to small-scale mining in Guinea. In partial recognition of this fact, the artisanal mining of gold was legalized in 1986. Nevertheless certain restrictions still apply to the mining and marketing of gold. By law, all mines must have a license to operate. Furthermore, the Central Bank is the only institution that may legally purchase gold, even though the BCRG has purchasing centers only in Conakry and Kankan. Moreover at the Conakry purchasing office the Central Bank will pay only up to 50 percent of the value of purchases in US dollars, the rest being paid in local currency plus a 5 percent premium on the local currency amount.[5]

Artisanal mining of diamonds, in contrast to gold, was legalized only in April 1992, being outlawed in 1985 when AREDOR was granted a monopoly. AREDOR's output of typically high-grade gem quality diamonds has fallen from a peak of 204,000 carats in 1981 to 125,000 carats in 1991, and the company has recorded losses for most of these years. In contrast, it is estimated that between 80,000 and 125,000 carats of artisanal diamonds leave Guinea each year (IMF 1993).[6] Since April 1992, when the purchase and export of artisanal diamonds was opened up to authorized buyers, ten buying-exporting companies have been licensed. Thus whether legally or illegally, there are significant prospects for small-scale diamond extraction and export in Guinea.

A third issue on the policy agenda with respect to the mining sector is related to the aforementioned focus on diversification and expansion. As in other sectors, mining expansion will depend on institutional and legal coherence that assures private investors that they will reap the benefits from their investments. Firms are currently not guaranteed extraction rights when they are given exploration rights to a concession. Moreover, discretionary powers given to the government and individual ministers have led to uncertainty in the eyes of investors. Also, the government's entitlement to a "free" 49 to 50 percent equity in mining firms creates a possible disincentive to foreign investment.[7] That is, the government controls large equity shares without being required to contribute capital. These drawbacks represent some of the reasons that Guinea continues to be unsuccessful in attracting new foreign investors into mining.[8]

Fourth, in addition to rectifying market failures due to the lack of linkage between exploration and extraction, the government must also address the profound negative consequences that mining has had on Guinea's environment.[9] Some measures are now being taken at the company level to mitigate pollution effects.[10] Clearly an integral component of an economic policy that intends to harness Guinea's mineral resources will be to ensure the sustainability of the rest of the nation's natural resource base. There is considerable scope for gains in this regard through the establishment of a regulatory framework, with little cost to productivity in mining.

A fifth reform issue centers around the possibility of future changes of the government's pricing and taxing of mineral exports. Considerations require weighing the improvement of incentives to mining firms by reducing taxes against improving the government's budget position by increasing taxes.[11]

GENERAL ECONOMIC CONSEQUENCES OF REFORMS

The mining sector was a pillar of the Guinean economy at the commencement of the adjustment program. In 1989 the mineral sector accounted for approximately 25 percent of Guinea's GDP. The value of total mineral exports rose by 24 percent between 1986 and 1990 (Table 48). This increase reflected in part high world prices for alumina and subsequent increases in both bauxite and aluminum production since 1985. The production increase was, in fact, a continuation of the trend extant prior to adjustment. Bauxite production increased by 15 percent between 1982 and 1985 and by 12 percent between 1985 and 1988 (World Bank 1990a). By 1988 total bauxite production was 16.5 million MT, bauxite exports being valued at US$ 361.2 million.

The effort to diversify mineral exploitation also contributed initially to higher levels of total exports after 1986 (Table 48). AREDOR commenced diamond production in 1986, adding an average US$ 52 million to total exports annually between 1986 and 1989. AUG commenced marketing its gold in 1988, exporting US$ 3.7 million worth in 1988 and an estimated US$ 13.5 million worth in 1989.

The partial liberalization of artisanal mining in 1986 further promoted growth in total mineral exports, as displayed in Table 49. The legalization of small-scale gold production immediately increased recorded exports of gold from zero to approximately US$ 95 million per year during the late 1980s. These statistics capture the rechanneling of previously illicit exports into now legalized conduits. Statistics since 1986 also reveal substantial artisanal diamond production, although it was banned between 1985 and 1992. The estimated value of exports from this artisanal activity ranges in value from US$ 12.4 million in 1986 to US$ 21.6 million in 1989 and US$ 28.9 million in 1992.

Despite the initial strengthening of mining exports with reform, between 1990 and 1992 the mining sector in Guinea experienced a sharp decline in revenue. In large part this revenue decline was due to a severe fall in the world prices of both bauxite and alumina. The price of aluminum fell by 16.7 percent in 1991 (GOG 1992a). However domestic production also dropped off for reasons other than the fall in world demand. CBG and SBK were affected by multiple technical problems such as train derailments, energy cuts, and equipment breakdowns. FRIGUIA, meanwhile, was involved in labor disputes. Consequently, between 1990 and 1992 bauxite export revenue fell by 19.6 percent and alumina export revenue by 38.2 percent (Table 48).[12]

As a result of price and output declines and expansions elsewhere, the share of mining revenues in total public revenues fell from 68 percent in 1988 to 45 percent in 1992 (World Bank 1994a). Even so, Guinea continues to rely substantially on the fiscal and foreign exchange revenues generated from mining. However the recent declines in mining revenue point to the vulnerability of Guinea's reform program to movements in world prices and to the production of mining output. Clearly the mining sector can and must continue to provide important foreign exchange and government revenue to Guinea. Continued investment in technology and infrastructure will be important if the mining sector is to continue to be the foreign exchange provider it has been.

The mining sector's future role can also be bolstered through further liberalization of artisanal mining and consequent diversification of mineral exports. This will not only increase and stabilize foreign exchange inflows and government revenues, but will also increase employment opportunities. Whereas the mining companies account for close to 80 percent of mineral exports, and create only nine thousand domestic jobs, artisanal mining contributes only 20 percent of mineral exports, but it provides employment to thirty thousand domestic workers, namely 77 percent of the domestic mining workforce. The mining sector as a whole cannot ever be expected to be the instrument for poverty alleviation in Guinea through employment creation, but artisanal mining holds some promise in generating income among the local poor. In contrast to other sectors, nevertheless, the mining sector in Guinea functions relatively efficiently and further gains in output or earnings from increasing efficiency are limited. In fact, the challenge that Guinea faces is that of relying less on mining by diversifying its exports, through the promotion of both agricultural policies and private sector participation in manufacturing and services.

NOTES

1. CBG's base price, for example, is determined on the basis of the bauxite's quality and of operating expenses, such as fuel and labor costs, as well as on world inflation (the U.S. wholesale price index for industrial commodities) and on the world price of aluminum and alumina. The agreement with CBG has also ensured the government of a guaranteed minimal income.

2. The labor force figure is based on the estimate that approximately 50 percent of the population is between the ages of 15 and 60.

3. If Guinea is to maintain its share of commanding approximately 20 percent of the world's bauxite production annually it would have to increase its production of bauxite. CBG has the reserves to increase production by the estimated 16 million MT required for Guinea to maintain its share of world bauxite production through the 1990s.

4. The project itself was first discussed over twenty years ago and would involve extracting up to nine million tons of iron ore and exporting it by rail through Liberia. The current initiative involves the governments of Guinea and Liberia, a French parastatal, and a private conglomerate. It has been slowed down, however, by inadequate assurances of external financing and the need to complete an environmental impact assessment. Additional difficulties include the division of risks and profits of the project between the governments of Guinea and Liberia, and coordination between the governments on tax, customs, and transit issues.

5. This 5 percent premium does not completely cover the premium that the parallel exchange rate has over the official rate. The former has recently been close to 10 percent higher than the latter (see chapter 3, "Trade and Exchange Rate Policy").

6. There are minor diamond deposits even within AREDOR holdings that prove to be too small for efficient industrial-scale extraction. The scope for artisanal mining is indicated by evidence that up to ten thousand artisans are active in extracting diamonds (World Bank 1990a). Presumably most of these diamonds are smuggled out of the country, although the Central Bank reportedly purchases some.

7. The disincentives from government participation may be less than they appear. It is argued in IMF (1993) that shareholders choose joint venture arrangements in part for the political protection and convenience they afford. Moreover in most companies' tax regimes, government revenues have been derived from special taxes or from income taxes, and not from dividend sharing.

8. Other reasons include the slow growth of the aluminum market, the lack of national geological survey data, and the inaccessibility of large tracts of land that were assigned indefinitely under the First Republic.

9. Mining results in the elimination of topsoil and vegetation on large tracts of land with deleterious implications for wildlife. The runoff of silt from mines, while adding to erosion, also affects the water quality of streams and rivers downstream. Dust from extraction, transportation, and processing contributes to air pollution.

10. At FRIGUIA, for example, attempts are being made at revegetation using topsoil stockpiled prior to mining, water quality is being monitored, and pollution control at the alumina plant is also being upgraded.

11. Pricing and tax issues are particularly pressing in the case of the bauxite firms. The government will be especially concerned with projections of declining tax revenues from CBG through the 1990s as a result of stable aluminum prices and a formula that discounts cost increases over time (World Bank 1990a).

12. The formal gold and diamond subsectors also experienced a fall in revenue of 38.7 percent and 13.0 percent, respectively.

7

FINANCIAL SECTOR POLICIES

HISTORICAL PERSPECTIVES

Soon after independence in March 1960, Guinea left the West African franc zone. The government subsequently launched an independent monetary policy in 1972 with its replacement of the CFA franc by the Guinea syli (which was replaced by the Guinean franc, at par in 1986). This policy financed and maintained an inefficient and unsustainable public sector over the next two and a half decades. Furthermore, the banking system was plagued by chaos due to financial mismanagement and corruption. These factors, in conjunction, contributed to the major crisis in finance and in faith in the banking system that became the focus of the reforms that commenced in 1986.

Restrictions and political pressures under the First Republic contributed to the banking sector's frailty. First, with one exception,[1] the Guinean government owned all banks and tightly controlled the operations of each. For example, certain banks could not accept deposits in sylis; others could only lend to public enterprises; and still others could not extend credit but instead had to deposit their funds with other banks. No bank could lend to the private sector until 1979, at which time only the Banque Central de la République de Guinée (BCRG) was permitted to do so. Also, as with most parastatals, the government expected the banks' assistance with its policy of assuring employment to all graduates. Consequently, banks were overstaffed. By 1984 there were approximately twenty-four hundred staff members in the banking sector, approximately one staff member for every fifty accounts.

Second, all profits, reserves, and depreciation allowances had to be transferred to the government. Therefore, the seed capital that state-owned banks were initiated with could not be augmented in step with their extension of credit.[2] Thus, by 1986, their capital was less than 0.5 percent of their total assets and liabilities (Tenconi 1988).

Third, as implementing agents of the Development Plan, banks were compelled to lend to public enterprise as per the directives of the Plan. As such, during the period 1960–1985, the banks extended short-term loans primarily to finance the working capital needs of parastatals. In most instances these loans covered recurring losses. In fact, at maturity the borrower's account was automatically debited, which usually just increased the debit balances of insolvent parastatals (Tenconi 1988). Similarly, after 1979, political and personal connections and bribery determined to whom in the private sector the banks lent. In general, banks did not use rate-of-return criteria.

Fourth, lax administrative practices, incompetence, and bad management exacerbated the disastrous condition of banks. The resulting accounting chaos, furthermore, was amenable to corruption. Items were often adulterated or not entered in the books at all; financial statements were infrequently prepared; documents were forged. Most significantly, a number of schemes created fictitious domestic assets and contributed to the expansion of the domestic money supply (M1). Certified checks drawn on other banks, for example, were deposited to individual accounts even though these checks were not always covered by the banks upon which they were drawn. By December 1985, state banks showed an estimated GF 40 billion of fictitious assets (Tenconi 1988).[3]

Statistics on monetary aggregates reveal these factors (Table 50). Domestic credit expanded rapidly, at an average annual rate of 17 percent between 1960 and 1980.[4] Moreover, the public sector garnered over 90 percent of this credit. The money supply expanded at an average annual rate of 41 percent over this period. Monetary policy, like exchange and trade policy, worsened the dichotomy between the official and parallel sectors of the economy. In fact, the inflationary pressure that resulted from expansionist monetary policy was not evident in the controlled movement of official prices and wages. Rather, it manifested itself in parallel market prices. The parallel exchange rate increased from GS 56 per US dollar in 1973 to GS 311 per US dollar in 1985, while the official rate remained constant at GS 20 per US dollar over the same period. As a result, most economic actors avoided the domestic monetary system. Firms in the mining sector, for

TABLE 50

Guinea: Financial Sector, 1960–1992.
(Billions of GF)

	1960	1965	1970	1975	1980	1986	1987	1988	1989	1990	1991	1992
Net foreign assets	0.5	-0.8	-1.9	-1.1	-6.7	7.9	25.1	-1.2	13.4	58.9	81.1	112.5
BCRG	—	—	—	—	—	-1.9	10.3	-4.6	6.4	44.3	57.0	74.2
Commercial banks	—	—	—	—	—	9.8	14.8	3.4	7.0	14.7	24.1	38.3
Net domestic assets	—	—	—	—	—	42.6	43.4	105.7	107.7	95.1	126.6	144.3
Domestic credit	1.0	5.3	9.9	12.8	21.8	37.2	42.1	92.1	92.6	95.1	122.7	156.3
Public sector (net)	1.0	5.1	9.3	11.7	20.6	25.8	17.1	47.5	39.5	23.5	42.4	54.0
Government (net)	0.4	1.3	4.0	0.9	6.1	37.2	36.4	47.3	39.3	23.1	39.9	51.9
State enterprises (net)	0.6	3.8	5.3	10.8	14.5	-11.4	-19.3	0.2	0.2	0.4	2.5	2.1
Private sector[a]	0.0	0.2	0.6	1.1	1.2	11.4	25.0	44.6	53.1	71.6	80.3	102.2
Other items (net)	—	—	—	—	—	5.4	1.3	13.5	15.1	0.0	3.9	11.9
Money and quasi-money (M1)	1.4	3.8	7.4	11.1	13.0	42.6	59.6	96.5	115.3	148.4	194.2	242.0
Currency	0.9	1.3	3.2	3.7	3.3	34.6	43.3	55.7	69.4	84.7	119.4	133.0
Deposits	0.5	2.5	4.2	7.4	9.7	8.00	16.3	40.8	45.9	63.7	74.8	109.0
Foreign currency deposits	—	—	—	—	—	7.90	8.9	8.0	5.7	5.8	13.5	14.8
Indices/ratios												
CPI (index 12/86=100)	—	—	—	—	—	100.0	133.7	168.9	212.8	240.5	287.6	335.4
CPI (percent)	—	—	—	—	—	—	33.7	26.3	26.0	13.0	19.6	16.6
Interest rates (percent)	—	—	—	—	—	11.0	15.0	17.0	24.0	24.0	25.0	25.0
GDP (billion FG current)	11.9	12.8	16.8	24.2	33.5	671.3	845.6	1081.6	1444.6	1820.4	2247.8	2684.3
Net domestic credit (as percent of GDP)	8.4	41.4	58.9	52.9	65.0	5.5	4.9	8.5	6.4	5.2	5.5	5.8
M1 (as percent of GDP)	11.8	29.7	44.1	45.9	38.8	6.4	7.1	8.9	7.9	8.2	8.6	9.0
Deposits (as percent of M1)	35.7	65.8	56.8	66.8	74.6	18.8	27.4	42.3	39.8	42.9	38.5	45.0

(Table continues on the following page.)

TABLE 50 (continued)

	1960	1965	1970	1975	1980	1986	1987	1988	1989	1990	1991	1992
Domestic bank deposits (in 1986 GF)	—	—	—	—	—	8.0	12.2	24.4	21.6	26.5	26.0	32.5
Growth in domestic bank deposits (percent)	—	—	—	—	—	—	52.4	100.3	-11.7	22.8	-1.8	24.9
Growth in deposits (percent)	—	400.0	68.0	76.2	31.1	-17.5	103.8	150.3	12.5	38.8	17.4	45.7
Private share of domestic credit (percent)	0.0	3.8	6.1	8.6	5.5	30.7	59.4	48.4	57.3	75.3	65.4	65.4
Private sector credit (in 1986 GF)	—	—	—	—	—	11.4	18.7	26.4	24.9	29.8	27.9	30.5
Growth in private sector credit (percent)	—	—	—	—	—	—	64.0	41.2	-5.5	19.3	-6.2	9.1
Growth in net domestic credit (real) (percent)	—	—	—	—	—	—	-15.4	7.3	-20.2	-9.1	7.9	9.3
Net domestic credit (1986 GF)	—	—	—	—	—	37.7	31.5	54.5	43.5	39.5	42.7	46.6

Sources: World Bank (1990); GOG (1992a); IMF (1993).

a. Includes non-performing loans.

example, utilized off-shore foreign exchange accounts. Other sectors held their savings either in foreign exchange or in real assets. This general lack of confidence in the financial system, and inflation, contributed to the increased reliance on barter trade throughout the country.

The few efforts to keep the financial system afloat and to restrain monetary expansion only further eroded confidence in the system. For example, a ceiling of GS 20,000 per month was set for cash withdrawals from any bank account. Several cash exchanges were also effected to eliminate some of the currency in circulation.[5] In practice these exchanges were sometimes counterproductive since the number of new bills issued actually exceeded the number of old bills exchanged. One such exchange was made by the party mechanism in April 1981 (Tenconi 1988).

POLICY REFORMS

Faced with a financial sector in shambles, the new government first moved slowly, then reacted drastically. Immediately upon the fall of the First Republic, the government liberalized trade, removed restrictions upon the hitherto specialized banks, and reduced fear of strong government sanction. In response, fictitious assets within the system grew dramatically from mid-1984 through 1985, contributing to the overall anarchy that overtook the banking system.

In response to the deteriorating conditions, the President ordered the immediate closing of all six state banks on December 22, 1985.[6] Banking from thereon has been open to private sector participation, including foreign interests. As a result, four commercial banks have opened in Guinea.[7] Most were founded with the help of foreign participation and foreign management.[8] Reform has contributed to the emergence, albeit restrained, of private sector investment in Guinea, including within the banking industry. Initially the government took a 51 percent share in the ownership of BIAG and BICIGUI, reflecting both the dearth of private capital then and a lingering nostalgia for *dirigisme*. By 1988, however, the government's share in BICIGUI's capital had declined to 39.5 percent as a result of capital increase. Fifty-five percent of the capital financing of SGBG, moreover, was private in 1988. Private investors now hold shares in three of the commercial banks.

Several factors made entry into the banking business attractive to the private sector. Special incentives, for instance, were provided by the government. Credit control and regulation by the Central Bank (BCRG) were minimal. For example, there was no reserve requirement. Banks were also allowed to import all necessary supplies without having to pay customs duties. Special tax exemptions were also granted on a case-by-case basis. Moreover, with few alternative savings options in Guinea, demand deposits at banks effectively cornered the savings market. In 1992 and 1993, the government began emphasizing regulation and organization of the banking sector. Issues included instituting and increasing reserve requirements, restructuring the financially troubled BIAG and BIG with the assistance of foreign capital, and defining the Central Bank's role in supervising private banks.

Although Guinea's monetary policy reform has focused on the overhaul of the banking system, the government has also reformed the interest rate structure in Guinea. A new interest rate schedule established in 1986 raised medium- and short-term interest rates (ceilings) to 14 and 16 percent respectively (Table 51). In 1981, comparable rates had been 3.5 to 7 percent (World Bank 1981c). Also part of these reforms, a deposit rate floor was established in 1987 for term deposits and deposits of convertible GF. In 1988, furthermore, a floor of 12 percent was established for savings and nonsight deposits.

Recognizing that these rates were well below the close to 30 percent inflation rate caused by exchange rate devaluation, the government increased nominal interest rates across the board every year from 1986 to 1991. By the end of 1992, all regulated interest rates were positive in real terms.[9] This has been true not only of commercial bank lending rates but also of deposit rates and the Central Bank's refinancing rates. As a result, the rates on savings and term deposits were 21 and 23 percent, respectively, by 1991 (Table 51). Moreover, by February 1990, both short- and medium-term lending rate ceilings were eliminated in commercial banks. Finally, the Central Bank introduced treasury bills, which since December 1993 have been sold by auction. Treasury bills have provided the Central Bank with a new instrument of monetary management and should also aid in setting a market-based flexible interest rate system (World Bank 1994a).

GENERAL ECONOMIC CONSEQUENCES OF REFORMS

Guinea's ability to reform its banking system so quickly is a credit to the government and a testimony to its will for change. Formal banking services, previously inaccessible, are now available to the private sector and to the public.

The positive consequences of these reforms are evident in the movements of monetary aggregates[10] (Table 50). First, domestic credit shifted away from state enterprises as they were liquidated and toward the private sector. From 1988 through 1992, net domestic credit to state enterprises averaged GF −1.22 billion per year whereas net domestic credit to the private sector averaged GF 56.48 billion. Whereas the share of private sector credit in total domestic credit was 5.5 percent in 1980, by 1986 it had increased to slightly over 30 percent, and by 1992 to over 65 percent. Second, as a result of the liberalization of the exchange

TABLE 51

Guinea: Structure of Interest Rates.
(percentage)

	May 1986	January 1987	January 1988	January 1989	February 1990	October 1990	July 1991	January 1993
Loan rates								
Central Bank refinancing								
Preferential (TREP)	9	10	10	11	14	15	19	17
Normal (TREN)	11	15	17	22	24	24	25	22
Commercial banks (ceilings)								
Short term	16	20	25	free	free	—	—	—
Medium term	14	15	15	16	free	—	—	—
External credit lines								
"Accord cadre"[a]	—	—	10	11	14	—	—	—
Other	—	—	9–11	10–11	12–14	—	—	—
Preferential[b]	—	12–15	15	16–18	18–20	—	—	—
Deposit rates (floors)								
Sight deposits	—	0	free	free	free	—	—	—
Savings deposits	—	—	12	12	16	17	21	18
Non-sight deposits	—	—	12	14	16	16	17	17
Term deposits[c]	—	15	17	19	21	21	23	—
Convertible Guinean Francs	—	17	19	21	23	23	—	—
Inflation (annual)	—	23.26	27.44	28.26	19.37	19.37	25.00	16.60[d]

Sources: World Bank (1990a, 1989c); GOG (1991b); BCRG (1992, unpublished data).

Note: Regulated interest rates only since free rates are not known.

a. For larger loans funded by Caisse Centrale de la Cooperation Economique's credit line.

b. For local currency loans complementing externally-funded credit lines.

c. Terms of over six months until January 1989 and over three months since then.

d. 1992 inflation rate.

regime, a new investment code, and an influx of donor credit, Guinea's net foreign asset position has turned positive for all years but one since 1986.[11] In 1992, net foreign assets (NFA) were GF 112.5 billion in contrast to the 1980 level of GF –6.7 billion. Commercial banks held 34 percent of NFA in 1992, while the Central Bank held the other 66 percent. Third, inflation has fallen substantially, from 27.44 percent in 1988 to 16.6 percent in 1992 (Table 51) and to an estimated 7.1 percent in 1993 (World Bank 1994a).

Reform's limits, however, are also revealed by the data in Table 50. The financial sector remains shallow. Money supply as a proportion of GDP remains relatively unchanged at approximately 7 to 8 percent, despite the large increases in currency printed in 1990 to help cover the budget deficit and in late 1991 to pay salaries.[12] Although deposits as a percentage of M1 have increased consistently from 18.78 percent in 1986 and have accelerated with positive interest rates, in 1991 this percentage was still only 38.52 percent. Estimates show that the private sector's local currency deposit base at the banking system was a low 2.1 percent of GDP in 1989 (World Bank 1990a).

This low base underscores the slow progress of interest rate reform. Even the increase of interest rates on deposits had a limited impact on savings, for two reasons. First, most deposits were still not interest-bearing by 1990. Since banks demanded high minimum balances for accounts to qualify for interest, only about 30 percent of deposits actually earned interest (World Bank 1990a). Second, even after nominal increases, interest rates remained negative in real terms until 1990. Even with a fall in the inflation rate, savings and sight deposits in 1990 carried a –3 percent real rate of interest. This fall resulted in the first positive interest rate (4 percent) on term deposits. The 1992 drop in the inflation rate to 16.6 percent led to positive interest rates across the board, an outcome not reversed by a subsequent reduction in nominal rates by the Central Bank in 1993.

Subsidized interest rates available to commercial banks have exacerbated distortions and have limited the efficient expansion of the banking system in Guinea. While banks sometimes lent at rates above the 25 percent interest ceiling through 1988, the actual average cost of funds that year was estimated at only 1.7 percent (World Bank 1990a). Importantly, commercial banks have been able to refinance GF-denominated loans through the Central Bank at highly subsidized rates. Both the preferential rate (TREP) of 11 percent and the regular rate (TREN) of 22 percent in 1989 were well below that year's inflation rate of 28 percent. Even with the decline in the inflation rate in 1990, the Central Bank refinancing rate (TREN) continued to be negative in real terms. While policy reform had led to the elimination in 1989 of interest rate ceilings for regular short- and medium-term loans by commercial banks, the availability of funds at cheap, subsidized rates through the Central Bank restrains banks from assuming higher risk loans or promoting interest-paying deposits. Moreover, the Central Bank accommodates the inefficiencies of Guinea's commercial banks. In addition to the high cost of delinquent loans, estimates for overhead costs are as high as 14.4 percent of outstanding portfolios, which is partly a result of the large expatriate staff at these banks (World Bank 1990a).

Commercial banks also face continuing disincentives to lend domestically. Also, constraints in the financial sector result from the institutional and legal void apparent in Guinea after the Sekou Touré years. The lack of credit records for clients and the absence of an enforced legal framework reduce information and increase risk for the lender. For instance, the lack of proper land registration titles denies banks the possibility of securing loans through real estate collateral. The inability to enforce creditor rights through foreclosure is also an outcome of an underdeveloped legal system and, often, collusion between debtors and judges (World Bank 1990a). As of 1992 a large portfolio of nonperforming bank loans reemerged, comprising 21 percent of total bank credit by the end of that year (IMF 1993).[13]

Apparently, institutional factors affected lending practices and the distribution of credit to the private sector. In effect, credit has been limited primarily to short-term loans. Eighty-five percent of all outstanding loans were short-term by the end of 1988 (World Bank 1990a). In 1992, short-term commercial credit accounted for a still high 80 percent of all credit to the private sector (BCRG 1993). Most of this credit financed commodity imports by large, well-known traders. Credit practices have thus reinforced the consumption-good orientation of the foreign exchange auction discussed earlier. Term-lending for investment purposes has been limited, and foreign investors usually must resort to external financing for their investments in Guinea.

Several steps in 1992 created a framework within which banks could extend credit, though the results have been limited. The government enacted the Land Tenure Code in March 1992, which legalized the private ownership of land and enabled borrowers to use land as collateral for bank loans. The final arrangements for a land registry were not yet worked out, however. Reforms of the legal system were also introduced in early 1992, including the establishment of a supreme court, training for magistrates, and more effective processing and enforcement of court decisions (IMF 1993).

Guinea's long-term growth depends on mobilizing and directing domestic savings, including personal savings, toward productive investment. To that end, however, efficient financial intermediation remains elusive. Gross domestic savings as a percentage of GDP has not increased beyond the 1986 level (Table 52). Gross fixed investment, however, has increased by 29 percent since 1986. This increase has been primarily due to a 47 percent increase in externally-

TABLE 52
Guinea: Consumption, Investment, and Savings, 1986–1992.
(percentage of GDP)

	1986	*1987*	*1988*	*1989*	*1990*	*1991*	*1992*
Gross domestic expenditure	96.48	100.60	105.30	100.80	101.54	101.71	106.34
Consumption	80.78	82.80	85.90	82.40	81.95	83.86	87.40
Private	71.18	72.00	75.30	71.90	72.45	73.44	77.36
Public	9.60	10.80	10.60	10.50	9.50	10.42	10.04
Gross fixed investment	13.30	16.40	17.70	16.40	17.47	15.68	17.14
Private	8.30	10.20	10.80	10.00	9.77	8.63	9.79
Public	5.00	6.20	6.90	6.40	7.70	7.05	7.35
Changes in stocks	2.40	1.40	1.70	2.00	2.12	2.17	1.80
Gross domestic savings	19.30	17.20	14.10	17.60	18.30	—	—
Gross national savings	13.40	13.00	9.70	12.20	13.00	—	—

Sources: IMF (1990a); GOG (1991b, 1993a).
Note: Excludes transactions with the USSR.

financed public investment. In fact, after an initial improvement in 1987, private sector investment declined between 1988 and 1991.

Clearly it will take time to regain the public's confidence in the banking sector. Increasing savings requires that real interest rates remain consistently positive and, possibly, that the subsidized refinancing of certain loans be eliminated. Small-scale personal savings need also to be mobilized. Formal financial institutions, however, will likely be unimportant in this regard. Instead, informal financial institutions should be promoted as a means of tapping the personal savings potential of households and microenterprises. On the investment side, the main limits to lending are high associated risks and the current lack of attractive opportunities. For savings and investment, however, a general improvement in business confidence is essential. Moreover, the shortcomings of the institutional and legal framework in Guinea will also have to be addressed. Legal measures that permit the use of collateral and the enforcement of contracts, for example, will be essential not only to lending but to business and investment in general.

NOTES

1.   Banque Islamique de Guinée (BIG) was the only private bank in Guinea prior to 1986. Established in 1983, it accounted for less than 5 percent of total deposits and credit.

2. In most instances, this seed fund amounted to GS 15 million.

3. The practice of depositing certified checks drawn on another bank continued even after it was deemed illegal in July 1985. Indeed, between July and December of 1985, certified checks comprised one-third of all private sector deposits (Tenconi 1988).

4. As a percentage of GDP, domestic credit grew from 8.4 percent in 1960 to 65.04 percent in 1980 (Table 50). As a percentage of GDP, M1 grew from 11.76 percent to 38.78 percent over that period. However, caution is necessary in interpreting GDP statistics, particularly prior to 1986. Gross domestic product was evaluated at official prices, undervaluing the official economy and probably seriously underestimating informal sector production.

5. For example, exchange of new notes was limited to a maximum of GS 20,000 in 1981, with all excess currency having to be deposited in the banking system.

6. Deposit balances were to be reimbursed only upon verification by the Liquidation Committee. Moreover, reimbursement on private accounts was to be phased out to reduce inflationary pressures while the government, as promised, furnished the financial requirements of public sector enterprises.

7. They are the Banque Internationale pour l'Afrique en Guinée (BIAG), the Banque Internationale pour le Commerce et l'Industrie en Guinée (BICIGUI), the Société Generale de Banques en Guinée (SGBG), and the Union Internationale de Banques en Guinée (UIBG). The Banque Islamique de Guinée (BIG), another commercial bank, had been established prior to the fall of the First Republic.

8. The BIAG, SGBG, BICIGUI, and UIBG's primary foreign partners are the Banque Internationale pour l'Afrique Occidentale, Société Generale, Banque Nationale de Paris, and Credit Lyonnais France, respectively. Other international financial institutions with partnership in Guinea's commercial banks include the International Finance Corporation, the European Investment Bank, and the Société Financiére pour les Pays d'Outremer.

9. Nominal interest rates actually decreased in 1993 following a fall in the inflation rate in 1992 (Table 51).

10. Given the large-scale changes in data methods, too much weight ought not be placed on the magnitude of changes in monetary aggregates between 1980 and 1986 in Table 50. Nevertheless, several observations regarding the direction of changes are noteworthy.

11. The new investment code of 1987 permits the future repatriation of capital, tax and customs exemptions for the import of intermediary goods required for foreign investment, and deductions of other taxes (GOG 1987a).

12. It is noteworthy that the M1-to-GDP ratios in the neighboring CFA countries of Mali and Côte d'Ivoire were 23 and 32 percent, respectively, and 14.5 percent in neighboring non-CFA Sierra Leone.

13. This problem has been particularly serious for two relatively small commercial banks.

8

PUBLIC SECTOR AND FISCAL POLICIES

HISTORICAL PERSPECTIVES

The First Republic did not formally document finances or the government budget. This lack of proper budgetary processes and expenditure control procedures again demonstrates the story of a state-run economy in crisis. Consequently, many expenditures went unrecorded; for example, much of government development expenditures were outside the budget (IMF 1987a). In addition, because the treasury generally had no knowledge of accounts being debited, it could not track the government's cash position.

Nevertheless, current estimates of the financial operations of the First Republic permit at least a general picture of government finances. Despite the public sector's domination of the domestic formal economy in Guinea, government expenditures accounted for a relatively small portion of GDP, on par with other African countries. In 1984 total revenues and grants were 23 percent of Guinea's GDP; total expenditures were 27.6 percent of GDP. The comparable figures for Sub-Saharan African countries on average were 24.8 and 31.2 percent respectively (UNDP and World Bank 1989). In addition to the fact that expenditures were low in absolute terms (US$ 9.8 per capita in 1984 estimated at the parallel exchange rate), the low ratio of government expenditures to GDP was also due to the increased importance of the enclave mining sector in Guinea.

Indeed government finances under the First Republic became highly dependent on revenue from the mining sector. Over the period 1974 to 1984, mining sector revenue grew at an average annual rate that was more than 20 percent above that of nonmining revenues (Table 53). In addition, public enterprises played an important role in generating nonmining income, reflecting their pervasive presence in the economy. Public enterprise contributed an average of 37 percent in nonmining revenue each year between 1980 and 1984 (Table 53). However, mismanagement and declining profitability lowered public enterprises' share in total revenue and grants to only 12 percent in 1984, about equal to its share 10 years earlier.

Current expenditures sustained the employment of an inflated civil service and the operation of an inefficient parastatal sector. Current expenditures had risen to account for 84 percent of total expenditures in 1984. Between 1981 and 1984, on average, 41 percent of current expenditures financed wages and salaries. Over the same period, on average, 28 percent was spent on subsidies and transfers to public enterprises (Table 53). Although little is known about sectoral breakdowns, evidence from the health and education sectors reveals that the large shares allocated to wages and salaries resulted in significant shortages in other sectoral expenditures, such as those on materials and supplies (discussed in the next section).

Capital expenditure levels during the First Republic were low, the government placing little priority on maintaining infrastructure and investing for the future. By 1984, development expenditures accounted for approximately 16 percent of total expenditures, down from 34 percent ten years earlier (Table 53). Much government investment, moreover, was allocated to unprofitable collectivized agriculture and to inefficient parastatals, consequently earning low rates of return (World Bank 1990a).

In summary, the imperatives of keeping parastatals afloat and of providing government employment to all graduates necessitated the budget deficits that characterized the First Republic. In 1983 the government deficit was estimated at over ten percent of GDP (Table 53). These deficits were funded, in part, by external financing. To a large extent, moreover, the government financed deficits by creating money. At least temporarily, therefore, Guinea's precarious fiscal situation was kept from collapsing by compromising monetary balance.

POLICY REFORMS AND THEIR GENERAL ECONOMIC CONSEQUENCES

The fiscal reforms undertaken by the Second Republic were both a response to the fiscal crisis that burdened the country in 1984 and also an integral part of

TABLE 53

Guinea: Financial Operations of the Central Government, 1974–1993.
(billions of nominal Guinean Francs)

	1974	1975	1976	1977	1978	1979	1980	1981	1982	1983
Revenue and grants	3.33	3.35	13.35	7.98	9.10	9.90	10.77	11.86	17.70	10.70
Mining sector revenues	0.00	0.40	1.50	1.37	2.18	1.97	2.53	3.43	3.30	3.20
Nonmining sector revenues	3.05	2.79	9.14	6.54	6.38	7.61	6.33	8.06	13.80	7.10
Taxes on income and profits	0.85	0.65	1.15	0.95	1.41	1.30	2.04	1.08	4.80	1.20
Payroll taxes	0.05	0.05	0.05	0.04	0.06	0.03	0.03	0.03	—	—
Taxes on domestic goods and services	0.29	0.26	0.48	0.25	0.34	0.15	0.15	0.12	1.10	0.20
Petroleum excise tax	0.05	0.04	0.06	0.05	0.05	0.05	0.00	0.08	0.40	—
Taxes on international trade	0.81	0.87	1.54	1.43	1.53	2.08	1.47	2.36	1.50	1.20
Nontax revenue and miscellaneous taxes	1.04	0.97	5.91	3.88	3.04	4.05	2.64	4.47	6.50	4.60
Grants	0.28	0.15	2.71	0.07	0.54	0.32	1.90	0.37	0.60	0.40
Expenditures	4.57	5.71	9.43	6.82	8.44	14.63	10.89	12.77	19.60	15.30
Current expenditure	3.01	3.26	4.54	4.34	6.45	6.44	7.19	7.04	15.80	12.40
Wages and salaries	1.83	1.87	2.41	2.19	2.42	2.84	3.40	3.79	4.30	4.60
Other goods and services	0.92	1.05	1.46	1.23	1.62	1.62	3.07	2.27	4.60	0.80
Subsidies and transfers	0.02	0.03	0.19	0.47	1.98	1.51	0.21	0.40	6.50	6.50
Public enterprises	—	—	—	0.47	1.66	1.22	0.00	0.17	5.50	5.80
Interest payments	0.24	0.31	0.49	0.44	0.44	0.46	0.51	0.59	0.50	0.50
Capital expenditure	1.56	2.45	4.89	2.48	1.99	8.20	3.70	5.73	3.80	2.80
Deficit (commitment basis)	-1.25	-2.37	3.92	1.16	0.66	-4.73	-0.13	-0.92	-1.90	-4.60
Net changes in expenditure arrears	—	—	—	—	—	—	—	—	0.20	0.50
Cash deficit (−)	—	—	—	—	—	—	—	—	-1.70	-4.10
Financing	1.98	0.03	10.88	5.04	2.34	6.55	6.25	10.29	1.70	4.10
Current budgetary surplus	0.20	-0.11	8.54	3.84	4.05	3.29	3.25	4.48	—	—
Net external financing	1.95	1.55	1.34	0.08	1.22	1.14	0.90	1.71	1.20	1.10
Drawings	2.17	1.89	1.88	1.07	2.07	2.41	2.20	2.86	1.90	1.80
Amortization	-0.85	-1.09	-1.70	-2.00	-1.83	-2.08	-2.04	-2.29	-1.30	-1.10
Changes in amortization arrears	0.62	0.75	1.16	1.02	0.98	0.81	0.74	1.14	0.60	0.40
Debt relief	—	—	—	—	—	—	—	—	—	—
Deferred payments	—	—	—	—	—	—	—	—	—	—
Debt rescheduling	—	—	—	—	—	—	—	—	—	—
Arrears (reduction −)	—	—	—	—	—	—	—	—	—	—
Short-term credit, net	—	—	—	—	—	—	—	—	0.50	—
Net domestic financing	-0.17	-1.41	0.99	1.12	-2.93	2.12	2.10	4.11		3.00

164

	1984	1985	1986	1987	1988	1989	1990	1991	1992 (Est.)	1993 Budget
Revenue and grants	11.10	9.30	103.40	170.7	199.6	274.9	362.1	412.5	478.4	548.0
Mining sector revenues	4.20	3.70	71.10	107.3	111.3	150.7	197.6	190.0	162.7	145.4
Nonmining sector revenues	6.80	5.40	19.50	28.6	51.5	71.7	96.3	140.0	198.4	254.9
Taxes on income and profits	1.50	0.90	1.10	1.6	3.0	5.0	6.3	13.9	24.6	25.4
Taxes on domestic goods and services	0.60	0.40	4.10	10.4	23.4	38.0	41.7	68.4	101.3	142.9
Petroleum excise tax	—	—	0.00	1.7	10.0	18.9	—	—	—	—
Taxes on international trade	2.50	2.60	6.00	8.4	11.1	14.2	25.7	38.2	46.3	64.7
Nontax revenue and miscellaneous taxes	2.20	1.40	8.30	8.2	14.0	14.5	22.6	19.5	26.2	22.0
Grants	0.10	0.20	12.80	34.8	36.8	52.5	68.3	82.5	117.3	147.7
Expenditures	13.30	21.40	136.20	205.6	276.3	347.5	458.4	515.2	597.1	650.3
Current expenditure	11.20	20.00	85.20	119.8	152.9	187.7	230.0	280.3	302.7	315.6
Wages and salaries	5.00	6.30	18.20	21.3	45.5	60.7	78.5	102.9	132.1	140.5
Other goods and services	1.80	2.30	45.00	61.5	50.1	67.5	86.7	96.2	89.4	94.7
Subsidies and transfers	3.90	10.80	9.50	14.0	21.5	24.4	17.2	28.0	32.6	24.7
Public enterprises	3.00	10.00	—	—	—	—	—	—	—	—
Interest payments	0.50	0.50	12.50	23.0	35.8	35.0	47.6	53.2	48.5	53.6
Capital expenditure	2.10	1.40	51.00	85.8	123.5	159.8	228.4	234.9	291.5	332.3
Net lending	—	—	—	—	—	—	—	—	2.8	2.5
Deficit (commitment basis)	-2.20	-12.10	-32.90	-34.9	-76.7	-72.6	-96.3	-102.7	-118.7	-102.3
Net changes in expenditure arrears	0.30	-0.40	3.20	-1.3	7.3	-1.6	37.7	12.1	-90.0	-12.6
Cash deficit (−)	-1.90	-12.50	-29.70	-36.2	-69.4	-74.2	-58.6	-90.6	-208.7	-114.9
Financing	1.90	12.50	29.70	36.2	69.4	74.2	58.6	90.6	208.7	68.0
Current budgetary surplus	0.40	0.90	36.70	37.6	58.5	83.7	75.7	74.5	216.9	74.1
Net external financing	1.00	1.00	59.00	62.9	94.3	124.1	120.0	147.3	178.9	220.3
Drawings	—	—	—	—	—	—	—	—	—	—
Amortization	-1.40	-1.90	-41.30	-42.5	-68.7	-73.7	-82.6	-117.3	-116.2	-92.6
Changes in amortization arrears	0.80	1.80	-7.90	—	—	—	—	—	—	—
Debt relief	—	—	26.90	0.0	0.0	0.0	0.0	0.0	28.0	-63.6
Deferred payments	—	—	—	13.6	11.0	44.8	30.8	45.4	346.8	14.2
Debt rescheduling	—	—	—	3.5	21.9	-11.4	7.6	-0.9	-219.4	-4.2
Arrears (reduction −)	—	—	—	—	—	—	—	—	-1.1	—
Short-term credit, net,	—	—	—	—	—	—	—	—	—	—
Net domestic financing	1.40	11.50	-7.10	-1.4	10.9	-9.6	-17.1	16.1	-8.2	-6.0

Sources: GOG (1991b); IMF (1987a, 1993); World Bank (1984b, 1990a).

the ideological move away from Touré-style socialism. One thrust of reform, such as the adoption of the government's first formal budget (*Loi de Finances*) in 1988, has been to get the fiscal house in order. Another thrust of public sector reform has been to get the state, at least partially, out of the economy. As such, the government has undertaken a series of reform measures within the public sector. These include improved budgetary control, increased efforts at revenue mobilization, privatization and liquidation of parastatals, civil service retrenchment, and the undertaking of a formalized public investment effort. These measures, in combination, have had a discernible impact on the aggregate finances of the government since 1986. In this chapter we shall consider the major reform measures in turn, except civil service retrenchment and reform, which is treated in chapter 5. We begin, however, by highlighting a number of general but important structural changes in the real finances of government occurring over the reform period (Table 54).

First, as per the objectives of the reform program, revenues and grants have grown since 1986, largely because of an increase in real nonmining sector revenue. Indeed, led by increased tax revenues from goods and services, real nonmining tax revenue increased at an average annual rate of 32.5 percent over the six-year period between 1986 and 1992 (Table 54). The share of nonmining tax revenue in total revenue rose from 12 to 55 percent over these years.[1] The rapid increase in the share of revenues from nonmining activities has been due in part to increases in the taxation of petroleum products since 1989 and to decreases in mining export revenue since 1991. With adjustment, the share of grants also increased rapidly, from 12 to 24 percent of total revenues and grants. Not surprisingly, the share of nontax revenue in nonmining revenue also declined with the shutdown of many parastatals.

Second, government expenditures have grown since 1986. In real terms, however, average annual expenditure growth has actually been contained to 6 percent between 1986 and 1990, about equal to the growth rate of revenues and grants over the same period.

Third, the growth in expenditures has been due primarily to the public investment program component of reform and to the ensuing influx of capital. Indeed capital expenditures increased on average by 10 percent annually in the six-year period between 1986 and 1992. The share of capital expenditures in total expenditures grew from 16 percent in 1984 to about 50 percent in 1992 (Table 54). Real current expenditures, on the other hand, grew by less than 2 percent during the period 1986 to 1992. This lack of growth was due to a real decline in expenditures on goods and services and on subsidies and transfers, despite real growth in expenditures on wages and salaries. Even at this aggregate level,

TABLE 54

Guinea: Financial Operations of the Central Government (Real GF), 1986–1993.
(billions of real GF, 1986)

	1986	1987	1988	1989	1990	1991	1992	1993
Revenues and grants	103.40	130.90	127.24	129.42	145.96	140.91	141.00	126.59
Mining sector revenues	71.10	82.29	70.95	70.95	79.65	64.90	47.95	37.49
Nonmining sector revenues	19.50	21.93	32.83	33.76	38.82	47.82	58.48	58.37
Taxes on income and profits	1.10	1.23	1.91	2.35	2.54	4.75	7.25	6.63
Taxes on domestic goods and services	4.10	1.30	6.37	8.90	—	—	—	—
Taxes on international trade	6.00	6.44	7.08	6.69	10.36	13.05	13.65	13.96
Nontax revenue and miscellaneous taxes	—	6.29	8.92	6.83	9.11	6.66	7.72	6.54
Grants	12.80	26.69	23.46	24.72	27.53	28.18	34.57	30.73
Expenditures	136.20	157.67	176.20	163.60	184.77	175.99	175.99	158.03
Current expenditure	85.20	91.87	97.47	88.37	92.71	95.75	89.22	80.02
Wages and salaries	18.20	16.33	29.00	28.58	31.64	35.15	38.93	38.25
Other goods and services	45.00	47.16	31.94	31.78	34.95	32.86	26.35	21.98
Subsidies and transfers	9.50	10.74	13.71	11.49	6.93	9.56	9.61	8.48
Interest payments	12.50	17.64	22.82	16.48	19.19	18.17	14.29	10.99
Capital expenditure	51.00	65.80	78.73	75.23	92.06	80.24	85.91	78.00
Deficit (commitment basis)	-32.90	-26.76	-48.89	-34.18	-38.82	-35.08	-34.98	-31.44
Net changes in expenditure arrears (reduction –)	3.20	-1.00	4.65	-0.75	15.20	4.13	-26.53	0.08
Cash deficit (–)	-29.70	-27.76	-44.24	-34.89	-23.62	-30.95	-61.51	-31.35
Financing	29.70	27.76	44.24	34.89	23.62	30.95	61.51	31.35
Net external financing	36.70	28.83	37.29	39.41	30.51	25.45	63.93	40.82
Drawings	59.00	48.24	60.11	58.43	48.37	50.32	52.73	52.89
Amortization	-41.30	-32.59	-43.79	-34.70	-33.29	-40.07	-34.25	-25.52
Changes in amortization arrears (reduction –)	-7.90	—	—	—	—	—	—	—
Debt relief	26.90	—	—	—	—	—	—	—
Net domestic financing	-7.10	-1.07	6.95	-4.52	-4.47	5.50	-2.42	-9.46

Sources: GOG (1991b, 1993a); IMF (1987a, 1993); World Bank (1984b, 1990a).

therefore, the numbers reflect an imbalance between nonwage recurrent expenditures and capital expenditures.

Fourth, a common side effect of adjustment and the consequent influx of financial capital, be it concessionary or commercial, is an increase in government interest expenditures. This has been true in Guinea. Between 1986 and 1990 interest payments increased on average by over 9 percent annually in real terms (Table 54). The share of interest payments in total expenditure increased to about 10 percent in 1990, as compared to a level closer to 5 percent in 1984.

Fifth, notably is the change in the means of financing the deficit since the commencement of the adjustment program. Under the First Republic, budgetary deficits were covered primarily by domestic financing, particularly by creating money. In 1984 net domestic financing accounted for close to 74 percent of total deficit financing.[2] Under the Second Republic, on the other hand, the deficit has been financed mainly from external sources. In 1992, for example, net domestic financing was actually –4 percent and external financing 104 percent of total financing. The principal sources of external deficit financing have been in the form of drawings (GF 122.7 billion in 1989) and of debt relief (GF 87.3 billion in 1989). In 1990, the budget deficit was additionally kept in check with the accumulation of expenditure arrears.

Several components of fiscal reform together have driven these structural changes in government finances. We turn now to discuss four of these in greater detail. They are: (1) tax reform, (2) public enterprise reform, (3) public investment reform, and (4) health and education sector reform. As mentioned previously, a fifth component, civil service employment and wage reform, merits its own section under the consideration of labor markets in chapter 5. While each of these components is far-reaching in its macroeconomic implications, the changes in health and education, particularly in the civil service, are important because of their more direct and critical impact on the welfare of certain segments of the Guinean population.

Tax Reform

Guinea's domestic tax system at the termination of the First Republic was "inadequate to meet even the most modest financing requirements" (World Bank 1988). Just as disconcerting was the fact that the mining sector accounted for approximately 40 percent of all government revenue and grants by 1984, making the government's finances extremely vulnerable to fluctuations in international mineral markets. The fall in the share of nonmining revenue was largely due to an eroding tax base consequent to the granting of frequent, uncontrolled, and often large-scale discretionary tax exemptions. Indeed opportunities and incentives existed for substantial corruption among low paid tax and customs officials. Exemptions were often granted for a fee.

Tax reform under the Second Republic has concentrated on diversifying the source of tax revenue beyond the mining sector. In particular, the reform effort has had as objectives: (1) an improvement in exploiting the available tax and customs base while avoiding large rate increases; (2) an equitable application of tax and customs codes; (3) the avoidance of high marginal tax and customs rates so as to lessen evasion, fraud, and disincentive effects; and (4) the application of a progressive income tax system that would exempt households under the poverty line (World Bank 1988). Specific reform objectives with respect to revisions of the *tax directorate* included broadening the tax base by including rental income and closing loopholes, entering all taxes into the budget, applying consumption surtaxes on domestically produced alcohol and tobacco, and increasing the excise tax on petroleum products. Equally important has been the focus on institutional reform. Central taxpayer files are being created, audit procedures improved, and legal sanctions enforced in such areas as fraud and evasion.

Customs and tax rates have been largely consolidated and simplified and in many cases even reduced. For example, the turnover tax was reduced to 2 percent, and the customs and fiscal taxes were reduced and combined. Currently most imports are charged a tax and customs duty at a rate of between 18 and 30 percent of their c.i.f. value. A 60 percent surtax also has been imposed on luxury items. The same tax levels apply to domestic goods of the same categories.

Significant progress has also been made in reducing the government's dependence on mining sector revenues. Between falling mining revenues and won revenue increases elsewhere, mining tax revenue has decreased from 68 percent of total government revenue in 1988 to 45.2 percent in 1992 (World Bank 1994a). Progress in raising the nonmining component of tax revenue, though substantial, has been slower than expected. Guinea's aggregate tax yield (tax revenue to GDP ratio) actually fell from 14 to an estimated 12 percent from 1986 to 1992 (Table 55).[3] Still, real tax revenue rose over the same years by 33 percent, or 5.5 percent annually. Given falling mining revenues, this net real increase has been due entirely to the increase in nonmining tax revenue, largely from a special tax on petroleum products (TSPP).[4] Estimates for 1992 show TSPP revenue reached 25 percent of total nonmining revenues. Even so, 1992 disbursements of Guinea's Enhanced Structural Adjustment Facility were suspended specifically because TSPP tax revenues had been falling well below target levels.

A number of factors account for the lower than expected tax yields. Shortcomings in management and evaluation skills, and in information technology, limit the government's ability to properly identify and track taxpayers. The larger problem is that discretionary exemptions, corruption, and other loopholes

TABLE 55
Guinea: Real Tax Revenue, 1986–1992.
(millions of 1987 real U.S. dollars)

	1986	1987	1988	1989	1990	1991	1992
Mining revenues[a]	213.0	250.5	225.8	234.8	264.4	213.9	149.2
Profit taxes + dividends	—	83.1	20.5	20.7	50.3	33.1	25.0
Special tax[b]	—	87.3	116.0	131.0	142.8	121.2	105.9
OBK's net surplus	—	72.8	79.1	63.7	66.8	57.6	15.4
Other	—	7.2	10.1	19.3	4.4	1.9	2.8
Nonmining revenues	35.3	66.8	104.5	111.7	128.9	157.6	182.0
Income taxes[c]	3.3	3.7	6.1	7.8	8.4	15.7	22.6
TSPP[d]	0.0	4.0	20.3	29.1	22.9	39.7	44.8
Turnover tax[e]	7.2	14.0	19.3	22.6	26.1	30.8	30.7
Excise surcharge	4.4	5.8	6.9	6.1	5.8	5.2	4.9
Others[f]	0.6	23.3	32.5	25.7	33.5	24.8	38.6
Import duties	19.2	15.4	19.1	20.1	32.0	41.2	40.3
Export taxes[g]	0.6	0.2	0.4	0.3	0.1	0.1	0.1
Total tax revenue	248.3	317.2	330.3	346.5	393.1	371.5	331.1
Tax yield (revenue/GDP)	14.1	14.9	14.0	13.7	14.8	13.8	12.4

Sources: IMF (1993); World Bank (1984b, 1990a, 1993b).
a. Formal mining sector only (including notional taxes of OBK).
b. Tax on mining products.
c. Taxes on profits and personal incomes.
d. Specific tax on petroleum products.
e. Includes turnover taxes on domestic production and imports.
f. Other taxes on domestic trade, international trade, and nontax revenue including fishing rights.
g. 1986 is an estimate.

continue to prevent the current tax base from being efficiently exploited. A 1988 Ministry of Planning and International Cooperation (MPCI) estimate put the percentage value of imports that were exempted from duty at 40 percent of total import value.[5] Even upon excluding these exempted imports the actual import and TCA tax revenues on taxed imports were only 5.5 percent of the estimated value of imports that year. This is despite the fact that most commodities were officially subject to TCA and duty tax levels of 20 percent (World Bank 1990a). Tax evasion, undercollection, and corruption additionally may have been encouraged by excessively high tax rates on certain commodities.[6] Specific priority was placed, starting in 1992, on reducing the number of beneficiaries of tax exemptions. Steps were also taken to computerize customs records and to offer customs agents incentive pay.

The low rate of effective tax collection has also partly been a manifestation of continued, nontransparent, budgetary cross-subsidization. For example, the petroleum distribution parastatal, ONAH, collected the TSPP on behalf of the Customs Service. However, ONAH was unable to remit the tax revenue back to the treasury since it has needed these revenues to absorb its losses. Several factors, in turn, accounted for ONAH's losses. In addition to theft, losses resulted from panterritorial petroleum pricing (which subsidizes gasoline consumers far from the capital) and from the underpayment and nonpayment for gasoline. In particular, government officials and agencies, the military, and several parastatals have been subsidized in this manner. ENELGUI and Air Guinée, for example, were chronically in debt to ONAH and were thus effectively cross-subsidized. The privatization of ONAH and of Enelgui in 1990/91 should thus greatly improve effective tax collection.

Efficient revenue mobilization and budgetary management is thus inextricably linked not only to public enterprise restructuring (to be discussed below) but also to the elimination of hidden subsidies. Like so many other aspects of Guinean reform, success will depend also on the elimination of the system of patronage and corruption, which remains a legacy of Guinea's First Republic. It has become clear that institutional reform with respect to tax and customs administration is likely to take much longer than policy reform. Nonetheless, reducing marginal tax rates and increasing civil service wages can reduce incentives for fraud.

Public Enterprise Reform

In 1981 over 180 public enterprises (PEs) were operating in Guinea, covering every aspect of economic activity.[7] In fact there was little formal enterprise other than public sector enterprise. These state-operated enterprises accounted for approximately 75 percent of all modern sector employment and 92 percent of all domestic credit.[8] Given the relative importance of private sector mining and agriculture to the national economy, however, PEs accounted for only about 25 percent of GDP. Two-thirds of PE-generated GDP (18 percent of national GDP) was accounted for by commercial enterprises, as opposed to industrial enterprises, which contributed only 5 percent of total GDP (World Bank 1981c).

Guinea's parastatals were subject to many of the same deficiencies and distortions faced by other economic entities during the First Republic. Infrastructure was poor, and employees were poorly trained. Moreover, public enterprises were required to transfer internally generated funds back to the government. As such, PEs faced a cash constraint, which, when coupled with general foreign exchange unavailability, meant a lack of funds for maintaining and replacing investment or purchasing many needed inputs. As a consequence, the PE capital stock depreciated over time. The inability to purchase needed variable inputs kept many PEs operating well below full capacity. For example, average capacity utilization at agroindustrial enterprises (excluding ENTA) was approximately 18 percent between 1977 and 1980 (World Bank 1981c). Among manufacturing firms, capacity utilization over this period was approximately 28 percent.

Nevertheless, the public enterprise sector served as an important source of revenue for the government. In the five-year period between 1977 and 1981, PEs contributed 80 percent of the Guinean government's nontax revenue, 42 percent of the its nonmining revenue, and 30 percent of total revenues and grants (Table 54).

These figures, however, mask some of the actual, but often implicit, costs and inefficiencies incurred by public enterprises. First and foremost, much of the "profit" accruing to public enterprises was in fact the collection of an implicit tax (on consumers and producers of tradables) inherent in the gross overvaluation of the exchange rate. Indeed 75 percent of the PE sector's total profits was generated by the parastatals that imported, exported, and distributed these internationally traded goods (World Bank 1981c). In particular, IMPORTEX, which had primary access to foreign exchange at the subsidized official exchange rate in order to undertake official imports, subsequently sold these imports to earn about 50 percent of total PE sector profits. Second, while public enterprises had their foreign exchange and other supplies rationed, the economy operated on the basis of favoritism so that state companies still had the most privileged access to rationed goods. Third, parastatal sales were additionally bolstered by virtue of the fact that they retained official monopolies in most markets. Fourth, although difficult to document given the oblique accounting practices, many parastatals benefited from additional implicit and explicit subsidies from the government.

For example, in 1979 explicit subsidies to public enterprises reached over GS 1.0 billion, partly in compensation for operating losses resulting from government pricing policy (World Bank 1981c).

The economic reforms under the Second Republic have called for a complete overhaul of the public enterprise sector. Some enterprises were slated for liquidation, others were to be privatized, and yet others were to be jointly operated with the private sector. In conjunction with privatization, monopoly rights have been rescinded. The Second Structural Adjustment Credit (World Bank 1988) stated that all enterprises slated for liquidation would be closed by the end of 1988 and liquidated during 1989. Enterprises slated for privatization were also to be sold, along with assets, during 1989.[9] The government expected the privatization program to improve not only efficiency, but the state of government finances through the sale of public enterprises and their assets as well. Certain essential services such as utilities and transportation and "strategic" (i.e., mining) enterprises, however, were to remain under state ownership and operation. However, these firms were also to be subject to significant restructuring in order to improve performance. Performance contracts stipulated that parastatal managers would be more accountable to the government yet more independent in their operations.

The government's adherence to reform guidelines with respect to public enterprise has been laudable, especially given the vested interests with which it has had to contend, as witnessed elsewhere in Africa. By the end of 1988, 25 of 131 original enterprises had been privatized, and 68 had been liquidated (World Bank 1990a).[10] Twenty enterprises remained to be privatized or liquidated. Of the remaining 18, 8 firms are to continue under complete government control.

In 1990 further progress was made with the liquidation of 5 commercial enterprises. Most importantly, the state petroleum company ONAH was the object of restructuring. ONAH was replaced by a mixed company, la Société Guinéene des Pétroles (SGP). In 1992, the government privatized the importation and distribution of petroleum products.[11] In addition, 6 other enterprises were also privatized in 1990.

Despite the speed of these reforms, several problems with respect to parastatal reform have emerged in practice. The government's slow progress in certain areas of parastatal reform is also partly responsible for the holdup of ESAF disbursements. First, very little was done initially to restructure enterprises that continued under government control, such as Air Guinée, SOGETRAG, ENELGUI, PTT, and SBK.[12] Second, the expected financial benefits to the government from the sale of parastatals have been far from met. Enterprises were often sold at low prices, payable over a number of years at zero interest. Assets were also sold at extremely low prices. The lack of transparency on these deals has raised substantial criticism.

In addition, some privatized companies were given significant tax breaks as well as temporary monopoly rights, often beyond the provisions of the new Investment Code (World Bank 1990a). Third, utility tariffs for utility companies that have remained under state management have remained low.

Public Investment Reform

Over the course of the First Republic, public infrastructure as well as the physical capital of public enterprises had suffered significant degeneration. Roads, railways, and sewer systems put in place during the colonial era fell into disrepair. Little new construction was undertaken as government expenditures were diverted to consumption needs.

A priority of the fiscal reform program has been to increase and improve public investment. To this end the government instituted a three-year rolling Public Investment Program (PIP) in 1987. Effectively the PIP formalized the government's investment priorities by sector and estimated financing needs. As such it represented an institutionalized programming and budgeting device as well as a consolidated investment plan intended to attract additional foreign financing.

From 1989 to 1991 PIP reflected the Guinean government's investment ambitions. Capital expenditures for 1988 were 45 percent higher in nominal GF terms than during the previous year (Table 54).[13] In 1989 capital expenditures increased by 29 percent in nominal terms. In 1988 capital expenditures had increased to 45.5 percent of total government expenditures; in 1990 capital expenditures accounted for as much as 51.1 percent of all government expenditures.

The sectoral allocation of the development budget reflects the government's immediate investment priorities. Of expenditures planned for the 1989-1991 period, 62 percent were allocated to infrastructure (almost all related to roads and bridges), 25 percent to rural development, and 15 percent to social services (9.6 percent to the health sector specifically) (World Bank 1989b).

The Guinean government has also been successful in securing foreign financing commitment for the PIP. Eighty-five percent of PIP projects in the 1989–1991 period were financed from external sources. Moreover, most of the financing was at extremely concessionary terms. Only 1 percent of financing was at commercial terms, whereas 70 percent was in the form of concessional loans and 29 percent in the form of grants (World Bank 1989b).

The rapid increase in investment expenditures in Guinea is essential in that it addresses some of the binding constraints to the nation's development (discussed elsewhere in this book). Rehabilitating the transport infrastructure is key to priming the agricultural and export sector; rehabilitating the health and educational infrastructure is key to improving the well-being and productivity of the population. The speed at which the Guinean government was able to raise investment levels since 1984 attests to both the government's and the donors' recognition of these facts.

Nevertheless the implementation of the PIP has encountered some difficulties. The government fell into arrears (GF 8.0 billion in 1990) in the payment of the local currency component of various projects that constitute the investment program. This slippage required a revision of the PIP budget, which resulted in a net increased commitment of funds to the locally financed component of the investment program (the *budget national de developpement*, or BND) as well as the elimination of some projects that were initially locally funded. The difficulties experienced in adhering to the budget highlight the need for the Ministries of Finance and Plan to apply strict budgetary procedures to development spending in addition to recurrent spending.

The speed of policy reform has also run into binding institutional constraints that go beyond the good intentions of both government and donors. In putting together and choosing projects for the PIP, little economic or technical project appraisal is done by the government (World Bank 1989b). In fact there is not much capacity nor experience at the technical ministerial planning units to do such work. Hence project cost/benefit analysis never really takes place. In particular, little attention is paid to the recurrent cost implications of projects. Recurrent costs should concern the Guinean government not only because they could constitute a major component of total project cost, but also because the burden of financing recurrent costs generally falls on the recipient country and is rarely borne by donors. In terms of efficiency, recurrent costs also are indispensable: a small, well-staffed hospital is more effective than a large, unstaffed one.

The institutional problems faced in Guinea are neither unexpected nor uncommon. They are encountered throughout sub-Saharan Africa as donors and governments push investments to make up for lost time. During a decade of structural adjustment financing, the constraints of "absorptive capacity" are being felt in Africa as they were rarely felt in Asia. In particular, these constraints are being encountered much earlier in the investment pipeline at the planning stage, even before the implementation stage. Bottlenecks are met at the Ministry before they are met on the field. These observations do not speak for a curtailment of investment or aid for Guinea. Rather they stress the imperative of investment in human capital as a medium-term solution and the role of technical assistance in the short run.

Social Services and Reform

Government policies and financing with respect to the provision of social services are of special relevance in considering the impacts of reform on vulnerable groups of the population. A detailed analysis of policy changes in the education and health sectors, however, is made impossible by the lack of consistent time-series data. Data on public expenditure levels and the shares of social spending as a percentage of the total over time are scarce. Even less is known about education and health outcomes (e.g., literacy and infant mortality rates) over time, and it is virtually impossible to relate public expenditure inputs to these health and education outputs. Nevertheless, an overview can be pieced together of the government's provision of social sector services, including its education and health sector policies. The resulting picture illustrates the failures of the past and reveals those reforms that will enhance the quality of human resources.

EDUCATION. The educational system inherited by the Second Republic was financially bankrupt, organizationally inefficient, and socially irrelevant. First, although the system was geared toward training cadres for the civil service, the content of education was highly politicized and dogmatic. Education was generally inconsequential to the needs of employers and those who were self-employed.[14] Second, both bad management and the lack of financing led to a contraction in recurrent expenditures. This too weakened both access and the quality of education. School buildings, libraries, and laboratories were dilapidated, and teaching materials and equipment were inadequate. Third, funds were spent disproportionately on the secondary and tertiary levels relative to the primary level. This top-heavy inefficiency was partly due to the vested interests of upper-level officials, whose families had access to higher level educational tiers and to the jobs to which their diplomas subsequently entitled them. Fourth, Guinea was faced with a lack of qualified teachers. As a consequence of brain drain, Guinea lost many of its educators. Faculties of the universities of Paris and Dakar were full of Guinean professors in the 1970s, for example, while the Polytechnique of Conakry was not fully functional because it lacked qualified teaching personnel (Azarya and Chazan 1987).

With the advent of the Second Republic, a number of reforms were undertaken. French was reintroduced in primary school as the medium of instruction for the first time since independence. Secondary school instruction was extended by one year. Education was placed under the administrative supervision of a single ministry.

The Guinean Government's Statement of Sector Policy approved in late 1989 formalizes the main policy thrusts for the next decade. It aims to reduce illiteracy by raising the primary admissions ratio to 50 percent by 2000. It targets quality and efficiency improvements with a commitment to increase the diffusion of teaching materials, to improve curricula, to upgrade and increase the number of schools (especially in rural areas), to stress in-service training of teachers, to improve training of skilled workers for the private sector, and to strengthen institutional and technical capabilities for sectoral analysis and management. The structure of the educational system in Guinea, however, has not changed significantly with reform, and it continues to parallel those in other francophone countries. In 1988 and 1989 approximately 382,000 students were enrolled in the educational system: 77 percent in primary school, 20 percent in secondary school, 1.4 percent in technical school, and 1.6 percent in universities (World Bank 1990a). At each of these educational levels, instruction has been free in Guinea: students do not have to pay direct fees.

Evidence on the current state of the educational system reveals mixed results; in many areas reform has yet to address the major problems within the sector. The illiteracy rate is still high at 74 percent.[15] Yet some encouragement comes from the growing percentage of children entering first grade. Although between the preadjustment years 1980 and 1985 this percentage fell by 4.7 percent, it subsequently rose by 5.6 percent between 1985 and 1989 (Serageldin et al. 1994). For the 1980s as a whole, however, the primary school gross enrollment ratio has shown little substantial improvement, having remained at approximately the same level throughout the decade (Table 56).[16] In 1987 and 1988 a primary school

TABLE 56

Guinea: Primary School Enrollment, 1980–1994.

Years	Primary School Enrollment	Primary School Gross Enroll- ment Ratio (percentage)	First Year Admissions	First Year Admission Rate (percentage)
1980/81	257,547	31.5	35,000	21.6
1981/82	249,905	29.6	38,500	23.3
1982/83	247,702	28.4	40,000	23.8
1983/84	246,129	27.3	49,500	28.9
1984/85	287,804	30.8	88,000	50.5
1985/86	276,438	28.6	38,000	21.4
1986/87	270,140	27.0	44,451	24.7
1987/88	287,586	28.0	64,350	35.2
1988/89	295,801	—	—	—
1989/90	310,074	—	—	—
1990/91	346,807	32.0	—	—
1991/92	—	—	—	—
1992/93	—	36.7	—	—
1993/94	—	44.0	—	—

Sources: BCRG (1992); GOG (1991b); Orivel and Perrot (1988); World Bank (1995a, b).

gross enrollment ratio of 28 percent placed Guinea among the worst ranked ten countries in the world and well below the average for the region. Sub-Saharan Africa's average gross enrollment ratio stands at 77 percent. Moreover, Guinea's secondary school enrollment rate of 8 percent is also well below the regional average (World Bank 1990a).

Coupled with these low average levels of enrollment, the primary school gross enrollment ratio varies significantly by region and by gender. In rural areas the primary school gross enrollment ratio is 18 percent, whereas in urban areas it is 54 percent. Furthermore, the educational system is utilized unequally by gender—a disparity that, in urban areas, increases with each level of education following primary school (del Ninno and Sahn 1990).[17] The national gross enrollment rate in 1992/93 was only 22.8 percent for girls, while it was 51.0 percent for boys (Table 57). In addition to lower enrollments, girls more frequently miss school, more often repeat grades, and perform less well on lower secondary entrance exams. In 1992/93, only one-quarter of the students in lower secondary school were girls, a figure that fell below 20 percent for upper secondary school.

Important differences also exist between the upper and lower 40 percent of the per capita expenditure distribution. As shown in Table 58, enrollment ratios are nearly four times higher for the highest than for the lowest 40 percent of the income distribution. Secondary school enrollment data reveal an even greater disparity in enrollments between income groups: overall, eight times more children are enrolled from the richest 40 percent of the population than from the poorest 40 percent. Furthermore, the discrepancy between income groups is significantly greater for girls than for boys.

TABLE 57
Guinea: Primary School Gross Enrollment Rates for Girls and Boys, by Region, 1992/93.
(percent)

	Total	*Girls*	*Boys*
Region			
Conakry	72.77	59.00	85.70
Lower Guinea	32.77	19.00	46.80
Middle Guinea	26.71	15.00	38.60
Upper Guinea	27.98	15.00	41.20
Forest Region	41.20	22.00	61.30
Total	36.70	22.80	51.00

Source: World Bank (1995a).

TABLE 58
Guinea: Gross Enrollment in Primary and Secondary Education,
by Expenditure Group, 1994.
(percent)

	Primary			Secondary		
	Poorest 40 Percent	Richest 40 Percent	Average	Poorest 40 Percent	Richest 40 Percent	Average
All groups	21	77	44	4	33	19
Boys	30	91	53	5	43	25
Girls	10	64	34	2	21	11
Rural	20	52	27	2	7	5
Urban	22	86	78	16	40	38

Source: World Bank (1995b).

A variety of factors explains the low enrollments, especially for girls. First, on the supply side, the schools are not equipped for more students. Schools lack places for students: the pupil-to-teacher ratio was 48 in 1992–1993, slightly higher than earlier in the decade (World Bank 1995; GOG 1988a).[18] Where places do exist, they are often in schools that are long distances from the communities that need them (GOG 1989d). Finally, despite government efforts to develop school infrastructure, basic necessities are also still lacking—ranging from latrines to classroom equipment, such as chairs and blackboards.

On the demand side, direct costs associated with schooling can be substantial and can serve as a deterrent to enrollments among poor households. These costs include uniforms, medical expenses, supplies, and registration fees—a total of GF 17,400 for first graders, according to Sow (1994). Willingness to pay these costs is weakened partly by the perception that education has limited returns in the labor market, especially in rural areas where the current curriculum is often seen as irrelevant.[19] Likely the most significant enrollment deterrent, however, is the high opportunity cost of foregone agricultural and household labor by children attending school. The foregone earnings of children attending school, particularly in rural areas, are especially substantial for girls, who assume a wide variety of chores and non-remunerated household production activities, from gathering wood and fetching water to preparing meals and caring for children. In addition to economic considerations, attitudes also interfere with girls attending school. Parents worry about their daughters having experiences that may reduce their desirability and marriage price and see few appropriate models of education leading to success in the labor market. The school system itself seems to reinforce the latter belief: less than one-quarter of primary-school teachers are females—a fact that may foster the perception that women are less likely to find employment opportunities, and will have lower returns to schooling, than men.

The low levels of government financing budgeted for the educational sector as well as the poor allocation of funds within the sector have been important factors in explaining the persistently weak educational system. In 1989, 12.9 percent of the government's recurrent budget was allocated to education, up from just 9.1 percent at the beginning of the reform program. This figure, however, was far lower than the Sub-Saharan African average of 20 percent (World Bank 1990a). Relative to GNP, public expenditure on education was 1.7 percent. Funding for education has increased markedly in 1990 and 1991 (Table 59). In 1990 the Guinean Government's budget to education increased by 26 percent in nominal terms to reach 15 percent of the total recurrent budget. In 1991 a 20 percent increase in the government's allocation to the sector was complemented by external funding from the first installment of a sectoral adjustment loan (from USAID and the World Bank). Whereas the domestic allocation to the sectoral budget was 15.1 percent of the recurrent budget, the total allocation to education (including external funds) raised this to 19.2 percent of the recurrent budget, more than twice the share in 1986.

In addition to these increases in total sectoral funding, special attention will be required to ensure adequate funding for operating expenditures and expenditures on materials and on goods and services. The share of these expenditures in the sector's recurrent expenditures was about 19 percent but may have experienced a decline in real terms (World Bank 1990a). Real operating expenditures are particularly vulnerable given the reluctance to cut salary expenses (which

TABLE 59
Guinea: Education Sector Expenditures.

	1986	1987	1988	1989	1990	1991
	Billions of GF					
Total education expenditures	5.19	7.79	12.12	18.29	22.77	35.13
Nationally funded	—	—	12.12	18.29	23.06	27.71
Externally funded	—	—	0.00	0.00	0.00	7.42
	Percentage of recurrent budget					
Total education expenditures	9.10	9.10	11.40	12.90	14.30	19.20
Nationally funded	—	—	11.40	12.90	14.30	15.10
Externally funded	—	—	0.00	0.00	0.00	4.10

Sources: World Bank (1990a) and unpublished government sources.

account for about three-quarters of sectoral recurrent expenses) and the low scope of recovering education costs through fees.[20] In Guinea, the risk of cutting operating expenditures is of particular concern since, in 1989, of the estimated annual cost of US$ 38 per student at the primary level, only US$ 0.20 was spent on teaching supplies (World Bank 1990a).

Inappropriate allocation of resources is evident not only functionally but also by educational tier. Allocation of education expenditures is still skewed toward higher levels. In 1993, recurrent expenditures continued to be heavily weighted toward secondary and vocational (22.3 percent of total operating expenditure) and higher (37.1 percent of total operating expenditure) education rather than toward primary education (40.6 percent of total operating expenditure), despite the fact that over three-quarters of all enrolled students are at the primary level (World Bank 1995b). Higher priority needs to be placed on primary education on the grounds of both equity and productivity.

Equity should also be considered in terms of who benefits from government subsidies. First, as shown in Table 58, wealthier households have much higher enrollment ratios, even for primary and secondary education. Second, those in the upper end of the income distribution are the predominant enrollees in vocational training, teaching training, and higher education—school levels with substantially higher unit costs per student. Overall, therefore, taking into account the distribution of enrollment by expenditure groups and the unit cost per student, the total per capita education expenditure for the wealthiest quintile of the income distribution is approximately nine times higher than the poorest quintile. Much of this skewing of education expenditures reflects the fact that education expenditures are concentrated in the urban areas, where the rich tend to live. For example, per capita primary school expenditures are nearly twice, and secondary education more than eight times, as high in the urban as rural areas (World Bank 1995). Thus, Guinea's education system continues to favor the non-poor and those who reside in the urban areas. These patterns have persisted, despite government statements of intent to reform the educational system, and substantial external support from the World Bank and bilateral donors to move toward a more equitable pattern of expenditure that favors primary education and the needs of Guinea's poor majority.

HEALTH. The First Republic's strategy of "health for the people, by the people" was incomplete in the people it covered in part because of a shortage in the people to implement the strategy. By 1984 Guinea's formal health care system had almost totally collapsed. Partly as a consequence of this, the general health status of the Guinean population has been poor, even by West African standards. An accurate picture of health in Guinea is impossible to present given the absence of a health monitoring system and of epidemiological surveys. Nevertheless, various estimates confirm the population's weak health status. The 1983 population census revealed a national infant mortality rate of 146, as compared to a sub-Saharan African average of 105 (Table 60). Life expectancy at birth for Guineans was forty-five years as compared to the sub-Saharan African average of fifty.[21]

The infant mortality rate is higher in rural areas than in urban ones. The infant mortality rate in rural Guinea is 163, compared with 104 in urban Guinea and 84 in Conakry. These variations reflect both lower educational levels and also more limited access to health facilities in rural as compared with urban areas. For instance, Conakry accounted for approximately 19 percent of the national population but housed up to 45 percent of the nation's doctors and 58 percent of the nation's pharmacists (UNICEF 1990b).[22]

Several main factors contributed to the population's poor health status. First, active community participation in health care did not work in practice. In fact, health education, sanitation, and health care provision by "health brigades" at the village level were often perceived by the population as yet another facet of the unpopular but mandatory requirements of the state in the area of community development.

Second, government policies to integrate preventive and curative health care at the local level were not supported with adequate resources. The health budget of the MOPH was approximately 1.5 percent of GNP between 1979 and 1984 (World Bank 1986a). Furthermore, the share of the national operating budget

TABLE 60

Guinea: Infant Mortality and Life Expectancy by Region and by Gender, 1983.

	Infant Mortality	Life Expectancy
Guinea	146	45.1
Lower Guinea	142	46.9
Middle Guinea	161	40.8
Upper Guinea	179	38.4
Forest Guinea	166	40.8
Urban	104	54.9
Rural	163	41.2
Conakry	84	59.2
Males	158	43.2
Females	139	45.7

Source: GOG (1989c).

allocated to health declined steadily to approximately 5 percent in 1984 (World Bank 1986a).

The drying up of operating funds led to shortages in medical equipment and essential drugs. Laboratories and vehicles fell into disuse due to the lack of chemicals and fuel. Moreover, the deteriorating quality of health education, both at the faculty of medicine and through in-service training, contributed to a further decline in the quality of health service. Meanwhile, both the Ministries of Public Health and Social Services were accorded less priority than most other ministries. Lacking management skills and expertise, they made inefficient use of already scarce resources. While data do not exist from the end of the First Republic, surveys from 1987 show a bed occupancy rate of only 13 percent; primary care facilities were used by only 7 percent of the population; and immunizations covered only 5 percent of the children (World Bank 1993a). Some health facilities were oversized, underused, dilapidated, and understaffed, problems that persisted into the Second Republic. Both Eniphargui and Pharmaguinée, the parastatals entrusted with producing and with importing and distributing drugs, respectively, were also mismanaged.

In light of the weakened state of the health system, the coming of the Second Republic resulted in an Action Plan for the health sector that outlined a large number of policy "tenets." The Second Republic committed itself to providing basic health care in rural areas, upgrading hospital administration, and improving and maintaining capital investment. The government also promised to fortify preventive services by upgrading training and staff skills and by guaranteeing the availability of medical supplies; improving health statistics and planning, as well as supervision and evaluation; providing basic prenatal and postnatal care for women and children including vaccinations; and, examining the potential role of traditional medicine in primary health care.

Specific reforms have also been undertaken. In 1985 the Ministries of Public Health and Social Affairs were consolidated into the Ministry of Health and Social Affairs (MSPP) so as to coordinate the formulation and implementation of health policy and eliminate duplication of tasks. The MSPP was partially restructured in 1988 in a civil service reform program, but in 1992 the Secretariat of State for Social Affairs was reintegrated into the Ministry after a temporary separation. The inefficient local production of drugs was also terminated in 1985. The government took steps to stem the costly mismanagement and leakage of drugs at Pharmaguinée. The 1990s witnessed efforts to restructure Pharmaguinée, which had been virtually inoperable since 1987, as a commercial public enterprise with interim financing from the African Development Bank. The private sector was permitted to enter the pharmaceutical market in 1985, though at the wholesale level one company, Laborex, has retained quasi-monopoly status with

90 percent of the market share (World Bank 1993a). Given the limited government revenues available for health, mechanisms for cost recovery became an important part of health reform. Cost recovery has begun at hospitals, though most are still required to remit recovery costs to the treasury and thus are prevented from directly covering their operating costs.[23]

Means of reducing public expenditures on drugs were also considered. The Action Plan allowed health facilities to procure drugs from suppliers through competitive bidding in an international tendering procedure. A team of national directors also revised the essential drug program to emphasize drugs that corresponded to priority diseases. These essential drugs were to be procured through nonprofit organizations from generic producers in bulk quantities, rather than from commercial producers in individual packaging (Knippenberg et al. 1990).

Reform with respect to the provision of primary health care has probably been the most significant element of health sector policy. Services have already been improved. By 1991, for example, primary care service coverage and vaccination protection for children under five years had reached 40 and 60 percent of the population, respectively, in some areas of the country (World Bank 1993a). The rate of utilization of the public health care system is still low, at less than one contact per inhabitant per year. However, a UNICEF evaluation shows utilization and effective coverage rates are rising. For example, 50 percent of expectant mothers used three-visit antenatal services in 1990, up from 20 percent just four years earlier (World Bank 1993a). Another objective of reform has been to increase access to health care by strengthening a decentralized, community-based network of subprefectural primary health care units. As at hospitals, these health centers (*Centres de Sante*) try to recover certain operating costs, and the funds collected are owned and managed by community-level committees responsible for health care planning at the subprefectural level.

The movement toward cost recovery has been carried out according to the principles of the Bamako Initiative, a framework of health reform launched by Ministers of Health of African states in 1987. The initiative seeks universal, permanent accessibility to maternal and child health services, stressing effectiveness, cost minimization, and sustainability. Generally, costs can be recovered at the community level through prepayment schemes, fixed consultation fees, or direct payment in proportion to cost. Each mechanism has different incentive effects upon health care users in terms of willingness to pay and willingness to complete treatment; each also differs in how it allocates the risk of bankruptcy between clinic and user (Knippenberg et al. 1990). Guinea's health centers have adopted a combination of flat consultation and proportional drug cost fees. Cost recovery based on a differential tariff structure for standard diagnoses has been implemented in two hundred health centers and in some prefectural and regional hospitals. While this pricing system has the advantage that revenues increase as health center use and costs increase, low-use centers may not be able to cover fixed operating costs. In terms of other costs, the program specifically calls upon the government to furnish the basic physical infrastructure and cover the wage bill of health personnel. UNICEF has been committed to covering the cost of initial training for health center staff. Other donors are providing the initial stock of medical supplies to each clinic as well as equipment such as refrigerators for the storage of vaccines.[24] Whereas vaccines are to be donated on a continual basis, other medicines as well as gasoline and office supplies are donated only initially, as a seed stock. Thus at the community level, clinics have instigated cost recovery for curative care to cover their own operating costs.[25] The charge for treatment is generally low: between GF 50 and 2,000 in 1990 and on average less than US$ 1 per treatment (UNICEF 1990b).

Experience with cost recovery to date is informative. Operating costs and revenues were analyzed for seventy-three health centers between November 1988 and April 1989. During this time frame clinics had been operating under Bamako Initiative principles for about a year. The ability to pay on the part of patients, a matter of potential concern under the pricing system, has not to date been considered a widespread problem.[26] In individual cases where cost has been an issue, patients or their families have obtained approval from health committees to be treated at no cost, or have received financial support from the local mosque. According to the World Bank (1993a), drug overprescription and overcharging appear to be more serious problems than patients' abilities to pay. Regarding the scope of cost recovery, the evaluation found that, overall, community financing revenue covered 47 percent of overall costs (Knippenberg et al. 1990). Some city health centers had recovered all costs except salaries when provided with an initial stock of drugs, materials, and other operating needs. Centers with lower utilization rates, however, had not been able to recover all nonsalary operating costs. Hospitals similarly have not been able to recover sufficient funds to cover expenditures beyond drugs and basic materials and will continue to depend on adequate funding from the public sector and donors (World Bank 1993a).

The belief that cost recovery is not a major obstacle to the implementation of a sound public health policy has recently received further support from household survey data that indicate the poor's willingness to pay significant amounts of money for health services, both private and public. More specifically, Table 61 indicates that the poor are already paying to use public, as well as private facilities, with the expenditures for private sector care, primarily the traditional sector, being substantially higher. It can be inferred that this higher expenditure in the private sector is explained by a combination of the perceived superior quality of and the greater ease of accessing private services. Regarding the latter,

TABLE 61

Guinea: The Burden of Household Expenditures on Health, 1994.
(percent)

| | Health Spending as a Share of Per Capita Nonfood Expenditures | | |
Quintiles	Public Sector	Private Sector	All Health
Poorest	0.48	0.75	1.23
2	0.62	0.84	1.46
3	0.82	0.41	1.23
4	0.73	0.45	1.18
Wealthiest	0.52	0.27	0.79
Average	0.63	0.43	1.06
Rural	0.59	0.56	0.76
Urban	0.54	0.26	0.31

Source: World Bank (1995b).

survey data indicate that, for example, the average time required to see a caregiver at a primary health care facility is nine hours in Guinea, inclusive of the time traveling to the facility and waiting for services. In contrast, the time involved in seeing a traditional caregiver in the private sector is one hour, on average. Thus, while the implementation of cost recovery schemes should be sensitive to the ability to pay, a more critical concern is ensuring that the quality of care is improved and that the accessibility of the services is increased.

In terms of progress in implementing the network of community-based health centers, by 1991 approximately 200 of 346 health centers were fully operational under the reform program put forward by the Ministry of Health. There have also been some preliminary indicators of success. A UNICEF report (1990b), for example, reports high utilization of prenatal care. The report estimates that two to three out of every four pregnant women utilize prenatal health care, that one-third to one-half of all pregnant women receive two doses of antitetanus vaccinations, and that one-quarter to one-third of children receive six recommended vaccines before their first birthday. Health centers have adopted the fairly successful strategy of providing unsolicited preventive care (i.e., vaccinations or growth monitoring) and the curative care that individuals demand, especially in the area of maternal and child health. To reinforce this preventive emphasis, incentive payments are made to health center staff based upon their performance as measured by coverage with preventive care (Knippenberg et al. 1990).

Despite these successes and innovations the health reform program faces external challenges and internal problems. The health sector has been reformed and coverage extended against the backdrop of pessimistic demographic indicators for Guinea's people. The population in 1991 stood at over six million, with an average life expectancy for Guineans of forty-four years. Forty-seven percent of the population is younger than fifteen years of age. With a growth rate at 2.8 percent per annum, Guinea's population could reach eight million by the year 2000 (World Bank 1993a). Along related lines, family planning through artificial contraceptives is negligible, approximately 1 percent.

Furthermore, while the fully operational health centers in 1990 were estimated to cover close to three million people, effective coverage is likely lower. In rural areas only 30 to 40 percent of the population live within a 5 kilometer radius of a health center, and the quality of care is not uniform. For example, the referral system that is set up in theory does not work in practice given the weakness of tertiary care. Moreover, no formal system is yet in place to provide care to the indigent. In urban areas, people reportedly have difficulty gaining access to care given high levels of demand (UNICEF 1990b). Migration to and population growth in Conakry (5 percent annually) places increasing pressure on parts of the capital's health care system. The creation of new infrastructure is not keeping pace with population growth. Thus, in aggregate terms the medical system's coverage of the population continues to be thin. In 1988 there was one doctor for every 9,700 people in Guinea, one pharmacist for every 50,300 people, one midwife for every 18,600 people, and one nurse for every 4,300 people nationally (Table 62). Moreover, health workers in Guinea continue to be disproportionately concentrated in Lower Guinea and in Conakry relative to other regions. Hopwood (1993) notes that some staff are reluctant to serve in rural health centers and are ingenious in finding ways to circumvent such appointments.

TABLE 62
Guinea: Health Coverage Ratios in 1988.

Categories	All Guinea	Lower Guinea	Middle Guinea	Upper Guinea	Forest Guinea
Doctor per person	9,700	4,700	21,500	17,800	19,200
Pharmacist per person	50,300	31,300	112,800	61,400	51,600
Dentist per person	384,700	161,200	—	450,100	1,290,000
Midwife per person	18,600	7,800	106,000	61,400	28,600
Nurse per person	4,300	2,500	12,100	7,400	3,700

Source: GOG Ministry of Health (1988c).

Despite some improvements in the financing of the health system, the health sector still receives inadequate funding to perform effectively. In part, health reform cost estimates at the outset of reform were weak, and planners had the difficult task of anticipating how utilization patterns would increase under a reformed system. Whatever the main reason, the health budget did not grow at all in real terms in 1988 after a real growth of 59 percent in 1987. Moreover, the share of the total government budget allocated to health, having increased in 1985, then decreased below its 1984 share of 3.4 percent for every subsequent year other than 1989 (Table 63). The 1993 per capita expenditure on health was US$ 3, which is low by African standards and inadequate to allow the sector to provide even basic minimum services for the population. To illustrate the scale of expenditures: the 1988 recurrent health budget was GNF 4.87 billion; in comparison, a 1988 WHO study on pharmaceuticals estimated that Guineans spent GNF 5.5 billion privately on drugs (World Bank 1993a).

The health sector's share in the investment budget had grown, however, from 4.8 percent to 6.8 percent between 1989 and 1990 as the government renewed the priority of the health sector (GOG 1991a). The share of the investment budget allocated to tertiary services in Conakry is declining, while the share allocated to primary and secondary care at health centers and provincial hospitals is increasing (World Bank 1993a). As of 1986 the recurrent budget for health stood at approximately 5.6 percent of the national recurrent budget (World Bank 1987b). While on par with other countries with the same standard of living, the level of public funds allocated to operating expenses in Guinea has been low given the negligible role of the private sector in health care provision in the country. Within the recurrent budget, salary increases brought the salary share to 72 percent in 1990 and 80 percent in 1991, while the share allotted to drugs fell from 9.6 to 7.6 percent between the same years (World Bank 1993a). The lack of recurrent funds and nonsalary funds is evident in shortages of medical equipment and essential drugs at hospitals. These shortages continue to constrain the proper functioning of some health centers. In addition, the sector continues to suffer from weak administration and management. This weakness often translates into the nonimplementation of policies.

A further weakness of the health care system is manifested in the distribution of government spending on health care. While equity and efficiency considerations would support progressive health sector spending, targeted to those at the bottom end of the income distribution, just the opposite is the case in Guinea. This is a result of, first, the neglect of primary health care. Budget data for the period 1991–1994 reveal an insufficient allocation of funds to primary care: this sector comprised only 28 percent of the total health budget. The remaining health care expenditures were disbursed as follows: secondary care facilities, which

TABLE 63

Guinea: Government Recurrent Health Budget, 1977–1991.
(millions of nominal Guinean Francs [millions of Guinean Syli at par prior to 1986])

	Personnel	Medicines	Materials	Equipment	Total Recurrent Health Budget	Health Budget Share of National Recurrent Budget
1977	—	—	—	71.5	357.6	5.2
1978	—	—	—	49.8	343.8	4.1
1979	—	—	—	39.9	441.0	3.7
1980	272.3	144.0	30.0	50.2	496.6	3.8
1981	295.9	145.2	66.4	65.0	572.6	3.2
1982	261.6	160.0	52.6	55.0	529.3	4.2
1983	298.0	165.0	55.2	55.0	573.2	3.4
1984	294.5	165.0	9.1	50.0	518.7	3.4
1985	296.4	200.0	18.1	442.8	957.4	5.3
1986	1,021.0	—	1,130.0	—	2,151.0	2.8
1987	1,014.0	1,473.3	518.8	239.7	3,246.9	2.2
1988	2,500.0	1,500.0	523.3	348.7	4,872.1	2.6
1989	—	—	—	—	4,752.8	3.5
1990	—	—	—	—	4,677.5	2.9
1991	—	—	—	—	8,980.0	2.2

Sources: Sodeteg, Credes, Juin (1987); UNICEF (1990c); WHO (1988); World Bank (1993a).

189

include small hospitals that also deliver primary health services, received 27 percent; tertiary care, comprised of large hospitals, accounted for 25 percent; administration received the remaining 20 percent. Second, household survey data reveal that 60 percent of the households in the lowest expenditure quintile did not use health facilities during the previous month, while this was the case for only 30 percent of the households in the highest quintile. When seeking treatment, the poor relied much more heavily on the lower level services, which are grossly underfunded, while the rich made disproportionate use of the secondary and tertiary care facilities, which have a substantially higher budgetary cost per visit. Taking into account the patterns of use and the cost per visit to public facilities, the lowest quintile captures only 4.1 percent of the benefits of government expenditures in the health sector, while the highest quintile captures nearly 50 percent of the spending (Table 64). There are also noteworthy differences between benefits by source of care. Specifically, the bottom 20 percent of the expenditure distribution receives 9.7 percent of the value of expenditures on health clinics, in contrast to only 1.4 percent for hospital spending (World Bank 1995b).

CHALLENGES AHEAD. The shortfalls with respect to policy implementation as well as the lack of significant improvements in health financing have meant a continued poor general health status among the Guinean population. Health indicators have yet to reflect the impact from health reform. Guinea's infant mortality rate was 136 as of 1991, which, though lower than the 1983 level of 146, remains tragically high. The mortality rate for children under age five remained at 237 as of 1991, meaning that almost one in four children die before the age of five (World Bank 1993a). Health and nutrition conditions in Guinea have also been exacerbated by the recent influx of Liberian refugees, many of whom are malnourished and place a heavy strain on health facilities in border

TABLE 64
Guinea: Per Capita Government Health Expenditures, by Expenditure Quintiles.

	Expenditure Quintiles				
	1	*2*	*3*	*4*	*5*
Hospital expenditures	1.4	5.7	15.1	23.2	54.5
Health clinic expenditures	9.7	12.9	18.5	23.3	35.6
All health expenditures	4.1	8.1	16.2	23.2	48.4

Sources: World Bank (1995b) and authors' calculations.

TABLE 65
Guinea: The Ten Major Causes of Morbidity among Children between
the Ages of 0 and 5 Years.

Rank	Disease	Number of Cases	Percent
1	Malaria	23,588	33
2	Respiratory disease	19,831	28
3	Diarrhea	10,602	15
4	Cutaneous infections	8,543	12
5	Malnutrition	1,679	2
6	Anaemia	1,671	2
7	Pernicious malaria	1,379	2
8	Eye infections	1,300	2
9	Measles	1,223	2
10	Traumas and burns	607	1

Source: UNICEF (1990a).

areas. Recent statistics on hospital deaths reflect a close relationship between mortality and morbidity. In 1988 diarrhea was cited as the cause of 12.5 percent of all hospital deaths. Cardiovascular diseases (10 percent of hospital deaths), malaria (9.7 percent), and broncho-pneumonia (9.5 percent) were the next highest ranking causes of hospital mortality (GOG 1988b).

Indeed these illnesses figure prominently on the list of the ten primary causes of morbidity among children between the ages of 0 and 5, as reported in 62 health centers of the PEV/SSP/ME program covering over 1.5 million people in 1988 (Table 65). Malaria accounted for 33 percent of all seen cases, respiratory diseases for 28 percent, diarrheal diseases for 15 percent, cutaneous infections for 12 percent, and malnutrition and anemia for 2 percent each.

High morbidity levels are also apparent from the results of the CFNPP Conakry Household Welfare Survey (ENCOMEC). Approximately 20 percent of all children less than 60 months old and 10 percent of older children and adults were reported sick within the previous month (del Ninno and Sahn 1990). These household-level data also reveal that intestinal problems, fever, and malaria are the primary causes of sickness. Most of these prevalent diseases are preventable, as are respiratory infections, measles, tuberculosis, whooping cough, poliomyelitis, and tetanus (World Bank 1993a). Hopwood (1993) notes in particular that the resurgence of malaria as a source of morbidity and mortality was facilitated by the former collapse of Guinea's environmental health programs.

Little in the way of comprehensive national data is available about the current incidence of malnutrition in Guinea. A 1990 study in Middle Guinea found that

27 percent of preschoolers are chronically malnourished. Another study found 20 percent of children in Middle Guinea to have visible goiter (World Bank 1993a). Iodine deficiency is also thought to be a serious nutritional problem in Guinea, leading to mental retardation in newborns. Seasonal malnutrition is also known to occur during the *soudure* period, especially in Upper and Middle Guinea and the Fouta Djallon (UNICEF 1990b). In addition to protein and calorie deficiency, iron deficiency anemia and malnutrition among expectant and lactating mothers (as proxied by low birth weights) have also been documented as important nutrition-related problems in Guinea (UNICEF 1990b).

The Conakry Household Welfare Survey (CFNPP/ENCOMEC) also sheds light on nutrition levels in Conakry. Results based on the first half of that survey's sample reveal that the incidence of chronic undernutrition in the capital is 18.2 percent, intermediate to that recorded for Accra (22 percent) and Abidjan (11.4 percent). The incidence of acute malnutrition, however, was recorded at approximately 12.9 percent in Conakry, higher than that recorded in both Abidjan (9.4 percent) and Accra (6.5 percent) (del Ninno and Sahn 1990).

In conclusion, the problems of limited service coverage and poor quality of even primary health care under the First Republic are being partially addressed under Guinea's Health Sector Policy. Initial experience with cost recovery at health centers and hospitals is encouraging, although there is little evidence of progress in reducing the opportunity cost of receiving treatment, in terms of travel and waiting time. This problem, however, is supposedly being addressed by the efforts underway to expand the coverage and quality of primary care, refocusing funds and training resources toward public health and rural health centers. The Guinean Government has committed itself to improving preventive and curative care and health promotion efforts, and hopes to double the coverage of primary care to 80 percent of the population by the year 2000. Nonetheless, health expenditures remain woefully skewed in favor of the rich, as the poor only make minimal use of publicly subsidized facilities, particularly hospitals and tertiary care. Likewise, improvements in the provision of health services provide Guinea's people with tangible signs of progress at a time when other benefits of reform have yet to be fully realized. At the same time, the poor health and nutrition indicators of the people of Guinea provide strong motivation for all concerned to address the health sector problems that remain.

NOTES

1. The apparent drop in the share of nonmining revenue between 1985 and 1986 may be a function of differing estimation methods for the two series, which are joined at those years.

2. The Sub-Saharan African average was only 25 percent domestic financing of deficits or surpluses in 1983 (UNDP and World Bank 1989).

3. This compares, for example, to tax yield levels of 24 and 32 percent for Zambia and Gabon respectively (World Bank 1990a).

4. The price of gasoline per liter was increased from GF 375 to GF 550 per liter in September 1990. The tax per liter, however, actually fell from GF 255 to GF 223. Petroleum prices were raised from GF 250 to GF 375 per liter in 1989, corresponding to a TSPP per liter increase from GF 135 to GF 255.

5. Corruption and the granting of exemptions were made easier by the vague rules regarding exemptions and by the fact that customs officers were not required to record reasons for granting exemptions (until the November 1989 establishment of an Exemptions Monitoring Unit).

6. The World Bank (1990a) cites the case of tobacco surtax revenue, which fell by 80 percent after an increase in the rate from 40 to 125 percent, while the availability of tobacco imports did not decline.

7. Some of these parastatals were born upon the nationalization of private companies after independence. For a detailed description of the inception of Guinea's parastatals, their early independence history, and the nationalization process, see World Bank (1981c).

8. Public enterprise employment was estimated at about 75,000 in 1981.

9. Including those that remained unsold.

10. "Privatization" here is taken, as in World Bank (1990a), to mean the reduction of the state's participation in an enterprise to less than 49 percent of the total share of capital.

11. However, the GOG has been burdened with substantial debt (on the order of US$ 26 million) from the losses of the pre-existing petroleum consortium.

12. Air Guinée was downsized and finally liquidated in August 1992 and replaced with a new company that was to be privatized in 1993. SOGETRAG, the interurban transport company that had been heavily subsidized, was also to be restructured in 1993. The Soviet-operated OBK has been liquidated and SBK, created in its place, will be privatized and liable for taxes in the amount of 30 percent of its bauxite export revenue. With the production and distribution of electricity to be privatized, state-owned ENELGUI will initially be privately managed.

13. Capital expenditures were 20 percent higher in U.S. dollar terms.

14. An indication of the lack of skills imparted even by vocational and technical schools is the fact that most skilled workers on the construction sites of Conakry were nonGuinean Africans (Olson 1986).

15. The illiteracy rate for the French language is 88 percent.

16. The inscription rate for the first grade of primary school was 35 percent in 1987/88 in contrast to an average of 24 percent during the period 1980 to 1984. It is notable that in 1984/85, when education was reverted to French, this ratio increased to 50.5 percent. Presumably the high ratio is due partly to the enrollment of a large number of students over the age of seven who chose to enter school to learn French.

17. In Conakry, while 29 percent of males above the age of six have no education, this figure is 51 percent for females (del Ninno and Sahn 1990).

18. This ratio too varies significantly across regions. There were sixty-seven pupils per teacher in the average class in Conakry and thirty-two in rural areas in 1987–1988 (GOG 1988a).

19. For example, it was estimated that in the 1970s the supply of agricultural university graduates was twice the actual demand in the civil service (Olson 1986). However, government policy entitled all graduates to automatic employment with the public sector, albeit at extremely low wages.

20. Parents have little capacity to pay for schooling, and imposing school fees is likely to depress the already low enrollment rates (World Bank 1990a).

21. More recent government estimates put the 1990 infant mortality rate at 139 and life expectancy at 47 (GOG 1992a).

22. The urban bias is evident also in statistics from a 1984 health survey, which showed that 77 percent of rural health centers have no doctor and 7 percent were staffed by untrained workers (World Bank 1986a). Whereas on average there were three functioning health care units per subprefecture in urban areas, there was less than one unit per every two subprefectures in rural areas (World Bank 1986a).

23. As of 1987 two prefectural hospitals were allowed to retain all their recovered costs while the two teaching hospitals in Conakry were permitted to retain recovered costs above a threshold level which, in practice, they were unable to reach (World Bank 1987b).

24. Each clinic is to receive an initial supply of essential medicines based on the size of the population it covers (US$ 0.50 per person).

25. Clinics are permitted to sell medicines at a price of up to 2.5 times their purchase price. This markup margin will go toward covering operating costs. Some subsidization was foreseen for those clinics located in less densely populated areas (UNICEF 1990). Revenue was projected under the hypothesis that 80 percent of users would effectively pay these fees (Knippenberg et al. 1990).

26. A system of internal subsidies has also been put in place for expensive treatments needed for severely ill patients (Knippenberg et al. 1990).

9

CONCLUSION

This book has surveyed the Guinean economy from crisis through reform. We have focused on the role of economic policy in precipitating the crisis and on the initial consequences of policy change. By overviewing the reform process, this study also raises specific, policy-relevant concerns regarding the impact of macro-level reform on micro- and household-level outcomes.

Guinea's economic crisis resulted primarily from an unmitigated failure in policy. Guinea has not experienced the droughts of Sudan and Ethiopia, the wars of Angola and Mozambique, the transport shock of Malawi, the terms-of-trade shock of oil-exporting Nigeria and Gabon, or the scarce resources of Sahelian countries such as Mauritania and Mali. Rather, Guinea's politically repressive state is responsible for the acute economic failures experienced. The state's attempts to replace all vestiges of price-clearing markets with state-controlled institutions led to egregious economic distortions and pervasive corruption. Upon commencement of Guinea's reform program in the early 1980s, the official monetized economy had collapsed, both financially and philosophically. The pervasive parallel markets were fragmented, badly integrated, inefficient, and characterized by risk and scarcity premia. Guinea resulting experienced shortages, high prices for consumers without access to subsidized goods, and low remuneration for producers. Only the mining enclave continued to function in the formal economy. Its success tellingly was owed to its relative insulation from the rest of the economy and from state policy.

Examples abound of command economies suffering the detrimental consequences of state control. Africa and Eastern Europe, even Latin America and Asia, have all experienced the lack of legal private sector initiatives, low productivity, and lack of innovation that characterized the Guinean economy. However, examples are scarce of state control leading to such total economic disarray and so thoroughly failing the social and welfare needs of the people. The virtual disregard of health care for all but a privileged few and an education policy that resulted in literacy below the most basic standards represent Guinea's potentially most pathetic legacy. By the end of the First Republic, these policies, combined with the exodus of the educated elite and entrepreneurial class, had depleted the human capital stock.

Guinea's story, however, further stands out due to the magnitude and speed of its reform program. Exchange rate policy of the 1970s and early 1980s that discouraged legal exportation underwent dramatic reform. The government liberalized domestic marketing, particularly the agricultural sector, where explicit taxation (through forced procurement) and implicit taxation (through an overvalued exchange rate) had eliminated incentives to producers of both food and cash crops. Furthermore, the government privatized banking, after the virtual failure of the state-run banking system, and either privatized or liquidated most parastatals in the service and manufacturing sectors. The government also made more rigorous its own budgeting and accounting procedures, in response to the First Republic's poor revenue mobilization outside the mining sector and general failure to prioritize expenditures in a way that would promote growth and equity.

Despite Guinea's rapid reforms, problems still persist. In some instances the implementation of planned reform has been incomplete or half-hearted; in others, infrastructural and institutional barriers have hampered reforms undertaken.

In terms of specific areas of policy reform, Guinea has moved to realign its economy with the world's through trade and exchange liberalization. In 1986, the exchange rate was dramatically devalued. Guinea also shifted from a fixed exchange rate system to a managed peg regime. Although the real effective exchange rate (REER) had some subsequent appreciation between 1986 and 1988, it nevertheless stabilized in 1991 at close to eight times its pre-adjustment level. The volume of foreign exchange officially traded increased, and the margin between the parallel and official exchange rates decreased.

Despite these advances, reform objectives in the external sector have not been completely realized. First, continued demand on the parallel market suggests that utilization of the official foreign exchange market can be improved. Necessary policy adjustments would include reducing administrative encumbrances of applying for foreign exchange and lessening high banking fees.

Second, Guinea's exchange rate has not been determined by an auction and is thus not directly linked to market forces. The managed peg system in place has not been devalued at the pace of Guinea's relative inflation rate. Consequently, after its initial dramatic devaluation, the real effective exchange rate appreciated in the latter half of the 1980s. This appreciation, coupled with continual balance-of-payments deficits, implies the need for further and more rapid discretionary devaluation.

Third, exports have not responded strongly to devaluation, certainly not as much as imports. The transport infrastructure must be further developed before export growth can truly take off. Likewise, related impediments to international trade need to be addressed, including a shortage of credit for exporters to their lack of knowledge and experience with regard to servicing potential overseas markets.

Fourth, private sector imports through the auction continue to consist primarily of consumer goods. Opening up trade and access to foreign exchange has had similar results elsewhere in Africa, reflecting the pent-up demand for consumer goods after years of shortages. Guinea's inability to procure longer-term trade credits also explains the consumption bias observed in imports and the low share of capital and intermediate goods in total commodity imports. Similarly, the lower risk nature of importing goods that can quickly be sold further encourages a consumption bias; higher uncertainty exists with the long-term investments that rely on imported intermediary and capital goods. Several facilitating factors will promote a shift in the composition of imports, including: tangible improvements in infrastructure (e.g., communications, electricity) and the banking system and intangibles, such as raising investor confidence through political stability. In the short run, however, the availability of consumer goods will build confidence in reform. The availability of goods can also facilitate reform if purchasing power serves as an incentive to generate a surplus, especially among farmers. Finally, what is often construed as a consumer good (e.g., auto parts, batteries, tools, cloth) is actually the raw material for a small-scale enterprise, thus further promoting economic growth.

Fifth, current levels of imports are financed primarily by public sector tax revenue from the mining sector and by balance-of-payments support. Until Guinea diversifies and increases its foreign exchange earning capabilities, import levels and the exchange rate itself will be vulnerable to future changes in the level of concessional financing from donors and in tax revenue from mining. Moreover, even if continued balance-of-payments support were assured, Guinea must pay careful attention to the potential of its current policies to accumulate excessive debt.

With respect to agricultural and food policy reform, the liberalization of producer prices for export crops increased incentives for farmers to market through official channels. The nominal protection coefficient for cash crops such as coffee, for example, has increased markedly since 1985. Consequently, estimated official export levels for coffee, as for most export crops, have increased. However, the level of these increases is disappointing for several reasons. The increases lag the export levels that pre-date the policies of the First Republic; they have not kept up with the increase in the value of imports; and it is unclear to what extent the increase reflects a redirection of exports from unofficial channels into official ones.

Faster agricultural export growth hinges on several factors. Of critical importance, again, is the development of infrastructure by, for example, improving roads and designing policies that enable and encourage imports of more trucks and spare parts. Lower transportation costs would allow for increased producer prices and would enable farmers to earn a higher share of the world market price. As another potential source of growth, markets for nontraditional exports such as fruits and vegetables should be identified and explored. A shorter-term solution would be to make exports more efficient and attractive by further streamlining the administrative procedure for processing and shipping exports. Increasing access to credit for traders and access to credit and inputs to farmers could also increase the supply responsiveness of export crop production to price liberalization. Similarly, developing a system of agricultural extension and research will promote innovation and substantially help raise output in a healthy price environment.

Incentives for the production of food crops have, like export crops, experienced improvements with the liberalization of producer prices. The nominal protection coefficient (NPC) on rice, for example, increased threefold between 1985 and 1987, to a level close to parity. However, high transport and marketing margins cause farmers to earn well below the international border price of rice. These factors have contributed to a slippage in the NPC since 1987. Nevertheless, the increase in producer prices has resulted in some increase in domestic rice production since 1985.

Here again, factors beyond prices may be muting a potential supply response. In addition to high transport and marketing margins, farmers rarely use fertilizer or improved variety seeds. Increasing farmers' access to credit and extension services will help in this regard, as will promoting the private sector's participation in the marketing of agricultural inputs. Just as important, moreover, is increasing the local and adaptive research on rice technology. Further study on the constraints and parameters of domestic rice production, including an estimation of its domestic supply elasticity, will be important in fully understanding the impacts of price liberalization on agriculture and rural food security.

The consumer market for rice has also been significantly affected by liberalization of internal and external marketing. However, the length of the marketing chain, coupled with the high cost of transportation, results in domestic marketing margins of up to three times the cost of international freight for imported rice. Multimarket model analysis by Arulpragasam (1994) indicates the beneficial effects of a lowered marketing margin on real incomes for rural and urban poor and nonpoor households. Factors that inflate the marketing margin include the inaccessibility of credit for traders, poor roads, and the national shortage of trucks and rice milling equipment. Eliminating these constraints should lower the consumer price of domestic rice and increase its competitiveness with imported rice.

The liberalization of rice imports, coupled with increased food aid, has particularly affected the consumer market for rice in the capital city. Imported rice, priced at close to import parity, now accounts for approximately four-fifths of all rice consumed in Conakry. Since imported rice costs approximately one-third less than domestic rice, imported rice has served an important food security function in the capital.

Liberalization of rice imports with the formal abandonment of the rice rationing system that existed under the First Republic has implied different welfare effects for different groups under the adjustment program. Those with previous access to rationed rice, subsidized at a price well below import parity, have now experienced an elimination of the effective income transfer they had previously garnered. These individuals were likely the more influential merchants and higher level *functionaries*. However, even these groups have likely gained from reform; because their ration purchases were inframarginal, they had faced high parallel market prices for a large part of their food purchases prior to reform. Other individuals, mainly smaller merchants, part-time workers, and the unemployed, have clearly gained from adjustment policies that have lowered the retail market price of rice. They can now buy free market rice at prices close to import parity, whereas they were obliged under the First Republic to purchase parallel market rice at costs far above import parity prices.

Although import liberalization and exchange rate reform have made food more available and accessible at cheaper real prices since 1986, the real relative price of imported foods has increased during the more recent reform period. Tendencies toward protectionism and creeping appreciation of the real effective exchange rate are to blame for these price movements. Poorer consumers have especially suffered from the increase, since imported foods such as rice and sugar are particularly important budgetary components for them and since income and price elasticities for these commodities are larger for them, relative to the average population. Adhering to a liberalized import regime benefits urban food security in Guinea.

While the effect of liberalization policies on food security in rural areas is less clear, farmers likely have not suffered a welfare loss with rice liberalization policies. First, the availability of imported rice has not diminished production of domestic rice, even in coastal areas. Second, since domestic production levels have remained relatively unchanged, the influx of imported rice has filled the greater food needs of an increased population. Unchanged domestic production and the availability of cheaper imported rice during the pre-harvest period suggest that food security may actually have improved among the rural poor. Third, producer prices for all cash crops have increased with reform. These increases have raised rural incomes, albeit not dramatically given the small supply response to date.

Discussion of food import liberalization inevitably raises the question of its consequences on domestic production. Although demand analysis reveals that domestic and imported rice are substitutes in consumption, local supply is not highly responsive to prices in the short-term due to supply bottle-necks: insufficient transport infrastructure, a shortage of credit for traders to purchase the rice, and possible input constraints such as land and labor. Raising rice import prices through a tariff or quotas may therefore result in an overall decline in demand, since higher prices for imports simply generate higher local prices. Additional tariffs on imported food would particularly increase the price of local and imported rice and decrease real incomes for both rural and urban households, multimarket analysis reveals. Reducing the tariff on rice was found to have opposite effects. Therefore, rather than raise trade barriers, domestic producers should be made more competitive. Such a strategy could improve the efficiency of marketing and foster technological change.

Reforms in Guinea's labor market have centered around civil service reform and reduction and on a recognition of the importance of small-scale enterprise. Between 1985 and 1989, approximately 35,000 people were taken off the government payroll, showing retrenchment as a pillar of public sector restructuring. Given the government's compensation scheme, however, these layoffs carried a substantial fiscal cost. Furthermore, for those remaining on the public payroll, the average real wage more than doubled between 1986 and 1990. This, coupled with the moderating price of rice, means, for example, that while a day's wage in 1986 could purchase 3.9 kilograms of rice, in 1990 it could buy 11.79 kilograms. As a result, the government's reduction of the public sector work force has not reduced payroll expenditures. Yet in absolute terms public sector wages continue to be low, currently constituting about 33 percent of the average household's monthly expenditures.

Among those retrenched workers who re-entered the labor market, mean wages are higher in real terms than those at the time they left the employ of the state. Thus, for those retrenched workers who found jobs, employment in the private sector compensated for losses due to public sector retrenchment. Survey results show, however, that public sector workers have had comparative difficulty finding work in the private wage sector. Most retrenched workers who re-entered the labor force have done so as self-employed workers, after short durations of unemployment. Lengthy unemployment spells among redeployed public sector workers are thus largely due to their queuing for wage-sector jobs, where remuneration is greater than the non-wage sector, conditional upon finding a job. Overall, the unemployment rate is slightly higher for redeployed public sector workers than for the general public. Those who find jobs in the private sector tend to be better educated and generally earn more than they did in the public sector.

The great potential of the small enterprise/self-employment sector to create employment and generate income should lead policymakers to consider measures to strengthen the sector. Research shows that in Conakry, over half of all households, especially poorer ones, are involved in at least one small-scale enterprise. Women own the majority of small enterprises, presiding over small operations, almost exclusively in the retail sector. Almost three-quarters of enterprises in Conakry entail retail commercial activity; very few entail manufacturing. While most enterprises are small in terms of revenue, those formed between 1988 and 1990 have higher revenues and expenses than ones formed between 1985 and 1987. Given the significant role of small enterprises in generating income and employment, especially for the poor and for women in Conakry, the government should explore ways to help stimulate these small businesses. Since enterprise profitability appears to be directly linked to level of education or experience, one way the government can assist is by improving the skills of Guinea's workforce, especially in terms of math skills and literacy. Programs for adults to develop entrepreneurial skills, for example, could also be established outside the school system.

Despite significant agricultural and labor market reforms, the enclave mining sector, historically an important source of foreign exchange for Guinea, has not been subject to substantial reform. Recent policy has focused on the promotion of artisanal mining, a further source of employment and incomes to domestic labor. Policy has also focused on ensuring the government's continuing reliance on the mining sector to furnish it with high levels of foreign exchange in renegotiating contracts with bauxite companies.

Reform of financial sector policy in Guinea, meanwhile, has been extensive, including complete privatization of the banking sector and issuance of a new currency in 1986. The closure of many parastatals, moreover, has significantly increased the share of credit extended to the private sector. Despite these reforms, the Guinean economy remains relatively unmonetized. Increasing the deposit base and personal savings requires consistently positive interest rates and the slow rebuilding of confidence in the banking system. Elimination of subsidized bank refinancing rates and tighter supervision of private banks by the Central Bank will help improve the efficiency of bank lending (as measured by delinquency rates) and promote more lending at higher interest rates. An institutional and legal framework is also essential for the development of the banking system, the extension of formal credit, and business itself. A departure from the current, consumption-oriented outlook of business depends on increased confidence in the investment climate and rests in part on properly functioning legal structures that assign and enforce creditor rights. The government's adoption of a Land Tenure Code and magistrate training program and the creation of a Supreme Court in 1992 were steps in this direction.

Given the dominance of the public sector under Guinea's First Republic, public and fiscal sector reform have also been far-reaching. Progress has been made in liquidating and privatizing government parastatals, although sometimes at the cost of not securing a worthy sale price for assets. Also, the government's Public Investment Program has garnered substantial foreign financing for an ambitious program that appropriately prioritizes infrastructure, rural development, and the social services. More attention, however, must be given to the recurrent cost implications of these projects. Moreover, Guinea's investment program will push absorptive capacity constraints. On the investment planning and management front alone, limited local absorptive capacity illustrates the need for technical assistance in the short term and training in the long term.

In addition, with fiscal reform, tax and tariff structures have been simplified and many rates reduced. Nevertheless, a low tax yield in Guinea continues, due to weaknesses in information, management, evaluation, and enforcement capabilities of the tax administration. Corruption, together with the widespread granting of discretionary tax exemptions, also lowers tax revenue. Subsidization by means of the nonpayment of taxes by inefficient parastatals such as Air Guinée, Enelgui, and ONAH also significantly drained potential budgetary resources in recent years. Guinea must address each of these problems if it is to rely less on unstable and declining tax revenue from the mining sector, an inflationary tradition of monetary financing, and balance-of-payments support.

A final element of public sector policy directly relevant to welfare is the public sector provision of social services. Policy reforms in the health and education sectors since the Second Republic have been slow. With education, the sectoral expenditure share had risen to 19 percent (inclusive of foreign financing) by 1991. Results, however, are slow to materialize. The primary school gross enrollment ratio has not improved since 1980. Improving enrollment will require not only increased education expenditure levels in general but an increased share of sectoral spending to primary education in particular. Moreover, improving enrollment ratios will depend on increasing the quality and relevance of education to today's labor market and, particularly, constructing positive perceptions of returns to education. In addition to potential returns in health and nutrition levels, the demand for education will thus be linked to the demand for labor. Special attention must be paid to fostering greater accessibility to education of females and rural inhabitants, groups which are currently under-represented in schools.

Improvements to health service provision have also been slow since the inception of the Second Republic. The share of the total government budget allocated to health remains at close to 3 percent. A conspicuous shortage of equipment and drugs remains, due to insufficient operating funds, and coverage of the formal health care system continues to be thin, especially in rural areas. Increased financing of the health sector from the treasury should be complemented, however, with cost recovery for health care and drugs. While the ability of potential health service users to afford care remains a concern, evidence of high levels of household expenditure on health even prior to reform, due to recourse to parallel markets for drugs and private sector producers, suggests that most potential health service users are willing and able to contribute to the cost of their care. Of course, appropriate criteria should be developed to define exceptions to service payment.

Many problems persist in Guinea despite rapid reform. Institutional and infrastructural bottlenecks are now the binding constraints to growth. The Guinea case is showing, as in most countries throughout sub-Saharan Africa, that price reform alone is not a panacea. Measures beyond price-oriented structural adjustment must be employed. Guinea's commitment to state disengagement, although essential to restoring the role of markets, is not sufficient to propel the economy into a rapid growth scenario. Although the reliance on market forces is not unfounded, state contraction will not automatically result in legitimate laws, the elimination of corruption, the restoration of markets, and growth of private sector institutions. Rather, the state needs to retain its crucial role in providing public goods and making investments where the social rate of return far outweighs private returns. Furthermore, the state must stay involved in rebuilding infrastructure, collecting and disseminating information, engaging in agricultural research, investing in neglected human resources, promoting foreign investment through appropriate statutes and regulations, and providing an income transfer to the poorest of the poor. The challenge for donors is to help the government redefine and facilitate this new role without reinforcing old notions of state control. At the same time, twenty-five years of decay and decline will not be reversed in four or five years. An urgency to implement reforms must be tempered with patience so as not to trigger detrimental policy reversals.

REFERENCES

AGRER. 1992. Macro-économie et Dimensions Sociales de l'ajustement—Rapport Définitif. Ministère du Plan et de la Cooperation Internationale, Conakry.

AGRER/GOG. 1991. Etude de Securité Alimentaire. Ministère du Plan et de la Cooperation Internationale, Conakry.

Alderman, Harold, David E. Sahn, and Jehan Arulpragasam. 1991. Food subsidies and exchange rate distortions in Mozambique. *Food Policy* 16(5): 395–404.

Appleton, S., Paul Collier, and P. Horsell. 1990. *Gender, education, and employment in Côte d'Ivoire*. Social Dimensions of Adjustment Working Paper No. 8. Washington, DC: World Bank.

Arid Lands Information Center. 1983. Environmental profile of Guinea.

Arulpragasam, Jehan. 1994. *The effects of trade and exchange policies on food consumption, and urban poverty in Guinea: A multimarket analysis*. Working Paper No. 65. Ithaca, NY: Cornell Food and Nutrition Policy Program.

Arulpragasam, Jehan, and Carlo del Ninno. 1993. Price changes and their effects on consumption in Conakry. ENCOMEC Findings Bulletin No. 12. Cornell Food and Nutrition Policy Program, Washington, DC.

Arulpragasam, Jehan, and Carlo del Ninno. Forthcoming. Do cheap imports harm the poor? In *Economic reform and the poor in Africa*, ed. David E. Sahn. Oxford: Clarendon-Oxford.

Associates for International Resources and Development (AIRD). 1989. *Agricultural sector assessment, Republic of Guinea*. Somerville, MA: AIRD.

AIRD and Government of Guinea. 1983. ONADER project: Study of prices and rural producer incentives—final report. Sommerville, MA: AIRD/Ministry of Agriculture, Water, Forests, and Processing.

Azarya, Victor, and Naomi Chazan. 1987. Disengagement from the state in Africa: Reflections on the experience of Ghana and Guinea. *Comparative Studies in Society and History* 29(1): 106–131.

Banque Central de la République de Guinée. 1989. Rapport Annuel D'Activites au 31 Décembre 1989. BCRG, Conakry.

_____. 1993. Rapport Préliminaire d'Activities 1992. BCRG, Conakry.

_____. Various years. Bulletin Trimestriel d'Etudes et de Statistiques. Nos. 4, 5, 7, 8, 9, and 15. BCRG, Conakry.

Barbier, Jean-Pierre. 1987. Guineé: Une Résurrection Laborieuse. *Afrique Contemporaine* 144 (April): 23–36.

Benz, Hélène. 1992. Quelques Élements sur les Importations et le Commerce du Riz en Guinée. CIRAD, Montpellier.

Braverman, Avishay, and Jeffrey S. Hammer. 1986. Multimarket analysis of agricultural pricing policies in Senegal. In *Agricultural household models: Extensions, applications, and policy*, eds. Inderjit Singh, Lyn Squire, and John Strauss. Baltimore, MD: Johns Hopkins University Press.

Braverman, Avishay, Jeffrey S. Hammer, and Choong Yong Ahn. 1987. Multimarket analysis of agricultural pricing policies in Korea. In *The theory of taxation for developing countries*, eds. David Newbery and Nicholas Stern. New York: Oxford University Press.

Bremer-Fox, Jennifer, Laura Bailey, Paola Lang, and Mary Mervenne. 1990. *Experience with auctions of food aid commodities in Africa.* Washington, DC: Robert Nathan Associates.

Caputo, E. 1991. Rapport d'Evolution d'un Programme National D'Appui à la Filière Riz en Guinée. CCCE, Conakry.

Chemonics International. 1986. Investment opportunities in the Guinean rice industry. Chemonics International, Washington, DC. Photocopy.

_____. 1987a. Investment opportunities in the Guinean coffee industry. Washington, DC: Chemonics International.

_____. 1987b. Investment opportunities in the Guinean tropical fruit industry. Washington, DC: Chemonics International.

Conde, Julien. 1976. "La Situation Démographique en République de Guinée." *Revue Française d'études Politiques Afraicaines* 123 (March): 102–125.

Cornell Food and Nutrition Policy Program (CFNPP). 1990. The Conakry household welfare survey 1989–90. Duplicated.

del Ninno, Carlo. 1994. *Welfare and poverty in Conakry: Assessments and determinants.* Working Paper No. 66. Ithaca, NY: Cornell Food and Nutrition Policy Program.

del Ninno, Carlo, and David E. Sahn. 1990. Survey methodology and preliminary results of household welfare in Conakry: A progress report. Cornell Food and Nutrition Policy Program, Ithaca, NY. Photocopy.

Dorosh, Paul A., Carlo del Ninno, and David E. Sahn. 1995. Poverty alleviation in Mozambique: A multi-market analysis of the role of food aid. *Agricultural Economics* 13: 89–99.

Dorosh, Paul, and David E. Sahn. 1993. *A general equilibrium analysis of the effect of macroeconomic adjustment on poverty in Africa.* Working Paper No. 39. Ithaca, NY: Cornell Food and Nutrition Policy Program.

Education Development Center (EDC). 1994. *Limited technical assessment: Selective analysis of elementary education sector reform in Guinea.* Washington, DC: USAID.

Filippi-Wilhelm, Laurence. 1987. *Circuits de Commercialisation et de Distribution en Guinée.* Vol. 1. Conakry: UNCTAD/UNDP.

———. 1988. *Circuits de Commercialisation et de Distribution en Guinée.* Vol. 2. Conakry: UNCTAD/UNDP.

Food and Agricultural Organization of the United Nations (FAO). 1990. Inventaire des Projets Administrés par la FAO en Republique de Guinée pour la période de Janvier à Decembre 1989. Conakry: FAO.

———. 1991a. *Production yearbook.* Rome, Italy: FAO.

———. 1991b. *Trade yearbook.* Rome, Italy: FAO.

———. Various years. *Food outlook.* Statistical supplement. Rome: FAO.

Forbeau, Francis, and Yannick Meneux. 1989. Riz Local ou Riz Importé en Guinée? Institute de Recherches Agronomique Tropicales (IRAT), Montpellier.

Glick, Peter, and David E. Sahn. 1993. *Labor force participation, sectoral choice, and earnings in Conakry, Guinea.* Working Paper No. 43. Ithaca, NY: Cornell Food and Nutrition Policy Program.

Greer, J., and Erik Thorbecke. 1986. A methodology for measuring food poverty applied to Kenya. *Journal of Development Economics* 24:59–74.

Guillaumont, Sylviane Jeanneney. 1985. Foreign exchange policy and economic performance: A study of Senegal, Madagascar and Guinea. In *Crisis and recovery in Sub-Saharan Africa*, ed. Rose Tore. Paris: OECD.

Guinea, Government of (GOG). 1985. Rapport Statistique de l'Activité Manufacturière en 1984. CEGIR and Ministère du Dévelopeement Industriel, Conakry.

_____. 1986. Enquête Légère sur la Consommation des Ménages de la Ville de Conakry, 30/09/84–3/11/84. Ministère du Plan et de la Coopération International, Conakry. Photocopy.

_____. 1987a. Code des Investissements et ses Textes d'Application. GOG, Conakry.

_____. 1987b. Etude du Secteur Informel en Guinée, Potentiels et Constraintes. CEGIR and Ministère des Ressources Humaines de l'Industrie et des PME, Conakry.

_____. 1987c. Situation Economique et Conjoncturelle au 30 Juin 1987. Ministère du Plan et de la Coopération Internationale, Conakry.

_____. 1987d. Situation Economique et Conjoncturelle au 31 Decembre 1985 et Elements sur la mise en oeuvre de la Reforme Economique au Cours du Premier Tremestre 1986. Ministère du Plan et de la Coopération Internationale, Conakry.

_____. 1987e. Enquete sur les depenses menages de la ville de Conakry. Ministere du Plan et de la Cooperation, Conakry.

_____. 1988a. Analyse Economique et Financière des Dépenses du Secteur Education en Republique de Guinée. Ministère de l'Education Nationale, Conakry.

_____. 1988b. Annuaire Statistique. Ministère de la Santé Publique et de la Population, Conakry.

_____. 1988c. Plan d'Action Sanitaire de la Guinée. Ministère de la Santé Publique et de la Population, Conakry.

_____. 1989a. Loi de Finances pour l'année 1989. Ministère de l'Economie et des Finances, Conakry.

_____. 1989b. Rapport Annuel 1988: Situation et Perspectives Economiques 1988–91. Ministère du Plan et del'Coopération Internationale, Conakry.

_____. 1989c. Recensement General de la Population et de l'Habitat, 1983, Analyse des Resultats Definitifs. Ministère du Plan et de la Coopèration Internationale and Direction Nationale de la Statistique et del'Informatique, Conakry.

_____. 1989d. Stratégies du Governement dans la Perspective de l'Education pour Tous en l'An 2000. Ministère de l'Education Nationale, Conakry. Photocopy.

_____. 1990a. Loi de Finances pour 1990. Ministère de l'Economie et des Finances, Conakry.

_____. 1990b. Rapport Economique et Social 1989. Ministère du Plan et de la Coopération Internationale, Conakry.

_____. 1990c. Resultats du Recensement National de l'Agriculture. Ministère du Plan et del'Coopération Internationale and Direction Nationale del'Statistique et del'Informatique, Conakry.

_____. 1991a. Dimensions Sociales de l'Ajustement Structurel (DSA) Enquête sur les Informations Prioritaires (ESIP)—Rapport Final. Ministère du Plan et des Finances, Conakry.

_____. 1991b. Rapport Economique et Social 1990. Ministère du Plan et de del'Coopération Internationale, Conakry.

_____. 1992a. Rapport Economique et Social 1991. Ministère du Plan et des Finances, Conakry.

_____. 1992b. Rapport Générale de l'Enquête Agricole Permanente Campagne 1991–1992. Volumes 1 and 2. Conakry: Ministère de l'Agriculture et des Ressources Animales (MARA). Photocopy.

_____. 1993a. Cadrage Macro-économique Annuel 1993. Ministère du Plan et des Finances, Conakry.

_____. 1993b. Synthese des Conclusions de la mission du Fonds sur l'execution du Programme 1992.

_____. Various Issues. Evolution de l'Indice des Prix à la Consommation des Ménages de Conakry. Ministère du Plan et de la Coopération International, Conakry.

_____. n.d. (a). Etude sur la Filière-Riz en Guinée Maritime. Ministère du Plan et de la Coopération Internationale and Ministère du Développement Rural, Conakry. Photocopy.

_____. n.d. (b). Enquête Filière-Riz Haute Guinée 1986–87. Ministère de l'Agriculture et Ressources Animales, Conakry.

_____. n.d. (c). Enquête sur les Dépenses des Ménages de la Ville de Conakry, December 1986–January 1987. Ministère du Plan et de la Coopération International, Conakry.

_____. n.d. (d). Rapport sur les Conditions de Vie des Menages de Conakry de 1986–88. Ministère du Plan et de la Coopération Internationale, Conakry. Photocopy.

_____. n.d. (e). Unpublished Data. Conakry: Ministry of Plan and Cooperation.

Hanrahan, Charles E., and Steven Block. 1988. *Food aid and policy reform in Guinea*. Prepared for USAID/Conakry. Cambridge, MA: Abt Associates.

Hirsch, Robert. 1986. Rapport d'un Mission Préliminaire sur le Secteur Rizicole Guinéen. Caisse Centrale de Coopèration Economique, Paris.

Hopwood, Ian. 1993. Policy Formulation and Health Sector Reform: Lessons from Zambia and Guinea.

International Labor Organization (ILO). 1986a. Rapport d'une Mission Sectorelle D'Emploi du PECTA en République de Guinée. ILO, Conakry. Photocopy.

_____. 1986b. Situation des Ressources Humaines en Guinée: Diagnostic et Priorités d'Action à Court et à Moyen Terms. Photocopy.

International Monetary Fund (IMF). 1986. *Guinea: Recent economic developments*. Washington, DC: IMF.

_____. 1987a. *Guinea: Recent economic developments*. Washington, DC: IMF.

_____. 1987b. Guinea—staff report for the 1987 Article IV consultation. Washington, DC: IMF.

_____. 1988a. Guinea—staff report for the 1988 Article IV consultation. Washington, DC: IMF.

_____. 1988b. *Guinea: Statistical annex*. Washington, DC: IMF.

_____. 1990a. *Guinea: Statistical annex*. Washington, DC: IMF.

_____. 1990b. Indicators of real effective exchange rates. Washington, DC: IMF.

_____. 1991. Guinea staff report. Washington, DC: IMF.

_____. 1992. Guinea staff report. Washington, DC: IMF.

_____. 1993. *Guinea: Recent economic developments*. Washington, DC: IMF.

_____. Various years. *International financial statistics*. Washington, DC: IMF.

Johnson, R.W. 1978. Guinea. In *West African studies: Failure and promise*, ed. John Dunn. London: Cambridge University Press. Cited in Victor Azarya and Naomi Chazan. Disengagement from the state in Africa: Reflections on the experience of Ghana and Guinea. *Comparative Studies in Society and History* 29(1, 1987): 106–131.

Kande, Mohamed Fallo. 1991. Politique D'Approvisionnement en Produits D'Importation de la Republique de Guinée. Paper presented at Seminaire National sur la Nouvelle Politique Commerciale de la Republique de Guinée et ses Imperatifs, Conakry.

Knippenberg, Rudolph, Daniel Levy-Bruhl, Raimi Osseni, Kandjoura Drame, Agnes Soucat, and Christine Debeugny. 1990. The Bamako initiative: Experiences in primary health care from Benin and Guinea. *Children in the Tropics*, No. 184/185.

Larfeuil, Bernard. 1990. Guinée: prèmier bilan d'une expérience de reconversion de fonctionnaires. *Afrique Contemporaine* 155 (3rd Quarter): 3–22.

Lee, Lung-Fei. 1983. Generalized econometric models with selectivity. *Econometrica* 51: 507–512.

Lowdermilk, Melanie. 1989. *Food needs assessment 1989–90*. Washington, DC: E/DI.

Mills, Bradford, and David E. Sahn. 1993a. *Is there life after public service? The fate of retrenched workers in Conakry Guinea.* Working Paper No. 42. Ithaca, NY: Cornell Food and Nutrition Policy Program.

_____. 1993b. Characteristics of small scale enterprises and proprietors in Conakry. Bulletin No. 9. Cornell Food and Nutritión Policy Program, Ithaca, NY.

_____. 1995. Reducing the size of the public sector workforce: Institutional constraints and human consequences in Guinea. *Journal of Development Studies* 31(4): 505–528.

Morice, Alain. 1987. Guineé 1985: Etat, corruption et trafics. *Les Temps Modernes.* 42(487): 108–136.

Nellum, A. L., and Associates. 1980. Guinea agricultural sector report. Photocopy.

O'Conner, Michael. 1972. Guinea and the Ivory Coast—contrasts in economic development. *Journal of Modern African Studies* 10(3): 425. Cited in Victor Azarya and Naomi Chazan. Disengagement from the state in Africa: Reflections on the experience of Ghana and Guinea. *Comparative Studies in Society and History* 29(1, 1987): 106–131.

Olivola, Kenneth J., and UNICEF. 1990. Children and women in urban Guinea (with special reference to Conakry). Rapid Situation Analysis.

Olson, Craig. 1986. Human resources and institutional development analysis for the USAID/Guinea country development strategy statement, fiscal years 1988–1990. Prepared for USAID. DAI, Washington, DC.

Paul, S. 1989. A model of constructing poverty lines. *Journal of Development Economics* 30:129–144.

Pick's currency yearbook. Various years. NY: Pick.

Porte Autonome de Conakry (PAC). 1993. Statistiques Comparées—Janvier à Décembre 1991 et 1992. Ministère du Commerce, des Transports et du Tourisme, Conakry.

Projet National d'Appuis à la Filière Riz (PNAFR). 1992. Note de Conjoncture 1992 Section Commercialisation. MARA/PNAFR, Conakry.

Pujo, Laurence. 1993. La Filière Riz en Guinée Forestière. CIRAD, Montpellier.

Ravallion, M., and B. Bidani. 1994. How robust is a poverty profile? *World Bank Economic Review* 8(1): 75–102.

Reveco. 1988. Les Cicuits d'Approvisionnement de Conakry Riz Importé—Riz Local. UNDP/UNCTAD, Conakry. Photocopy.

Rivière, Claude. 1977. *Guinea: The mobilization of a people.* Ithaca, NY: Cornell University Press.

Sahn, David E., and Harold Alderman. 1987. The role of the foreign exchange and commodity auctions in trade, agriculture, and consumption in Somalia. Washington, DC: International Food Policy Research Institute. Photocopy.

Sahn, David E., and C. Delgado. 1989. The nature and implications for market interventions of seasonal food price variability. In *Seasonal variability in Third World agriculture: The consequences for food security*, ed. David E. Sahn. Baltimore: Johns Hopkins University Press.

Serageldin, Ismail, Christiaan Grootaert, and Fernando Reimers. 1994. Education and structural adjustment in Africa in the 1980s.

SScetagri/Agroprogress. 1986. Etude de Restructuration des Services, Agricoles, et de Schémas Directeurs Regionaux de Développement Rural Programmes Nationaux.

Sodeteg/Credes. 1987. Financement du Secteur Santé.

Suret-Canale, J. 1970. *La République de Guinée*. Paris: Editions Sociales.

Tenconi, Roland. 1988. Restructuring of the banking system in Guinea. World Bank, Washington, DC. Photocopy.

Thenevin, Pierre. 1988. Politique de Relance de la Filière Rizicole et Approvisionnement en Riz Local de la Guinée; Identification et Feasibility de Quelques Actions. Photocopy.

UNICEF. 1990a. Les Femmes et les Enfants en République de Guinée, une Analyse de la Situation dans la Contexte Socio-Economique. Conakry: UNICEF. Photocopy.

———. 1990b. Women and children. Conakry: UNICEF. Photocopy.

———. 1990c. Plan Quinquennal de Cooperation: Programme Santé et Nutrition. Programme de Cooperation Gouvernement—UNICEF. Conakry: UNICEF.

United Nations Development Programme (UNDP). 1991. *Human development report 1991*. Oxford: Published for UNDP by Oxford University Press.

———. 1992. *Human development report 1992*. Oxford: Published for UNDP by Oxford University Press.

UNDP and World Bank. 1989. *African economic and financial data*. Washington, DC: World Bank.

United States Agency for International Development (USAID). 1987a. An evaluation of United States food aid in Guinea. USAID, Conakry. Photocopy.

———. 1987b. Guinea foreign exchange system. USAID, Conakry. Photocopy.

———. 1989. Guinea grant food assistance programs second mid-term evaluation. Conakry: USAID. Photocopy.

———. 1990. Guinea foreign exchange system report for CY 1989." USAID, Conakry. Photocopy.

Weaver, Robert D. 1987. *Comparative advantage in food production in Guinea: A study of smallholders.* Washington, DC: World Bank.

World Health Organization. 1988. Examen de l'Utilisation des Ressources dans les Pays, République de Guinée. Draft/Confidential.

World Bank. 1981a. *Accelerated development in sub-Saharan Africa: An agenda for action.* Washington, DC: World Bank.

_____. 1981b. *Revolutionary People's Republic of Guinea: Country economic memorandum.* Washington, DC: World Bank.

_____. 1981c. *Revolutionary People's Republic of Guinea—Survey of the public enterprise sector.* Washington, DC: World Bank.

_____. 1983. *African development indicators.* Socio-economic time service retrieval system (STARS). Washington: World Bank.

_____. 1984a. *Guinea agricultural sector review: Western African region.* Washington, DC: World Bank.

_____. 1984b. *Guinea: The conditions for economic growth, a country economic memorandum.* Washington, DC: World Bank.

_____. 1986a. *Guinea: Population, health, and nutrition sector review.* Washington, DC: World Bank.

_____. 1986b. *Guinea: Structural adjustment credit, credit summary.* Washington, DC: World Bank.

_____. 1987a. *Côte d'Ivoire country economic memorandum.* Washington, DC: World Bank.

_____. 1987b. *Staff appraisal report—Guinea: Health services development project.* Washington, DC: World Bank.

_____. 1988. *Guinea: Structural adjustment credit.* Washington, DC: World Bank.

_____. 1989a. *Cameroon agricultural sector review.* Washington, DC: World Bank.

_____. 1989b. *Guinea: Public investment review, 1986–1991.* Washington, DC: World Bank.

_____. 1989c. *Memorandum of the President on a proposed credit to the Republic of Guinea for a socio-economic development support project.* Washington, DC: World Bank.

_____. 1990a. *Republic of Guinea: Country economic memorandum.* Vols. 1 and 2. Washington, DC: World Bank.

_____. 1990b. *World debt tables 1989/90.* Washington, DC: World Bank.

_____. 1990c. *World development report 1990.* Washington, DC: World Bank.

_____. 1993a. *Staff appraisal report—Republic of Guinea health and nutrition sector project.* Washington, DC: World Bank.

_____. 1993b. *World tables.* Baltimore: Johns Hopkins University Press for the World Bank.

_____. 1994a. Special program of assistance status report for Guinea. Prepared for the April 1994 Multidonor Meeting. World Bank, Washington, DC.

_____. 1994b. *World debt tables 1993/1994.* Washington, DC: World Bank.

_____. 1995a. *Developing girls' education in Guinea: Issues and policies.* Report No. 14488-GUI. Washington, DC: World Bank.

_____. 1995b. Guinea public expenditure review. World Bank, Washington, DC.

Yansané, Aguibou Y. 1984. *Decolonization in West African states with French colonial legacy.* Cambridge, MA: Schenkman Publishing Company, Inc.

_____. 1990. Guinea: The significance of the coup of April 1984 and economic issues. *World Development* 18(9): 1231–1246.

Zorick, Michael P. 1989. Report updating current budgetary procedures and decision making processes in the Republic of Guinea. USAID, Conakry.

INDEX

Age
in labor force participation rate, 114–115
in small-enterprise sector, 137–138
Agricultural cooperatives, 51
Agricultural exports, 36, 38, 52–54, 60, 68–71, 198
Agricultural gross domestic product, 49
Agricultural landholding sizes, 47–49, 51–52
Agricultural marketing, 68–80, 99–101
Agricultural policy. See Food and agricultural policy
Agricultural pricing, 62–64, 67–80
Agricultural production. See also Crops
reforms affecting, 1–2, 68–80
retail prices for, 62–64, 67–68
stagnating, 54, 57, 58
terms of trade in, 61
and urban-rural dichotomy, 13

Agricultural products purchased by government, 58–60
Agricultural research center, 67
Agricultural resources, 5–7
Agriculture, subsistence, 14
Agroecological zones, 5–7, 46–49
Almost Ideal Demand System (AIDS), 81, 84
Aluminum mining, 143, 144, 147, 148
Artisanal mining, 146, 148–149
Auctioning of foreign exchange, 22–29, 38–40

Balance of payments, 30–37, 41–42
Bamako Initiative, 184
Banking system, 151–160, 202
Barter trade, 61
Bauxite mining, 142–144, 147, 148
Budget deficits, 162–165, 167, 168

Cash crops, 46–49
Civil service. See Public wage sector

Coffee exports, 68–69
Comité Militaire de Redressement
    Nationale (CMRN), 14
Constitution, 14
Consumer goods import taxes, 25–26
Consumer markets, 60–68
Consumer prices, 2, 60–68, 78–80,
    86–87, 103
Conte, General Lansana, 14–15
Cooperatives, agricultural, 51
Cost recovery in health system,
    184–186
Credit availability, 72, 77
Crops
    cash, 46–49
    export, 36, 38, 52–54, 60, 68–71,
        19
    food, 46–49, 52–54, 71–80,
        99–101. *See also* Rice *entries*
    taxes on, 54
Customs taxes, 169

Debt crisis, 35–37
Diamond mining, 142, 144, 146, 148
District Agro-Pastoral Farms
    (FAPAS), 50–51
Drugs in health system reform,
    183–185
Economic centralization, 11
Economic reform
    conclusions about, 195–204
    evolution of, 1–4
    history of, 15
    structural adjustment in, 1–3,
        14–16, 22, 66–68, 146
Economic stagnation, 7–14
Education
    and gender, 178–180, 203
    health, 183

and labor market sectors, 117–120
in small-enterprise sector, 135–139
Educational system
    government expenditures on,
        180–181
    performance of, 10
    reforms in, 176–181, 203
Employment. *See also* Labor *entries*
    in banking sector, 152
    in mining sector, 145, 148–149
    in private wage sector, 12, 115–
        120, 123, 128, 130, 201
    in public wage sector. *See* Public
        wage sector
    self-, 115, 121, 128. *See also*
        Small-enterprise sector
Enclave mining sector, 143, 201–202
Exchange rate indices, 27
Exchange rate policy, 18–42
    and balance of payments, 30–37
    history of, 18–21
    and private sector, 19–23
    reforms in, 21–42
Exchange rates. *See also* Foreign ex-
    change and balance of payments,
    33, 41–42
    devaluation of, 15, 26, 29, 33, 36,
        38–41, 54, 56, 196–197
    and exports, 36, 38
    and imports, 28–29, 38–41, 88
    and monetary system, 152, 155
    overvaluation of, 12–14, 18–21,
        172
    parallel, 19–21, 24, 26–29, 41–42,
        54, 56, 152, 155
    and producer prices for crops, 54,
        56
    real, 103–105
    real effective, 27, 29–30

Export crops, 36, 38, 52–54, 68–71, 198
Export licenses, 21
Export taxes, 20, 25, 67, 69–70
Exports
  agricultural, 36, 38, 52–54, 60, 68–71, 198
  composition of, 38
  in economic reform, 197, 198
  and exchange rates, 36, 38
  mining sector, 36, 38, 143–145, 147–149
  parastatal control of, 52
  quality control of, 69–70

Ferme Agricole Commune (FAC), 51
Financial sector policies, 151–160, 202
First Republic, 10–14, 51–66
Fiscal policies, 162–192, 202, 203
Food aid, 67, 77, 78, 80
Food and agricultural policy
  analyzing, multimarket model in, 88–105
  failure of, 49–52
  history of, 13, 46–66
  reforms in, 66–101, 198
  rice pricing in, 81–88
Food commodity elasticities, 84
Food consumption patterns, 81–85
Food crops, 46–49, 52–54, 71–80, 99–101. *See also* Rice *entries*
Food imports, 59–60, 90–98
Food marketing margins, 99–101
Food product taxes, 25
Food security, 81–88
Food shortages, 60
Foreign assistance, 15–16, 29. *See also* Food aid

Foreign exchange. *See also* Exchange rate *entries*
  auctioning, 22–29, 38–40
  in mining sector, 143, 145, 148
Foreign exchange budget, 22–24
Forest Guinea, 7, 47, 49, 61–62, 72, 87
Formal-informal sector division, 13–14

Gender
  and education, 178–180, 203
  infant mortality and life expectancy by, 182
  and labor force participation, 114–120
  in small-enterprise sector, 135–137, 139, 201
Ghost workers, 122
Gold mining, 142, 144, 146, 148
Government expenditures, 162, 166–168. *See also* Budget deficits; Fiscal policies; Public *entries*
  for agricultural products, 58–60
  on drugs, 184
  on educational system, 180–181
  on health system, 184, 188–190
  on interest, 168
Government revenues, 163–171. *See also* Tax *entries*
Gross domestic product (GDP), 7–10, 49

Health education, 183
Health system, 181–192, 203
Household consumption of rice, 81–88
Household welfare, 64–66, 90, 93–98, 128–130
Human Development Index, 9–10

Illegal economy (parallel market systems), 12–13, 64–66, 78–80
Illiteracy rate, 10, 177
Import licenses, 21, 24
Import taxes, 20–21, 25–26, 30, 90–98, 170, 171
Imports
    composition of, 40, 41
    in economic reform, 197–200
    and exchange rates, 28–29, 38–41, 88
    of food, 59–60, 90–98. *See also* Food aid
    in mining sector, 143
    of rice, 74–81, 84–88, 90–98, 199–200
Income distribution. *See also* Poverty and education, 178–179, 181
    and health system reform, 185–187, 190
Independence, consequences of, 10
Infant mortality rate, 9–10, 182
Inflation, 156, 158
Informal sector, 12–14
Infrastructure
    and agricultural exports, 70, 73, 74
    in health system, 183, 187, 203
    history of, 10
    maintaining, 163
    in mining sector, 142, 148
    reforms affecting, 174–175, 203–204
    regional differences in, 6, 7
    rural, 13
Interest expenditures, 168
Interest rate reforms, 156–160
Iron ore mining, 146

Labor, availability of, 72. *See also* Employment
Labor force participation rates, 114–121

Labor market sectors. *See* Private wage sector; Public wage sector; Self-employment sector; Small-enterprise sector
Labor markets, 113–139, 200–201
Land Tenure Code, 159, 202
Landholding sizes, 47–49, 51–52
Legal system, 13, 159, 202
Life expectancy, 9–10, 182
Livraisons obligatoires, 58
Lower (Maritime) Guinea, 6, 7, 46–47, 61, 71, 72, 87
Luxury taxes, 26

Malnutrition, 190–192
Market clearing, 103
Marketing margins for food, 99–101
Merchant class, 12
Middle Guinea, 6–7, 47–48, 72
Mineral resources, 5–7
Mining code, 146
Mining sector, 14
    and balance of payments, 30–33
    enclave, 143, 201–202
    government revenues from, 163–165, 168, 169
    and monetary system, 152, 155
Mining sector exports, 36, 38, 143–145, 147–149
Mining sector policies, 141–149
Ministry of Reform and Civil Service (MRAFP), 125–126
Monetary aggregates, 152–155
Monetary policy, 11, 152, 155–156
Monopoly rights, 173, 174
Morbidity rates, 191
Mortality rates, 9–10, 182, 190, 191
Multimarket model, 88–105
Multiple jobs, 12

Natural resources, 5–7
Net foreign assets (NFA), 158
Nominal protection coefficient
  (NPC), 54, 56, 198
Nonwage sector, 131, 132, 135. *See
  also* Self-employment sector;
  Small-enterprise sector

Parallel exchange rate, 19–21, 24,
  26–29, 41–42, 54, 56, 152, 155
Parallel market systems, 12–13,
  64–66, 78–80
Parastatals
  and budget deficits, 163
  export control by, 52
  history of, 11
  loans to, 152
  reforms of, 67, 172–174, 202
  subsidies to, 172–173, 202
Paris Club agreements, 16, 35–36
Parti Démocratique de Guinée
  (PDG), 10–11
Petroleum company privatization,
  173
Petroleum product taxes, 169, 171
Political history, 10–14
Political reform, 14–15
Pollution from mining, 147
Population and population density,
  5–7, 48, 187
Poverty
  and food import taxes, 90–98
  and food marketing margins,
  99–101
  and health system reform,
  185–187, 190
  and labor market sectors, 116–117
  and mining sector, 145, 149
  and rice consumption, 81, 84–85

Poverty line, 90, 95
Private sector
  and banking system, 152, 155–156
  in economic reform, 2, 3
  and exchange rate policy, 19–23
  and exchange rate reform, 24–25
  mining companies in, 142
  and trade reform, 24
Private wage sector, 12, 115–120,
  123, 128, 130, 201
Privatization program, 173–174
PRL (village-level) councils, 50–52
Producer prices, 2, 52–60, 71–80,
  103
Production costs of crops, 54, 55
Programme de Redressement
  Economique et Financier (PREF),
  15–16
Programme Intérimaire de Redressement Nationale (PIRN), 15
Public enterprises, 163–165, 171–
  174. *See also* Parastatals
Public Investment Program (PIP),
  166, 174–175, 202
Public investment reform, 174–175
Public sector. *See also* Fiscal policies; Government *entries*
  in economic reform, 2, 3
  history of, 10–14
Public wage sector, 11–12, 115–131,
  163
  reform in, 121–131, 200–201
  rent-seeking in, 121–122
  retirement from, 126, 127, 129, 130
  wages in, 121, 124–125, 128

Quality control of exports, 69–70

Ration system, 62–67, 84, 199

Redeployment program, 121–131, 200

Rent-seeking in public wage sector, 121–122

Retail prices, 62–68, 78–80

Retirement from public wage sector, 126, 127, 129, 130

Rice consumption, 81–88

Rice imports, 74–81, 84–88, 90–98, 199–200

Rice marketing liberalization, 73–80

Rice price policy, 81–88

Rice prices, 71–88

Rice technology, 198–199

Rural areas
  credit availability in, 72
  food consumption patterns in, 84–85
  health system in, 186, 187
  infrastructure of, 13
  versus urban areas, 13–14

School enrollments, 10, 177–181, 203

Second Republic, 14–16, 66–68

Secondary market for foreign exchange, 22

Secondary sector, 6

Self-employment advisory service, 123

Self-employment sector, 115–121, 128, 200, 201

Service sector, 6

Small-enterprise sector, 131–139, 200, 201

Smallholder farms, 51–52

Smuggling, 12, 14, 61–62

Social service reforms, 175–191, 203

Social stagnation, 9–10

Structural adjustment program, 1–3, 14–16, 22, 66–68, 146

Subsidies to parastatals, 172–173, 202

Subsistence agriculture, 14

Subsistence ratio, 61

Tax reform, 67, 69–70, 168–171, 202

Taxes
  on crops, 54
  customs, 169
  export, 20, 25, 67, 69–70
  on food products, 25
  history of, 11
  import, 20–21, 25–26, 30, 90–98, 170, 171
  on luxury items, 26
  in mining sector, 143, 145, 147
  on petroleum products, 169, 171
  revenues from, 166, 167, 170, 171
  turnover, 169

Technological innovation, 72

Terms of trade, 34, 61

Time lags in economic reform, 3

Touré, Sekou, 10–11, 14

Trade. *See also* Export *entries;* Import *entries;* Smuggling
  barter, 61
  terms of, 34, 61
  triangular, 61

Trade balances, 30, 31, 33–35

Trade liberalization, 21, 74–77, 196–197, 199–200

Trade policy reforms, 24–26, 39, 41

Trade restrictions, 33

Transport of agricultural exports, 70–71, 73–74

Treasury bills, 156

Triangular trade, 61

Turnover taxes, 169

Upper Guinea, 7, 47, 49, 71, 72, 87
Urban areas
  food consumption patterns in,
    81–84
  health care in, 186, 187

  labor markets in, 113–139
  versus rural areas, 13–14

Wages
  by gender, 119–120
  by labor market sector, 119–121,
    124–125, 128, 201